Intro

With over 200 fully featured services available in Amazon Web Services (AWS), it can be a daunting task if you want to know about every service. Each AWS Service has its own Overview Page, Use Case, Documentation, FAQs, and Pricing pages, which can also contain detailed explanations of how each service works, coupled with its interdependencies with other services. This can lead to your learning focus being derailed into multiple technological areas that you may not have been initially aiming for.

This series is an attempt to cut down on that complication. You will find Service Summary Cards (SSC) describing all the W questions (What, Why, When, Where, Who, How, How much?) organized based on services covered in an AWS Certification Exam.

These cards are designed to provide the key information and can be useful to anyone who wants to learn about different AWS services, including someone who is not preparing for a certification exam.

Disclaimer

The information provided within this book is for general informational purposes only. While author try to keep the information up-to-date and correct, there are no representations or warranties, express or implied, about the completeness, accuracy, reliability, suitability or availability with respect to the information, products, services, or related graphics contained in this book for any purpose. Any information described within this book is the author's personal thoughts. They are not intended to be a definitive set of instructions.

The author does not claim any copyright on content, images, web links, or any other material in the book. All the information is compiled from the AWS official documentation. The purpose of this book is to present the detailed information available on the AWS official website in a concise, bite-sized information and answer common questions related to an AWS service or a feature. The author understands how important it is to provide accurate information to readers, but even with the author's best efforts an error may occur. If you believe you've found a mistake in this book, please bring it to the author's attention. You can contact the author by scanning the QR Code on the back of this book.

The advice and strategies contained herein may not be suitable for every situation. This work is sold with the understanding that the publisher is not engaged in rendering legal, accounting, or other professional services. If professional assistance is required, the services of a competent professional person should be sought. Neither the publisher nor the author shall be liable for any damages arising here from. The fact that an organization or Website is referred to in this work as a citation and/or a potential source of further information does not mean that the author or the publisher endorses the information the organization or Website may provide or recommendations it may make.

Further, readers should be aware that the information presented in the book may have changed between when this work was written and when it is read. AWS Services are always evolving, so in case of conflicting or confusing information, please refer to AWS documentation. - https://docs.aws.amazon.com/

Views shared are my own, not those of my employer

AWS Certified Cloud Practitioner (CLF-C01)

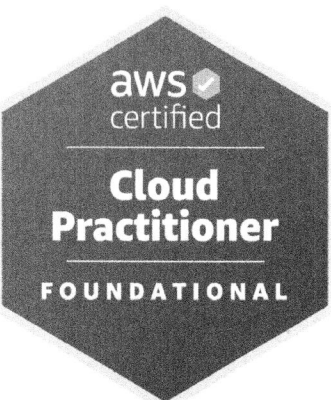

Domain:	% of Exam
Domain 1: Cloud Concepts	26%
Domain 2: Security and Compliance	25%
Domain 3: Technology	33%
Domain 4: Billing and Pricing	16%

Exam Level	Length	Cost	Questions
Foundational	90 Minutes	100 USD	65 Questions

AWS Certified Cloud Practitioner (CLF-C01)

Domain 1: Cloud Concepts

1.1 Define the AWS Cloud and its value proposition

1.2 Identify aspects of AWS Cloud economics

1.3 Explain the different cloud architecture design principles

Domain 2: Security and Compliance

2.1 Define the AWS shared responsibility model

2.2 Define AWS Cloud security and compliance concepts

2.3 Identify AWS access management capabilities

2.4 Identify resources for security support

Domain 3: Technology

3.1 Define methods of deploying and operating in the AWS Cloud

3.2 Define the AWS global infrastructure

3.3 Identify the core AWS services

3.4 Identify resources for technology support

Domain 4: Billing and Pricing

4.1 Compare and contrast the various pricing models for AWS (for example, On-Demand Instances, Reserved Instances, and Spot Instance pricing)

4.2 Recognize the various account structures in relation to AWS billing and pricing

4.3 Identify resources available for billing support

Table of Content

Analytics:
Amazon Athena	9
Amazon Kinesis	10
Amazon QuickSight	11

Application Integration:
Amazon SNS	15
Amazon SQS	16

Compute and Serverless:
AWS Batch	19
Amazon EC2	20
Amazon Elastic Beanstalk	21
AWS Lambda	22
Amazon Lightsail	23
Amazon WorkSpaces	24

Containers:
Amazon ECS	27
Amazon EKS	28
AWS Fargate	29

Customer Engagement:
Amazon Connect	33

Database:
Amazon Aurora	37
Amazon DynamoDB	38
Amazon ElastiCache	39
Amazon RDS	40
Amazon Redshift	41

Developer Tools:
AWS CodeBuild	45
AWS CodeCommit	46
AWS CodeDeploy	47
AWS CodePipeline	48
AWS CodeStar	49

Management, Monitoring, & Governance:
AWS Auto Scaling	55
AWS Budgets	56
AWS CloudFormation	57
AWS CloudTrail	58
Amazon CloudWatch	59
AWS Config	60
AWS Cost and Usage Report	61
Amazon EventBridge	62
AWS License Manager	63
AWS Managed Services	64
AWS Organizations	65
AWS Secrets Manager	66
AWS Systems Manager	67
AWS Systems Manager Parameter Store	68
AWS Trusted Advisor	69

Networking and Content Delivery:
Amazon API Gateway	73
Amazon CloudFront	74
AWS Direct Connect	75
Amazon Route 53	76
Amazon VPC	77

Security, Identity, and Compliance:
AWS Artifact	83
AWS Certificate Manager	84
AWS CloudHSM	85
Amazon Cognito	86
Amazon Detective	87
Amazon GuardDuty	88
AWS IAM	89
Amazon Inspector	90
AWS License Manager	91
Amazon Macie	92
AWS Shield	93
AWS WAF	94

Storage:
AWS Backup	97
Amazon EBS	98
Amazon EFS	99
Amazon S3	100
Amazon S3 Glacier	101
AWS Snowball Edge	102
AWS Storage Gateway	103
Additional Resource	107

Analytics

Amazon Athena

Serverless, interactive query service

Amazon Kinesis

Work with real-time streaming data

Amazon QuickSight

Fast, easy to use business analytics

Amazon Athena

What?
- Amazon Athena is an interactive query service that makes it easy to analyze data in Amazon S3 using standard SQL.
- Amazon Athena uses Presto with ANSI SQL support and works with a variety of standard data formats, including CSV, JSON, ORC, Avro, and Parquet.

Why?
- Athena is serverless, you don't need to worry about configuration, software updates, failures or scaling your infrastructure as your datasets and number of users grow.
- With Athena Federated Query, you can run SQL queries across data stored in relational, non-relational, object, and custom data sources.

When?
- You want to tap into your data without setting up complex processes to extract, transform, and load the data (ETL).
- You want to process logs, perform data analytics, and run interactive queries.

Where?
- Amazon Athena is a regional service, but it can access data in other regions or other AWS accounts.
- Athena works directly with data stored in S3.
- It also natively supports the AWS Glue Data Catalog.

Who?
- Athena is serverless service, so you don't have to setup or manage any infrastructure.
- Amazon Athena allows you to control access to your data by using AWS IAM policies, Access Control Lists (ACLs), and Amazon S3 bucket policies.

How?
- To get started, Just point to your data in Amazon S3, define the schema, and start querying using the built-in query editor.
- Results are displayed in the console, and automatically written to a location of your choice in S3. You can also download them to your desktop.

How Much?
- Amazon Athena is priced per query and charges based on the amount of data scanned by the query.
- It queries data directly from Amazon S3, so your source data is billed at S3 rates.

Category: Analytics

Amazon Kinesis

What?
- Amazon Kinesis makes it easy to collect, process, and analyze real-time, streaming data.
- Amazon Kinesis capabilities - Amazon Kinesis Data Streams, Amazon Kinesis Data Firehose, Amazon Kinesis Data Analytics and Kinesis Video Streams.

Why?
- Amazon Kinesis enables you to process and analyze data as it arrives and respond instantly.
- It can handle any amount of streaming data and process data from hundreds of thousands of sources with very low latencies.

When?
- When you want to ingest real-time data such as video, audio, application logs, website clickstreams, and IoT telemetry data for machine learning, analytics, and other applications.

Where?
- Amazon Kinesis is a regional service.
- Kinesis Data Streams and Kinesis Data Firehose synchronously replicate data across three Availability Zones, providing high availability and data durability.

Who?
- Amazon Kinesis is fully managed and runs your streaming applications without requiring you to manage any infrastructure.

How?
- After you create a Kinesis Data Firehose delivery stream or a Kinesis Data Streams, configure your data producers to continuously add data to your data stream.
- You can process streaming data through Kinesis Data Analytics using SQL or Apache Flink.

How Much?
- Amazon Kinesis Data Streams - on-demand and provisioned option.
- Amazon Kinesis Data Firehose - pay for the volume of data you ingest.
- Amazon Kinesis Data Analytics - hourly rate based on the number of Kinesis Processing Units (or KPUs) used.

Category: Analytics

Amazon QuickSight

What?
- Amazon QuickSight is a cloud-powered business analytics service that makes it easy to build visualizations, perform ad-hoc analysis, and quickly get business insights from data.

Why?
- You can connect to any of the data sources discovered by Amazon QuickSight and get insights from this data in minutes.
- Amazon QuickSight lets you quickly embed interactive dashboards and visualizations into your applications without needing to build your own analytics capabilities.

When?
- You want to ask business questions in natural language and receive accurate answers with relevant visualizations to gain insights from the data.
- You want to gain deeper insights through ad-hoc analysis and machine learning capabilities such as anomaly detection, forecasting, and natural language queries.

Where?
- Amazon QuickSight is a regional service but you can also explicitly connect to other AWS data sources that are not in your account or in a different region by providing connection details for those sources.

Who?
- Amazon QuickSight is a fully managed service.
- It supports native IAM permissions for Amazon S3 and Amazon Athena with fine-grained access control for serverless data exploration.

How?
- Create a new analysis. Add new or existing datasets then choose fields to create the first chart.
- QuickSight automatically suggests the best visualization or you can add more charts, tables, or insights to the analysis.
- Publish the analysis as a dashboard to share it with other people.

How Much?
- You pay month-to-month pricing for Authors and Readers.
- You pay for SPICE (Super-fast, Parallel, In-memory Calculation Engine) capacity used.
- Accounts enabled with Q are charged a $250/month Q base fee plus Q questions capacity pricing.

Category: Analytics

Application Integration

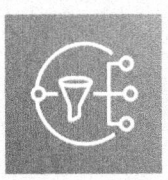

Amazon SNS

Managed message topics for Pub/Sub

Amazon SQS

Managed message queues

Amazon Simple Notification Service (Amazon SNS)

What?
- Amazon Simple Notification Service (Amazon SNS) is a fully managed push-based messaging service for both application-to-application (A2A) and application-to-person (A2P) communication.
- It provides message delivery from publishers to subscribers (also known as producers and consumers).

Why?
- Amazon SNS is a highly available, durable, secure, fully managed pub/sub messaging service that enables you to decouple microservices, distributed systems, and event-driven serverless applications.
- Amazon SNS provides topics for high-throughput, push-based, many-to-many messaging.

When?
- You can use Amazon SNS to support a wide variety of needs including event notification, monitoring applications, workflow systems, time-sensitive information updates, mobile applications, and any other application that generates or consumes notifications.

Where?
- Amazon SNS is a regional service.
- A2A destinations - Amazon Kinesis Data Firehose, AWS Lambda, Amazon SQS, AWS Event Fork Pipelines, HTTP/S.
- A2P destinations – SMS, Email, Platform endpoint, AWS Chatbot, PagerDuty

Who?
- Amazon SNS is a fully managed service.
- Amazon SNS has its own resource-based permissions system that uses policies written in the same language used for IAM policies. This means that you can achieve similar things with Amazon SNS policies and IAM policies.

How?
- Developers must first create a *topic* which is identifying a specific subject or event type for publishing messages and allowing clients to subscribe for notifications. Topic owner can set policies for it, such as limiting who can publish messages or subscribe, or specifying which protocols will be supported (i.e. HTTP/HTTPS, email, SMS).

How Much?
- Standard topic - number of monthly API requests made, and the number of deliveries to various endpoints.
- FIFO topic - pricing is based on the number of published messages, the number of subscribed messages, and their respective amount of payload data.

Category: Application Integration

Amazon Simple Queue Service (Amazon SQS)

What?
- Amazon Simple Queue Service (SQS) is a fully managed message queuing service that enables you to decouple and scale microservices, distributed systems, and serverless applications.

Why?
- SQS eliminates the complexity and overhead associated with managing and operating message-oriented middleware, and empowers developers to focus on differentiating work.
- SQS scales elastically with your application so you don't have to worry about capacity planning and pre-provisioning.

When?
- You want to send, store, and receive messages between software components, without requiring other services to be available.
- Use SQS standard queues for maximum throughput, best-effort ordering, and at-least-once delivery. Use SQS FIFO queues to guarantee that messages are processed exactly once, in the exact order.

Where?
- Amazon SQS is a regional service.
- Amazon SQS stores all message queues and messages within a single, highly-available AWS region with multiple redundant Availability Zones (AZs), so that no single computer, network, or AZ failure can make messages inaccessible.

Who?
- AWS manages the backend for Amazon SQS service, including scaling and durability.
- Customers can control who can send messages to a message queue and who can receive messages from a message queue. Amazon SQS has its own resource-based permissions system.

How?
- Messages are sent from producers (applications, microservices, and other AWS services) to SQS Queue.
- It stores messages and waits for consumer to poll.
- Consumer applications (Lambda Functions, EC2 Instances and other AWS services) pull/poll the messages and process it.

How Much?
- The cost of Amazon SQS is calculated per request, plus data transfer charges for data transferred out of Amazon SQS.
- Each 64 KB chunk of a payload is billed as 1 request (for example, an API action with a 256 KB payload is billed as 4 requests).

Category: Application Integration

Compute and Serverless

AWS Batch
Fully managed batch processing at any scale

Amazon EC2
Virtual servers in the Cloud

Amazon Elastic Beanstalk
Run and manage web apps

AWS Lambda
Run code without thinking about servers

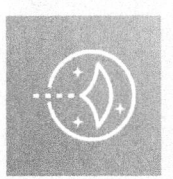
Amazon Lightsail
Launch and manage virtual private servers

Compute and Serverless

Amazon WorkSpaces

Desktops in the Cloud

AWS Batch

What?
- AWS Batch enables you to run batch computing workloads of any scale on AWS using Amazon EC2 and Amazon EC2 Spot.
- It supports any job that can execute as a Docker container.
- Batch computing is the execution of a series of programs (*jobs*) on one or more computers without manual intervention.

Why?
- AWS Batch eliminates the need to operate third-party commercial or open source batch processing solutions. There is no batch software or servers to install or manage.
- It is natively integrated with the AWS platform to securely retrieve and write data to and from storage services in AWS.

When?
- You want to dynamically scale compute resources to run your batch jobs, freeing you from the constraints of fixed-capacity clusters.
- You want to utilize Spot Instances to reduce the cost of running your batch jobs.

Where?
- AWS Batch is a regional service.
- It runs jobs using Amazon EC2 and EC2 Spot Instances and AWS Fargate.
- AWS Batch is natively integrated with the AWS platform to run jobs that safely and securely retrieve and write data to and from AWS data stores, such as Amazon S3 or Amazon DynamoDB.

Who?
- AWS Batch manages all the infrastructure for you.
- You simply define and submit your batch jobs to a queue and AWS Batch chooses where to run the jobs, launching additional AWS capacity if needed.

How?
- User creates the Job Definition and submits it to a managed AWS Batch job queue.
- AWS Batch evaluates the CPU, Memory, and GPU needs of the jobs and launches compute resources.
- After job completion, it writes the results to user-defined storage.

How Much?
- There is no charge for AWS Batch itself; you pay only for the resources it launches on your behalf.
- You can use your Reserved Instances, Savings Plan, EC2 Spot Instances, and Fargate with AWS Batch by specifying your compute-type requirements when setting up your AWS Batch compute environments.

Category: Compute and Serverless

Amazon EC2

What?
- Amazon Elastic Compute Cloud (Amazon EC2) is a web service that provides resizable computing capacity—literally, servers in Amazon's data centers—that you use to build and host your software systems.
- An Amazon EC2 instance is a virtual server in the AWS Cloud.

Why?
- Amazon EC2 reduces the time required to obtain and boot new server instances to minutes, allowing you to quickly scale capacity, both up and down, as your computing requirements change.
- Amazon EC2 changes the economics of computing by allowing you to pay only for capacity that you actually use.

When?
- You want to run cloud-native and enterprise applications, scale for High Performance Computing (HPC) applications, develop for Apple platforms.
- You want complete control of your computing resources and run it on Amazon's proven computing environment.
- You want to import your virtual machine images to Amazon EC2.

Where?
- Amazon EC2 is a regional service.
- Amazon EC2 instances run in an Availability Zone.
- You can protect your applications from failure of a single location by launching instances in separate Availability Zones.

Who?
- Customer must take care of OS patches, high availability, and scaling.
- AWS provides tools and services for patch management, auto-scaling, monitoring, backup and vulnerability scanning.
- AWS maintains the underlying system powering your instances.

How?
- Get started by selecting an Amazon Machine Image (AMI) followed by Instance Type selection.
- You can also select additional settings like, disk size, security group, network, start-up script etc.

How Much?
- On-Demand Instance – Pay per second / hour.
- Reserved Instances / Savings Plan – Commitment for 1-year / 3-year term.
- Spot Instances – Supply and Demand based pricing.

Category: Compute and Serverless

Amazon Elastic Beanstalk

What?
- Amazon Elastic Beanstalk is an application management platform.
- It is an easy-to-use service for deploying and scaling web applications and services developed with Java, .NET, PHP, Node.js, Python, Ruby, Go, and Docker on familiar servers such as Apache, Nginx, Passenger, and IIS.

Why?
- You can simply upload your code and Elastic Beanstalk automatically handles the deployment, from capacity provisioning, load balancing, auto-scaling to application health monitoring.
- Elastic Beanstalk provides a unified user interface (UI) to monitor and manage the health of your applications.

When?
- You want to focus on developing applications, not on deployment-oriented tasks, such as provisioning servers, or managing scaling.
- You want your developers to retain full control over the AWS resources powering their application instead of being forced to live with decisions predetermined by the vendor – with no opportunity to take back control.

Where?
- Amazon Elastic Beanstalk is a regional service.
- You can save configuration of your environment as an object in Amazon S3 bucket. Saved configuration can be applied to other environments during environment creation, or applied to a running environment.

Who?
- You select the AWS resources, such as Amazon EC2 instance types including Spot instances, that are optimal for your application.
- You can choose to automatically get the latest platform updates and new patches using managed platform updates.

How?
- Elastic Beanstalk uses proven AWS features and services, such as Amazon EC2, Amazon RDS, Elastic Load Balancing, Auto Scaling, Amazon S3, and Amazon SNS, to create an environment that runs your application.
- You can deploy your code through the AWS Management Console, Elastic Beanstalk Command Line Interface, Visual Studio, and Eclipse.

How Much?
- There is no additional charge for AWS Elastic Beanstalk.
- You pay for AWS resources (e.g., EC2 instances or S3 buckets) you create to store and run your application.

Category: Compute and Serverless

AWS Lambda

What?
- AWS Lambda is a serverless, event-driven compute service that lets you run code for virtually any type of application or backend service without provisioning or managing servers.
- AWS Lambda functions run for a maximum of up to 15 minutes per invocation

Why?
- With Lambda, you can run your code with zero administration overhead.
- AWS Lambda takes care of everything required to run and scale your code with high availability.
- You can set up your code to automatically trigger from other AWS services or call it directly from any web or mobile app.

When?
- Lambda is best suited for shorter, event-driven workloads, such as processing streaming data stored in Amazon Kinesis, or custom events generated by your applications.
- You want to build data-processing triggers for AWS services such as Amazon S3 and Amazon DynamoDB.

Where?
- AWS Lambda is a regional service. It runs your code on high availability compute infrastructure in a region.
- It maintains compute capacity across multiple AZs in each AWS Region to help protect your code against individual machine or data center facility failures.

Who?
- Lambda performs all the administration of your compute resources including server and operating system maintenance, capacity provisioning and automatic scaling, code and security patch deployment, and code monitoring and logging.
- All you need to do is supply the code.

How?
- The code you run on AWS Lambda is uploaded as a *Lambda function*.
- Each function has associated configuration information, such as its name, description, entry point, and resource requirements.
- Lambda will run your function by launching and managing compute resources as needed based on incoming requests.

How Much?
- Billing is metered in increments of one millisecond. You are charged based on the number of requests for your functions and the duration it takes for your code to execute.
- With Provisioned Concurrency, you pay for the amount of concurrency you configure and the duration that you configure it.

Category: Compute and Serverless

Amazon Lightsail

What?
- Amazon Lightsail is the easiest way to get started with AWS for developers, small businesses, students, and other users who need a solution to build and host their websites and web applications in the cloud.
- Lightsail offers simplified services such as instances, containers, databases, storage, and more.

Why?
- Lightsail includes everything you need to launch your project quickly – virtual private server (VPS) instances, containers, databases, CDN, load balancers, DNS management etc. – for a low, predictable monthly price.
- Common use cases include running websites, web applications, blogs, e-commerce sites, simple software, and more.

When?
- Lightsail is best suited for projects that require a few virtual private servers (VPS) and users who prefer a simple management interface.
- You want to use pre-configured development stacks like LAMP, Nginx, MEAN, and Node.js. to get online quickly and easily.

Where?
- Lightsail creates resources in a region.
- The DNS zones used by Lightsail are global resources. They are created only in the US East (N. Virginia) (us-east-1) region, but they can reference any instance in any AWS Region.

Who?
- Lightsail offers a number of pre-configured, stacks, including WordPress, Plesk, LAMP, Node.js and more.
- You are responsible to patch, update, and secure OS and applications on your Amazon Lightsail instances. You can enable automatic snapshots to have Lightsail create daily snapshots for you.

How?
- The Lightsail console guides you through the configuration process, and in many cases, has components already configured.
- First, select an OS platform (Linux/Unix or Windows); next, select a blueprint for your instance. You can choose an App (e.g. WordPress, MEAN) + OS or an OS Only blueprint.

How Much?
- Lightsail bundles resources like memory, vCPU, and SSD storage into one plan, so budgeting is easy and straightforward.
- Lightsail plans are charged on an hourly, on-demand basis, so you only pay for a plan when you're using it. A plan includes a low, predictable cost and a machine configuration (RAM, SSD, vCPU), and data transfer.

Category: Compute and Serverless

Amazon Workspaces

What?
- Amazon WorkSpaces enables you to provision virtual, cloud-based Microsoft Windows or Amazon Linux desktops for your users, known as WorkSpace - a cloud-based virtual desktop.
- Amazon WorkSpaces utilizes streaming protocols to provide users with a secure and high-quality virtual desktop experience.

Why?
- Unlike traditional on-premises Virtual Desktop Infrastructure (VDI) solutions, you don't have to worry about procuring, deploying, and managing a complex environment.
- Amazon WorkSpaces takes care of the heavy lifting and provides a fully managed service.

When?
- You want your users to access their virtual desktops from multiple devices or web browsers from any location and optimize costs with on-demand, pay-as-you-go scaling with various compute, memory, and storage options.
- You want to strengthen security by storing user data on AWS instead of vulnerable endpoint devices.

Where?
- Amazon Workspace is a regional service.
- It requires a directory service to store and manage information for your WorkSpaces and users.
- You can use one of the following options: AD Connector, AWS Managed Microsoft AD, Simple AD, Cross trust.

Who?
- You can select an Amazon WorkSpaces bundle for the user. The WorkSpaces bundle specifies the resources you need.
- Amazon WorkSpaces takes care of managing inventory, OS versions and patches, and VDI.

How?
- To get started, select from a choice of Amazon WorkSpaces bundles that offer different hardware and software options, and launch the number of WorkSpaces you require.
- Users download the WorkSpaces client applications and connect to their WorkSpace.

How Much?
- Amazon WorkSpaces provides monthly or hourly usage-based pricing based on the bundle you selected (OS, CPU, Memory, Storage).
- With monthly billing, you pay a fixed monthly fee for unlimited usage during the month. With hourly billing, you pay a small fixed monthly fee per WorkSpace and an hourly rate for each hour the WorkSpace is used.

Category: Compute and Serverless

Containers

Amazon ECS
Highly secure, reliable, and scalable way to run containers

Amazon EKS
Managed service to run Kubernetes on AWS

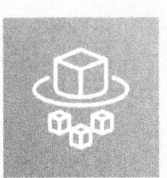
AWS Fargate
Serverless compute engine for running containers

Amazon Elastic Container Service (Amazon ECS)

What?
- Amazon Elastic Container Service (ECS) is a highly scalable, high performance container management service that supports Docker containers and allows you to easily run applications on a managed cluster of Amazon EC2 instances.

Why?
- Amazon ECS eliminates the need for you to install, operate, and scale your own cluster management infrastructure.
- You can use Amazon ECS to schedule container placement across your cluster based on your resource needs and availability requirements.

When?
- You want to schedule long-running applications, services, and batch processes using Docker containers.
- You want to maintain application availability and need the ability to scale your containers up or down to meet your application's capacity requirements.

Where?
- Amazon ECS is a regional service which can run and scale your container workloads across Availability Zones.
- It also supports running Docker containers on your infrastructure with Amazon ECS Anywhere.

Who?
- Amazon ECS is a fully managed container orchestration service, with AWS configuration and operational best practices built-in, and no control plane, nodes, or add-ons for you to manage.
- You define Tasks, Service, Capacity Providers, and deployment process based on your application requirements.

How?
- Your containers are defined in a task definition that you use to run an individual tasks or task within a service. Amazon ECS launches these tasks and services on a managed cluster of Amazon EC2 instances.
- Amazon ECS is integrated with familiar features like Elastic Load Balancing, EBS volumes, Amazon VPC and AWS IAM.

How Much?
- There is no additional charge for Amazon ECS.
- You pay for AWS resources (e.g. Amazon EC2 instances or EBS volumes) you create to store and run your application.

Category: Containers

Amazon Elastic Kubernetes Service (Amazon EKS)

What?
- Amazon Elastic Kubernetes Service (Amazon EKS) is a managed service that makes it easy for you to run Kubernetes on AWS without installing and operating your own Kubernetes control plane or worker nodes.
- Kubernetes is an open-source container orchestration system allowing you to deploy and manage containerized applications at scale

Why?
- Amazon EKS provisions and scales the Kubernetes control plane, including the API servers and backend persistence layer. It automatically detects and replaces unhealthy control plane nodes and patches the control plane.
- Amazon EKS is integrated with many AWS services to provide scalability and security for your applications.

When?
- You don't want the operational burden of managing the Kubernetes control plane.
- You want to maintain existing applications that run on upstream Kubernetes and want to use plugins and tooling from the Kubernetes community.

Where?
- Amazon EKS is a regional service.
- It runs and scales the Kubernetes control plane across multiple AWS Availability Zones to ensure high availability.

Who?
- Amazon EKS handles provisioning, scaling, and managing the Kubernetes control plane. It provides automated version upgrades and patching for control plane nodes.
- Customers provision an EKS cluster, deploy compute nodes, connect to EKS, and run Kubernetes applications.

How?
- You can get started by creating an Amazon EKS cluster.
- When your cluster is ready, you can configure your favorite Kubernetes tools, such as *kubectl*, to communicate with your cluster.
- Afterwards, you can deploy and manage workloads on Amazon EKS cluster the same way that you would with any other Kubernetes environment.

How Much?
- You pay a per hour charge for each Amazon EKS cluster you create and for the AWS resources you create to run your Kubernetes worker nodes.
- If you are using AWS Fargate, pricing is calculated based on the vCPU and memory resources used.

Category: Containers

AWS Fargate

What?
- AWS Fargate is a serverless compute engine compatible with Amazon ECS or Amazon EKS that allows you to run containers without having to manage servers or clusters.

Why?
- Fargate removes the need to own, run, and manage the lifecycle of a compute infrastructure so that you can focus on your applications.
- You define your application content, networking, storage, and scaling requirements. There is no provisioning, patching, cluster capacity management, or infrastructure management required.

When?
- You want to deploy and manage your applications, not your infrastructure.
- You want to support common container use cases including microservices architecture applications, batch processing, machine learning applications, and migrating on-premises applications to the cloud.

Where?
- AWS Fargate is a regional service.
- Both ECS and EKS use containers provisioned by Fargate to build and operate containerized application.

Who?
- Fargate handles the infrastructure management aspects of your workload for you.
- Customers package application in containers, specify the CPU and memory requirements; define networking and IAM policies, and launch the application.

How?
- On Amazon ECS by launching your services or tasks on AWS Fargate.
- On Amazon EKS by defining at least one Fargate profile that specifies which pods will use Fargate when launched. Fargate profiles are defined as part of your Amazon EKS cluster.

How Much?
- With AWS Fargate, you pay only for the amount of vCPU, memory, and storage resources consumed by your applications.
- vCPU and memory resources are calculated from the time your container images are pulled until the Amazon ECS task or EKS pod terminates, rounded up to the nearest second. A minimum charge of 1 minute applies.

Category: Containers

Customer Engagement

Amazon Connect
A contact center that enables engagement at any scale

Amazon Connect

What?
- Amazon Connect enables you to create an omnichannel cloud-based contact center to support your customers: a contact center that provides a unified experience across multiple channels, such as voice, interactive chat, and tasks.

Why?
- You can set up a contact center in a few steps; scale it up, or down to meet demand, with the flexibility to onboard agents working from anywhere.
- Amazon Connect is an open platform that you can integrate with other enterprise applications, such as Salesforce. In addition, you can take advantage of integration with the AWS ecosystem.

When?
- You want to set up a contact center in minutes that can scale to support millions of customers.
- You want to automate interactions, understand customer sentiment, enable capabilities like interactive voice response (IVR), chatbots with embedded artificial intelligence (AI) and machine learning (ML).

Where?
- Amazon Connect is a regional service.
- Agents can be based anywhere. Agents use the Contact Control Panel (CCP) website to communicate with contacts.

Who?
- Amazon Connect manages a network of telephony providers from around the world, removing the need for you to manage multiple vendors, negotiate complex multi-year contracts, or commit to peak call volumes.

How?
- Create an Amazon Connect instance which contains all the resources and settings related to your contact center. For voice, either us a phone number AWS provides, or port your current phone number. Establish a contact flow to define the customer experience with your contact center and add users (managers and agents), and configure their settings.

How Much?
- For Amazon Connect Voice - voice service charges (billed on a per-second basis) and telephony charges (toll-free phone numbers). For Chat usage – per message. For Task usage – per task.
- Additional charges apply for Customer Profiles, Contact Lens, Voice ID and Wisdom.

Category: Customer Engagement

Database

Amazon Aurora
MySQL and PostgreSQL compatible relational database

Amazon DynamoDB
Managed NoSQL database

Amazon ElastiCache
Managed caching service for Redis and Memcached

Amazon RDS
Managed relational database service

Amazon Redshift
Fully managed, Petabyte-scale data warehouse service

Amazon Aurora

What?
- Amazon Aurora (Aurora) is a fully managed relational database engine that's compatible with MySQL and PostgreSQL.
- It is built for the cloud, and combines the performance and availability of traditional enterprise databases with the simplicity and cost-effectiveness of open source databases.

Why?
- Aurora automates time-consuming administration tasks like hardware provisioning, database setup, and backups while providing the security, availability, and reliability of commercial databases at 1/10th the cost.
- It features a distributed, fault-tolerant, and self-healing storage system that is decoupled from compute resources.

When?
- You want to migrate your MySQL and PostgreSQL workload to a managed relational databases service in AWS cloud.
- You need a high-performance distributed storage subsystem for your workloads that grows automatically as needed.

Where?
- Amazon Aurora is a regional service; it automatically maintains six copies of your data across three AZs.
- Amazon Aurora Global Database feature supports cross-region replicas. You can create up to five secondary regions for an Aurora Global Database.

Who?
- Amazon Aurora is fully managed by RDS and it automatically and continuously monitors and backs up your database to Amazon S3, enabling granular point-in-time recovery.
- Customers can scale the compute resources allocated to their DB Instance by changing the DB Instance class.

How?
- You choose Aurora as the DB engine option when setting up new database servers through Amazon RDS.
- After launching an Aurora instance, you can connect to it using any database client that supports MySQL or PostgreSQL.

How Much?
- For Amazon Aurora On-Demand Instances, you pay by the hour. You can also choose Reserved Instances for additional savings.
- Aurora storage is billed in per GB-month increments, while I/Os consumed are billed in per million request increments.

Category: Database

Amazon DynamoDB

What?
- Amazon DynamoDB is a fully managed, serverless, NoSQL database designed to support key-value and document data models.
- DynamoDB has a flexible schema, to easily adapt the tables as your business requirements change, without having to redefine the table schema as you would in relational databases.

Why?
- DynamoDB offers built-in security, continuous backups, automated multi-Region replication, in-memory caching, and data export tools.
- You can scale up or scale down your tables' throughput capacity without downtime or performance degradation.

When?
- You want to build internet-scale applications supporting user-content metadata and caches that require high concurrency and connections for millions of users, and millions of requests per second.
- You want to support high-traffic, extreme-scaled events, encryption at rest with no operational overhead.

Where?
- DynamoDB is a regional service.
- All of your data is stored on SSDs and is automatically replicated across multiple Availability Zones in an AWS Region.
- You can use global tables to keep DynamoDB tables in sync across AWS Regions.

Who?
- Amazon DynamoDB is a fully managed service.
- It automatically scales tables to adjust for capacity and maintains performance with zero administration.
- Availability and fault tolerance are built in and it also provides on-demand backup capability.

How?
- DynamoDB stores data in a table. A table is a collection of items, and each item is a collection of attributes. An attribute is a fundamental data element, which does not need to be broken down further.
- It uses primary keys to uniquely identify each item in a table and secondary indexes to provide more querying flexibility.

How Much?
- DynamoDB charges are calculated for reading, writing, and storing data in tables, along with any optional features you choose to enable.
- DynamoDB has two capacity modes, which come with specific billing options for processing reads and writes on your tables: on-demand and provisioned.

Category: Database

Amazon ElastiCache

What?
- Amazon ElastiCache is a fully managed, in-memory caching service supporting flexible, real-time use cases.
- Amazon ElastiCache makes it easy to deploy and run Memcached or Redis protocol-compliant server nodes in the cloud.

Why?
- Amazon ElastiCache improves the performance of web applications by allowing you to retrieve information from a fast, managed, in-memory system, instead of relying entirely on slower disk-based databases.
- Amazon ElastiCache automates common administrative tasks and eliminates the operational overhead of self-managed caching.

When?
- Use Amazon ElastiCache for Memcached for simplest model possible, large nodes with multiple cores or threads.
- Use Amazon ElastiCache for Redis for complex data types (strings, hashes, lists, sets, and bitmaps); sort or rank in-memory datasets, persistence, automatic failover, pub/sub capabilities, backup and restore capabilities.

Where?
- Amazon ElastiCache is a regional service.
- When creating a cluster or adding nodes to an existing cluster, you can choose the availability zones for the new nodes.

Who?
- Amazon ElastiCache is a fully managed service. You do not need to perform management tasks such as hardware provisioning, software patching, setup, configuration, monitoring, failure recovery, and backups.
- You have access to monitoring metrics of your nodes, enabling you to diagnose and react to issues quickly.

How?
- You start using Amazon ElastiCache by creating a cluster. A cluster is a collection of one or more cache nodes, all of which run an instance of the cache engine software (either Redis or Memcached).
- Your application connects to your cluster using endpoints. An endpoint is a node or cluster's unique address.

How Much?
- You are charged hourly based on the number of nodes, node type, and pricing model you select.
- ElastiCache supports both on-demand nodes (pay by hour), and reserved nodes (commit to either one-year or three-year terms).

Category: Database

Amazon RDS

What?
- Amazon Relational Database Service (Amazon RDS) is a managed service that makes it easy to set up, operate, and scale a relational database in the cloud.
- Amazon RDS supports Amazon Aurora, MySQL, MariaDB, Oracle, SQL Server, and PostgreSQL database engines.

Why?
- You want to focus on your applications and business instead of managing time-consuming database administration tasks.
- Once your database is up and running, Amazon RDS automates common administrative tasks, such as performing backups and patching the software that powers your database.

When?
- You need the capabilities of a familiar MySQL, MariaDB, Oracle, SQL Server, PostgreSQL or Amazon Aurora database
- You want the flexibility of being able to easily scale the compute resources or storage capacity associated with your relational database instance.

Where?
- Amazon RDS can be deployed in a Single AZ or Multi-AZ. When you provision a Multi-AZ database instance, Amazon RDS synchronously replicates your data to a standby instance in a different AZ.
- Amazon RDS Read Replica can be deployed in the same or different AWS Region than the Amazon RDS Instance.

Who?
- Amazon RDS is a managed service.
- It manages the work involved in setting up a database, from provisioning the infrastructure capacity you request to installing the database software.
- You manage the database settings that are specific to your application.

How?
- The basic building block of Amazon RDS is the DB instance. You can get started by creating a DB instance that can contain one or more databases.
- You can access your DB instance by using the same tools and applications that you would use with a standalone database instance.

How Much?
- You are billed based on: DB instance hours, Storage (per GB per month), Provisioned IOPS per month, Backup Storage and Data transfer.
- Either you could use a on-demand instance and pay hourly rate or purchase reserved instances (commit to either one-year or three-year terms).

Category: Database

Amazon Redshift

What?
- Amazon Redshift is a fully managed, petabyte-scale data warehouse, designed to analyze data and run complex queries.
- Amazon Redshift supports client connections with many types of applications, including business intelligence (BI), reporting, data, and analytics tools.

Why?
- The compute and storage capacity of on-premises data warehouses are limited by the constraints of the on-premises hardware. Amazon Redshift gives you the ability to scale compute and storage independently.
- Amazon Redshift is a fully managed service, making it easy for you to run and scale analytics without having to manage your data warehouse.

When?
- You want to get real-time insights and predictive analytics on all your data across your operational databases, data lake, data warehouse, and third-party datasets.
- You want the benefit of massively parallel processing (MPP), columnar data storage, and columnar data compression.

Where?
- Amazon Redshift is a regional service, but the Amazon Redshift cluster is created in a Single AZ which consists of a leader node and one or more compute nodes.
- Clusters can also be relocated to alternative AZs without any data loss or application changes.

Who?
- Amazon Redshift service manages all of the work of setting up, operating, scaling a data warehouse, provisioning capacity, monitoring, backing up the cluster, applying patches, and upgrades to the Amazon Redshift engine.
- You can use the default database to load data and run queries on your data or you can create additional databases as needed.

How?
- As a first step, you launch a set of nodes, called an Amazon Redshift cluster. Each cluster runs an Amazon Redshift engine and contains one or more databases.
- Afterwards, you can upload your data set and then perform data analysis queries using the same SQL-based and BI tools.

How Much?
- Simply pay an hourly rate based on the chosen instance type (Reserved or On-Demand) and number of nodes in your cluster.
- When you choose on-demand pricing, you can use the pause and resume feature to suspend on-demand billing when a cluster is not in use.

Category: Database

Developer Tools

AWS CodeBuild

Build and test code

AWS CodeCommit

Store code in private Git repositories

AWS CodeDeploy

Automate code deployments

AWS CodePipeline

Release software using continuous delivery

AWS CodeStar

Quickly develop, build, and deploy applications

AWS CodeBuild

What?
- AWS CodeBuild is a fully managed continuous integration service that compiles source code, runs tests, and produces software packages that are ready to deploy.
- It provides pre-packaged build environments for popular languages and build tools such as Apache Maven, Gradle, and more.

Why?
- CodeBuild is a fully managed service so you don't have to set up, patch, and maintain the build server software yourself.
- You can integrate CodeBuild into your existing CI/CD workflow. For example, you can use CodeBuild as a worker node for your existing Jenkins server setup for distributed builds.

When?
- You want to build and test code with elastic scaling and pay only for the build time you use.
You want to immediately process each build you submit and run separate builds concurrently, without leaving your builds waiting in a queue.

Where?
- AWS CodeBuild is a regional service.
- You can plug CodeBuild into AWS CodePipeline, which automates building and testing code in CodeBuild each time you commit a change to your source repository.

Who?
- AWS CodeBuild is a fully managed service.
- You just specify the location of your source code and select settings for your build, such as the build environment to use and the build commands to run during a build.

How?
- You submit your build jobs to CodeBuild and it will create a temporary compute container of the class defined in the build project, load it with the specified runtime environment, download the source code, execute the commands configured in the project, upload the generated artifact to an S3 bucket, and then destroy the compute container.

How Much?
- You are charged for compute resources based on the duration it takes for your build to execute. The per-minute rate depends on the selected compute type.
- You may incur additional charges if your builds transfer data or use other AWS services. For example, Amazon S3 for storage.

Category: Developer Tools

AWS CodeCommit

What?
- AWS CodeCommit is a fully managed source control service to host secure and highly scalable private Git repositories. Source control (or version control) is the practice of tracking and managing changes to code.
- You can use CodeCommit to store anything from code to binaries.

Why?
- It supports repositories with no size limits; supports pull requests, the ability to review and comment on code changes; notify users about pull requests and comments; encryption at rest as well as in transit, and more.
- AWS CodeCommit stores code, binaries, and metadata in a redundant fashion with high availability.

When?
- You want to eliminate the need to operate your own source control system or to worry about scaling its infrastructure.
- You want the standard functionality of Git to seamlessly work with your existing Git-based tools. CodeCommit supports Git commands and its own AWS CLI commands and APIs.

Where?
- CodeCommit repository is a regional entity.
- AWS CodeCommit is built on highly scalable, redundant, and durable AWS services such as Amazon S3 and Amazon DynamoDB.
- You can migrate to CodeCommit from any Git-based repository.

Who?
- AWS CodeCommit is a fully managed service. It automatically scales to meet the growing needs of your project.
- You can implement workflows that include code reviews and feedback by default, and control who can make changes to specific branches.

How?
- CodeCommit provides a console for the easy creation of repositories and the listing of existing repositories and branches.
- Users can clone repositories to their computer, creating a local repo where they can make changes and then push them to the CodeCommit repository from the command line on their local machines or use a GUI-based editor.

How Much?
- CodeCommit charges are calculated based on three dimensions: Active users per month, used storage, and Git requests/month.
- Git requests include any push or pull that transmits repository objects, including a direct edit in the console.

Category: Developer Tools

AWS CodeDeploy

What?
- AWS CodeDeploy is a fully managed deployment service that automates software deployments to compute services such as Amazon EC2, AWS Lambda, AWS Fargate, Amazon ECS and your on-premises servers.
- CodeDeploy can also integrate with your existing software release process or continuous delivery toolchain (e.g., AWS CodePipeline, GitHub, Jenkins).

Why?
- AWS CodeDeploy makes it easier for you to rapidly release new features, helps you avoid downtime during application deployment, and handles the complexity of updating your applications.
- It helps you maximize your application availability by using blue/green or rolling updates with health tracking.

When?
- You want to automate application deployments, eliminating the need for error-prone manual operations, and consistently deploy your application across your development, test, and production environments.
- You want centralized control of your deployments to launch, control, and monitor your deployments.

Where?
- AWS CodeDeploy is a regional service.
- It supports Amazon S3, GitHub or Bitbucket repositories as source.
- The CodeDeploy agent is required only if you deploy to an EC2/On-Premises compute platform. The agent is not required for deployments that use the Amazon ECS or AWS Lambda compute platform.

Who?
- AWs CodeDeploy is a fully managed service.
- The service scales with your infrastructure so you can easily deploy to one instance or thousands.
- You can launch and track the status of your deployments and can also create push notifications to receive live updates about your deployments.

How?
- Get started by uploading your *Revision* (code, dependencies, AppSpec file) to a supported repository.
- CodeDeploy, deploys the Revision on one or more deployment groups which contains settings and configurations used during the deployment.

How Much?
- There is no additional charge for code deployments to Amazon EC2 instances through AWS CodeDeploy. You pay $0.02 per on-premises instance update using AWS CodeDeploy.
- You pay for any other AWS resources (e.g. S3 buckets) you may use in conjunction with CodeDeploy.

Category: Developer Tools

AWS CodePipeline

What?
- AWS CodePipeline is a continuous delivery service that automates the building, testing, and deployment of your software.
- Continuous delivery is a software development methodology where the release process is automated. Every software change is automatically built, tested, and deployed to production.

Why?
- Using AWS CodePipeline you can use pre-built plugins or your own custom plugins in any step of your release process. For example, you can pull your source code from GitHub, use your on-premises Jenkins build server, run load tests using a third-party service, or pass on deployment information to your custom operations dashboard.

When?
- You want to automate your build, test, and release processes, to increase the speed and quality of your software updates by running all new changes through a consistent set of quality checks.
- You want to model, visualize, and automate the steps required to release your software.

Where?
- AWS CodePipeline is a regional service.
- It can pull source code from AWS CodeCommit, GitHub, Amazon ECR, or Amazon S3. It can run builds and unit tests in AWS CodeBuild. It can deploy your changes using AWS CodeDeploy, AWS Elastic Beanstalk, Amazon ECS, or AWS Fargate.

Who?
- CodePipeline is a fully managed continuous delivery service. There are no servers to provision or set up.
- A pipeline can be as simple or as complex as your release process requires. You can integrate partner tools and your own custom tools into any stage of the release process to form an end-to-end continuous delivery solution.

How?
- When developers commit changes to a source repository, CodePipeline automatically detects the changes.
- Those changes are built, configured tests are run; the built code is deployed to staging servers for testing. After approval (manual or automated) it deploys the code to production instances.

How Much?
- AWS CodePipeline costs $1.00 per active pipeline per month.
- You may incur additional charges for storing and accessing your pipeline artifacts in Amazon S3 and for triggering actions from other AWS and third-party services that you connect to your pipeline.

Category: Developer Tools

AWS CodeStar

What?
- AWS CodeStar is a cloud-based service for creating, managing, and working with software development projects on AWS.
- AWS CodeStar guides you through the setup experience with project templates that set up real applications.

Why?
- AWS CodeStar provides an easy way to coordinate your day-to-day development activities through a unified user interface, reducing the need to switch between various service consoles.
- You can centrally manage activity for your CI/CD pipeline, such as code commits, builds, tests, and deployments and take remedial action.

When?
- You want to use project templates to help you quickly start developing applications for deployment on Amazon EC2, AWS Lambda, and AWS Elastic Beanstalk with support for many popular programming languages.
- You want to manage access for project owners, contributors, and viewers without manually configuring policies.

Where?
- AWS CodeStar is a regional service, but the console displays all of your development projects across all regions.
- AWS CodeStar stores your application code securely on AWS CodeCommit or on a GitHub repository.

Who?
- You select one of the available CodeStar project templates, which will automatically provision all of the needed resources.
- You can assign project team members the roles they need to access tools and resources. These permissions are applied automatically across all AWS services, so you don't need to create or manage complex IAM policies.

How?
- Start new software projects using templates (e.g. web applications, web services) for various project types and programming languages.
- After you create a project in AWS CodeStar, you can begin developing your code directly in AWS Cloud9 or use other popular IDEs such as Microsoft Visual Studio and Eclipse.

How Much?
- There is no additional charge for AWS CodeStar.
- You pay for AWS resources (e.g., EC2 instances, Lambda executions, or S3 buckets) used in your CodeStar projects.

Category: Developer Tools

Management, Monitoring, and Governance

AWS Auto Scaling

Scale your entire application on AWS

AWS Budgets

Set custom budgets and receive alerts

AWS CloudFormation

Create and manage resources with templates

AWS CloudTrail

Track user activity and API usage

Amazon CloudWatch

Monitor resources and applications

Management, Monitoring, and Governance

AWS Config

Track resource inventory and changes

AWS Cost and Usage Report

Most comprehensive set of cost and usage data

Amazon EventBridge

Serverless event bus to decouple event producers and consumers

AWS License Manager

Manage, discover, and report third-party license usage

AWS Managed Services

IT operations management for AWS

Management, Monitoring, and Governance

AWS Organizations
Central governance and management across AWS accounts

AWS Secrets Manager
Rotate, manage, and retrieve secrets throughout their lifecycle

AWS Systems Manager
Centrally manage application and resource in hybrid environments

AWS Systems Manager Parameter Store
AWS Systems Manager capability for secure, hierarchical storage for configuration data management and secrets management

AWS Trusted Advisor
Optimize performance and security

AWS Auto Scaling

What?
- AWS Auto Scaling enables you to quickly discover all of the scalable resources underlying your application and set up application scaling in minutes using built-in scaling recommendations.
- AWS Auto Scaling automatically creates all of the scaling policies and sets targets for you based on your preferences.

Why?
- It simplifies the scaling experience and enables unified scaling for multiple resources, and has predefined guidance to configure scaling.
- You can quickly see the average utilization of all of your scalable resources without having to navigate to other consoles.

When?
- You should use AWS Auto Scaling if you have an application that uses one or more scalable resources and experiences, variable load. A good example would be an e-commerce web application with ELB for distributing incoming traffic, Amazon EC2 for the compute layer, and DynamoDB for the data layer.

Where?
- AWS Auto Scaling is a regional service.
- It supports automatic scaling for Amazon EC2, Amazon EC2 Spot Fleets, Amazon ECS, Amazon DynamoDB and Amazon Aurora.

Who?
- AWS Auto Scaling scans your environment and automatically discovers the scalable cloud resources underlying your application, so you don't have to manually identify these resources.
- You can optimize for availability, for cost, or a balance of both.

How?
- With AWS Auto Scaling, you configure and manage scaling for your scalable AWS resources through a scaling plan. It lets you choose scaling strategies to define how to optimize your resource utilization.
- It creates target tracking scaling policies for all of the resources in your scaling plan, using your selected scaling strategy.

How Much?
- AWS Auto Scaling is free.
- AWS Auto Scaling is enabled by Amazon. Service fees for your application resources and Amazon CloudWatch apply.

Category: Management, Monitoring, and Governance

AWS Budgets

What?
- Using AWS Budgets, you can set a budget that alerts you when you exceed (or are forecasted to exceed) your budgeted cost or usage amount.
- You can also set alerts based on your RI or Savings Plans Utilization and Coverage using AWS Budgets.

Why?
- Businesses and organizations need to plan and set expectations around cloud costs. However, cloud agility requires you to adapt your forecasting processes and tools to match the dynamic nature of your usage.
- Budget keeps you informed of how your cost and usage progress and responds quickly when cost or usage exceeds threshold.

When?
- When you want to set custom budgets to track your cost and usage and want to be alerted by email or SNS notification when actual or forecasted cost and usage exceed your budget threshold.

Where?
- AWS Budget is a global service.
- While creating a Budget you can select specific dimensions to budget against. For example, you could select only few AWS services, Tags, Region, Linked account etc. to track as part of this budget.

Who?
- You can set Budget based on your business requirements.
- You can configure Budget Actions with IAM policies, Service Control Policies (SCPs), and target running instances.

How?
- You can get started by selecting a Budget type - Cost budget, Usage budget, Savings Plans budget, Reservation budget.
- Afterward, set budget amount and optionally scope your budget by adding dimensions of data to narrow on a set of cost information, set alert thresholds, and budget actions.

How Much?
- Budgets without actions are free. You can create two actions-enabled budgets for free.
- AWS Budgets Reports allow you to monitor the performance of your budget portfolio on a daily, weekly, or monthly basis by receiving an emailed report. Each report delivered will incur a cost of $0.01.

Category: Management, Monitoring, and Governance

AWS CloudFormation

What?
- AWS CloudFormation is a convenient provisioning mechanism for a broad range of AWS and third-party resources.
- It allows you to manage your provisioned resources in an orderly and predictable fashion by treating infrastructure as code (IaC).

Why?
- You can use a template to create, update, and delete an entire stack as a single unit, as often as you need to, instead of managing resources individually.
- You can build your own resource providers and provision third-party resources too.

When?
- You want to use a declarative way to scale your infrastructure worldwide and manage resources across all AWS accounts and regions through a single operation.
- You want a predictable, controlled approach for managing resources across your application portfolio.

Where?
- AWS CloudFormation is a regional service, but it can deploy stacks across multiple accounts and regions using StackSets.
- A CloudFormation template is stored in an Amazon S3 bucket.

Who?
- When you use AWS CloudFormation, you work with templates and stacks. You create templates to describe your AWS resources and their properties.
- Whenever you create a stack, AWS CloudFormation makes underlying service calls to AWS to provision and configure resources.

How?
- Use the AWS CloudFormation Designer or your own text editor to create or modify a CloudFormation template in JSON or YAML format that describes all the AWS resources that you need, and CloudFormation takes care of provisioning and configuring those resources (stack) for you.

How Much?
- There is no additional charge for using AWS CloudFormation, you pay for AWS resources created by it as if you had created them manually.

Category: Management, Monitoring, and Governance

AWS CloudTrail

What?
- AWS CloudTrail records actions taken by a user, role, or an AWS service as events across your AWS infrastructure.
- When activity occurs in your AWS account, that activity is recorded in a CloudTrail event. Events include actions taken in the AWS Management Console, AWS Command Line Interface, and AWS SDKs and APIs.

Why?
- Visibility into your AWS account activity is a key aspect of security and operational best practices. AWS CloudTrail monitors and records account activity, giving you control over storage, analysis, and remediation actions.
- You can use CloudTrail to view, search, download, archive, analyze, and respond to account activity across your AWS infrastructure.

When?
- You want to identify who or what took which action, what resources were acted upon, when the event occurred, and other details.
- You want to capture and consolidate user activity and API usage across AWS Regions and accounts on a single, centrally controlled platform.

Where?
- Activity information for services with regional end points (EC2, RDS etc.) is captured and processed in the same region as the action is made, and delivered to the region associated with your Amazon S3 bucket.
- You can create two types of trails - A trail that applies to all regions and a trail that applies to one region.

Who?
- CloudTrail is enabled on your AWS account when you create it.
- If you have created an organization in AWS Organizations, you can create a trail that will log all events for all AWS accounts in that organization.
- CloudTrail publishes log files multiple times an hour, about every five minutes.

How?
- You can view and search the last 90 days of events recorded by CloudTrail in the CloudTrail console or by using the AWS CLI without setting up a trail.
- For an ongoing record of activity and events in your AWS account, create a trail. A trail is a configuration that enables delivery of CloudTrail events to an Amazon S3 bucket, CloudWatch Logs, and CloudWatch Events.

How Much?
- You can deliver one copy of your ongoing management events to Amazon S3 for free by creating a trail. You are charged for data events or additional copies of management events.
- Once a CloudTrail trail is set up, Amazon S3 charges apply based on your usage.

Category: Management, Monitoring, and Governance

Amazon CloudWatch

What?
- Amazon CloudWatch allows you to collect, access, and correlate metrics, logs, and events data on a single platform from across all your AWS resources, applications, and services running on AWS and on-premises.
- It breaks down data silos to better understand the health and performance of your resources.

Why?
- Amazon CloudWatch helps you detect anomalous behavior in your environments, set alarms, visualize logs and metrics side by side, take automated actions, troubleshoot issues, and discover insights to keep your applications running smoothly.

When?
- You want to use a single platform for observability and to collect metrics for AWS and on-premises resources.
- You want to improve operational performance and resource optimization, get operational visibility and insight to derive actionable insights from logs.

Where?
- Amazon CloudWatch is a regional service.
- It supports creation of cross-account, cross-region dashboards too.
- You can also collect metrics from on-premises systems by deploying an agent.

Who?
- It natively integrates with more than 70 AWS services.
- You can create alarms based on metric value thresholds, or use alarms that can watch for anomalous metric behavior.
- You can install a unified CloudWatch agent to collect logs and metrics.

How?
- CloudWatch is basically a metrics repository. It correlates your metrics and logs to better understand the health and performance of your resources.
- You can create alarms based on metric value thresholds, or alarms for anomalous metric behavior based on ML algorithms.

How Much?
- Charges are calculated for number of Metrics (including detailed and custom metrics), APIs, Logs Ingested, Log Storage/Archival, Logs Insights Queries (analyze Log Data), Events, dashboards, alarms, Contributor Insights, Lambda Insights and Canaries.

Category: Management, Monitoring, and Governance

AWS Config

What?
- AWS Config provides a detailed view of the resources associated with your AWS account, including how they are configured, how they are related to one another, and how the configurations and their relationships have changed over time.

Why?
- AWS Config makes it easy to track your resource's configuration without the need for up-front investments and avoiding the complexity of installing and updating agents for data collection or maintaining large databases.
- This enables you to simplify compliance auditing, security analysis, change management, and operational troubleshooting.

When?
- You want to discover resources that exist in your account, record their current configuration, and capture any changes to these configurations to analyze potential security weaknesses.
- You want to assess compliance with your internal policies and regulatory standards.

Where?
- AWS Config is a regional service.
- It can collect configuration and compliance data from multiple accounts and multiple regions using an aggregator.
- It stores configuration information in an Amazon S3 bucket.

Who?
- AWS Config provides predefined rules (managed rules) and you can create custom rules backed by AWS Lambda functions.
- You can also use conformance packs (a collection of AWS Config rules and remediation actions) that can be easily deployed as a single entity in an account or across an organization in AWS Organizations.

How?
- AWS Config first discovers the supported AWS resources and generates a configuration item for each resource.
- When configuration changes occur, it records and normalizes the changes into a consistent format, and automatically evaluates the recorded configuration against the configuration you specify.

How Much?
- With AWS Config, you are charged based on the number of configuration items recorded, the number of active AWS Config rule evaluations, and the number of conformance pack evaluations in your account.
- Standard rates for Amazon S3 and Amazon SNS apply for storage and notification.

Category: Management, Monitoring, and Governance

AWS Cost and Usage Report

What?
- The AWS Cost & Usage Report (CUR) is your one-stop shop for accessing the most detailed information available about your AWS costs and usage.
- It contains AWS cost and usage data, including additional metadata about AWS services, pricing, credit, fees, taxes, discounts, cost categories, Reserved Instances, and Savings Plans.

Why?
- Dive deeper into your AWS cost and usage data, understand cost drivers at the resource-level, and identify opportunities for cost optimization.
- Organize cost and usage data with your own AWS Cost Categories and Cost Allocation tags.

When?
- You want the most comprehensive report for AWS cost and usage data at the management or member account level with hourly, daily, or monthly granularity.
- You want reports to be stored in a CSV (GZIP) format to use in analytics tools of your choice.

Where?
- AWS Cost & Usage Reports are global.
- It collects information across all regions, itemizes usage at the account or organization level by product code, usage type and operation.

Who?
- AWS updates the report files at least once a day.
- AWS builds on previous reports until the end of the billing period. AWS finalizes your reports usage charges after issuing an invoice at the end of the month.

How?
- Reports are delivered to Amazon S3 bucket, based on the time granularity you have selected during setup.
- When setting up an AWS Cost & Usage report, you can select the option to integrate with Amazon Athena, Amazon Redshift, Amazon QuickSight.

How Much?
- There is no cost for AWS Cost & Usage report.
- You pay storage cost for Amazon S3 bucket and for any other AWS resources you use (e.g., Amazon Athena, Amazon Redshift and Amazon QuickSight).

Category: Management, Monitoring, and Governance

Amazon EventBridge

What?
- EventBridge is a Serverless event bus service that enables you to create scalable event-driven applications by routing events between your own applications, third-party SaaS applications, and other AWS services via built-in integrations.
- EventBridge expands on the capabilities of CloudWatch Events.

Why?
- EventBridge ingests data from supported SaaS applications without writing custom integration code. It also reduces operational overhead as there are no servers to provision, patch, and manage and no software to install.
- EventBridge enables you to build event-driven architectures that are loosely coupled and distributed.

When?
- You want to build event-driven applications without the overhead of managing event ingestion and delivery, security, and error handling.
- You want to monitor and audit your AWS environments and respond to operational changes in your applications in real-time to prevent infrastructure vulnerabilities.

Where?
- Amazon EventBridge is a regional service.
- It also supports Global endpoints. Global endpoints allow you to fail over event ingestion automatically to a secondary region during service disruptions.

Who?
- Amazon EventBridge is a managed service.
- EventBridge automatically scales based on the number of events ingested. With EventBridge, there are no servers to provision, patch, and manage. There is no additional software to install, maintain, or operate.

How?
- EventBridge receives an event (an indicator of a change in environment) and applies a rule to route the event to a target.
- You can define a filtering rule to filter events and route events to AWS service targets and API destinations (via HTTP endpoints).

How Much?
- You are charged per million events published, which includes custom events, third-party events, and events to another bus.
- Customers may incur additional data transfer charges between regions for cross-Region invocations. There is no additional charge for global endpoints.

Category: Management, Monitoring, and Governance

AWS License Manager

What?
- AWS License Manager lets administrators create customized licensing rules that mirror the terms of their licensing agreements.
- License Manager supports tracking any software that is licensed based on virtual cores (vCPUs), physical cores, sockets, or number of machines.

Why?
- It reduces the risk of licensing overages and penalties with inventory tracking that is tied directly into AWS services.
- With rule-based controls on the consumption of licenses, administrators can set hard or soft limits on cloud deployments. Based on these limits, License Manager helps stop non-compliant server usage before it happens.

When?
- You need a built-in dashboard to provide ongoing visibility into license usage and assistance with vendor audits.
- You want to centrally distribute, activate, and track software licenses across accounts and throughout an organization.

Where?
- AWS License Manager is a regional service.
- AWS License Manager is integrated with Amazon EC2, AWS Systems Manager, AWS Organizations, AWS Service Catalog, and AWS Marketplace.

Who?
- You can manage your software licenses from software vendors centrally across AWS and your on-premises environments (using AWS Systems Manager Agent).
- Independent software vendors (ISVs) can also use AWS License Manager to easily distribute and track licenses.

How?
- You can get started by creating licensing rules. Afterwards, you attach the rules to the organization's specific AMIs, AWS CloudFormation templates, Amazon EC2 launch templates, or to applications in AWS Service Catalog.
- You can set hard or soft limits to control license usage and prevent the launch of a non-compliant instance.

How Much?
- There is no additional charge for AWS License Manager.
- You pay for AWS resources (e.g. EC2 instances) you create to run your application.

Category: Management, Monitoring, and Governance

AWS Managed Services

What?
- AWS Managed Services (AMS) operates AWS on your behalf. It monitors your AWS services 24x7x365 with proactive alarms and a complete incident management lifecycle—from response to resolution.
- AMS can take on full or partial operational responsibility for your environment during and post migration.

Why?
- AMS automates common activities, such as change requests, monitoring, patch management, security, backup services for your infrastructure.
- AMS can help augment your cloud operations skills and experience as a short term accelerator or long term solution; letting you focus on transforming your applications and business in the cloud.

When?
- You need a consistent operating model for your entire AWS fleet leveraging detective guardrails, monitoring, security, and incident management best practices to reduce your operational overhead and risk.
- You want to help your IT operators with the knowledge and resources needed to handle infrastructure and operations.

Where?
- Based on your use case, you can select an AMS Operation Plan at AWS account level. You can select an operation plan just to augment your operational capabilities, or for a full end-to-end operational solution.
- AMS can augment and optimize your operational capabilities in both new and existing AWS environments.

Who?
- AMS provides routine infrastructure operations such as patching, continuity management, security management, troubleshooting assistance for infrastructure issues, and IT management processes such as incident, change and service request management.
- AMS does not operate, access, or validate your application configurations.

How?
- After you complete onboarding, the AMS environment is available to receive requests for change (RFCs), incidents, and service requests.
- Your interaction with the AMS service revolves around the lifecycle of an application stack which is monitored and maintained by AMS by leveraging a growing library of automations, configurations, and run books.

How Much?
- AWS Managed Services offers you a pay-as-you-go approach for pricing for cloud services.
- The price of AWS Managed Services is calculated based on the number of instances and the usage fees of all other AWS services within the accounts managed by AMS.

Category: Management, Monitoring, and Governance

AWS Organizations

What?
- AWS Organizations is an account management service that enables you to consolidate multiple AWS accounts.
- You can organize the accounts in a hierarchical, tree-like structure (that you create and centrally manage) with a root at the top and organizational units (OUs) nested under the root organization.

Why?
- Using AWS Organizations, you can programmatically create new AWS accounts and allocate resources, group accounts to organize your workflows; apply policies to accounts or groups for governance, and simplify billing by using a single payment method for all of your accounts.

When?
- You want to centrally implement and enforce audit and compliance policies to ensure that users in your accounts only perform actions that meet your security and compliance requirements.
- You want to simplify costs and take advantage of quantity discounts with a single bill.

Where?
- AWS Organizations is a global service.

Who?
- You must first decide which of your AWS accounts will become the management account (formerly known as the master account). You can either create a new AWS account or select an existing one.

How?
- Select (or create) a management account to manage your organization and then create new accounts or invite existing accounts to your organization.
- Group accounts into OUs by use-case or workstream, apply Service Control Policies (SCP) and enable integrated services.

How Much?
- There is no additional charge for using AWS Organizations.
- You are charged only when you access other AWS services from the accounts in your organization.

Category: Management, Monitoring, and Governance

AWS Secrets Manager

What?
- AWS Secrets Manager is a secret management service that rotates, manages, and retrieves secrets throughout their lifecycle.
- A secret can be a password, a set of credentials such as a user name and password, an OAuth token, or other secret information that you store in an encrypted form in Secrets Manager.

Why?
- Secrets Manager enables you to replace hardcoded credentials in your code, including passwords, with an API call to Secrets Manager to retrieve the secret programmatically.
- It eliminates the investment and on-going maintenance costs of operating your own secrets management infrastructure.

When?
- You want to easily rotate secrets and enable users and applications to retrieve the secret without a code deployment.
- You need to audit and monitor secrets usage through integration with AWS logging, monitoring, and notification services such as AWS CloudTrail and Amazon CloudWatch.

Where?
- AWS Secrets Manager is a regional service.
- It allows you to replicate secrets in multiple AWS regions to support your multi-region applications and disaster recovery scenarios.

Who?
- AWS Secrets Manager is a fully managed service.
- You can attach AWS IAM permission policies to your users, groups, and roles that grant or deny access to specific secrets, and restrict management of those secrets.

How?
- You can get started by storing a secret in Secrets Manager. To retrieve secrets, you simply replace secrets in plain text in your applications with code to pull in those secrets programmatically using APIs.
- For rotation you can use a ready-to-use feature for supported AWS services or write a custom AWS Lambda function.

How Much?
- You pay for the number of secrets managed in Secrets Manager (per secret per month) and the number of Secrets Manager API calls made (per 10,000 API calls).
- A replica secret is considered a distinct secret and charged accordingly.

Category: Management, Monitoring, and Governance

AWS Systems Manager

What?
- AWS Systems Manager centralizes operational data from multiple AWS services and automates tasks across your AWS resources.
- It is comprised of capabilities (a set of tools and features) that you can use to perform operational tasks related to Operations Management, Application Management, Change Management, and Node Management.

Why?
- AWS Systems Manager provides you with a centralized and consistent way to gather operational insights and carry out routine management tasks.
- Systems Manager simplifies application and resource management; shortens the time to detect and resolve operational problems, and helps you manage your AWS resources securely at scale.

When?
- You want to automate management tasks such as collecting system inventory, applying OS patches, automating the creation of AMIs, and configuring OS and applications at scale.
- You want to group resources across different AWS services and automate operational actions across the group.

Where?
- AWS Systems Manager is a regional service.
- It supports multi-account and multi-region architectures too.

Who?
- You can install AWS Systems Manager Agent (SSM Agent) on Amazon EC2 instances, edge devices, and on-premises servers, virtual machines.
- Systems Manager provides a central place to view and manage your AWS resources, so you can have complete visibility and control over your operations.

How?
- To get started, create logical groups of resources such as applications, different layers of an application stack, or production versus development environments.
- You can then take action on each resource group depending on your operational needs.

How Much?
- Some of the System Manager features are provided at no additional charge. Following features have their own pricing dimensions - OpsCenter, AWS AppConfig, Parameter Store, On-Premises Instance Management, Distributor, Automation, Incident Manager.

Category: Management, Monitoring, and Governance

AWS Systems Manager Parameter Store

What?
- Parameter Store, a capability of AWS Systems Manager, provides secure, hierarchical storage for configuration data management and secrets management. You can store values as plain text or encrypted data.
- You can store data such as passwords, database strings, AMI IDs, and license codes as parameter values and control access.

Why?
- AWS Systems Manager Parameter Store offers a secure, scalable, hosted secrets management service with no servers to manage.
- It offers a centralized way to manage configuration data, store different logins, and reference streams.

When?
- You want to improve your security posture by separating your data from your code and
- You want to control and audit access to your parameters at granular levels.
- You want to store configuration data and encrypted strings in hierarchies and track versions.

Where?
- AWS Systems Manager Parameter Store is a regional service.
- It stores parameters reliably as Parameter Store is hosted in multiple Availability Zones in an AWS Region.

Who?
- You create a new parameter by specifying the parameter type and values.
- You can encrypt your sensitive data using your own AWS KMS key or the default key provided by AWS KMS.

How?
- You can store sensitive data as a parameter in the AWS Systems Manager Parameter Store, rather than storing it in plain text.
- Afterwards, you can reference parameters in scripts, commands, and automation workflows.

How Much?
- AWS Systems Manager Parameter Store consists of standard and advanced parameters. Standard parameters are available at no additional charge.
- When you create advanced parameters, you are charged based on the number of advanced parameters stored each month and per API interaction.

Category: Management, Monitoring, and Governance

AWS Trusted Advisor

What?
- AWS Trusted Advisor provides recommendations that help you follow AWS best practices.
- Trusted Advisor evaluates your account using checks. These checks are performed for cost optimization, performance, security, fault tolerance, and service limits.

Why?
- Trusted Advisor draws upon best practices learned from serving hundreds of thousands of AWS customers.
- The Trusted Advisor notification feature helps you stay up-to-date with your AWS resource deployment.

When?
- You want recommendations to optimize your AWS infrastructure, improve security and performance, reduce costs, and monitor service quotas.

Where?
- AWS Trusted Advisor is a global service.
- You can set up the organizational view feature to create a report for all member accounts in your AWS organization.

Who?
- AWS Trusted Advisor performs automated weekly refresh of checks for accounts with AWS Business Support, AWS Enterprise On-Ramp, and AWS Enterprise Support.
- You need to trigger these checks for accounts with AWS Developer Support and AWS Basic Support.

How?
- Trusted Advisor scans your AWS infrastructure, compares it to AWS best practices. You can use the Trusted Advisor console to review check results for your AWS account and then follow the recommended steps to fix any issues.

How Much?
- There are no additional charges for Trusted Advisor.
- AWS Basic Support and AWS Developer Support customers can access core security checks and checks for service quotas.
- AWS Business Support and AWS Enterprise Support customers can access all checks.

Category: Management, Monitoring, and Governance

Networking and Content Delivery

Amazon API Gateway

Build, deploy and manage APIs

Amazon CloudFront

Global content delivery network

AWS Direct Connect

Dedicated network connection to AWS

Amazon Route 53

Scalable DNS and Domain Name registration

Amazon VPC

Logically isolated virtual network

Amazon API Gateway

What?
- Amazon API Gateway acts as a "front door" for applications to access data, business logic, or functionality from your backend services.
- Amazon API Gateway allows developers to create, publish, maintain, monitor, and secure REST, HTTP, and WebSocket APIs.

Why?
- Amazon API Gateway provides developers with a service that handles all aspects of creating and operating robust APIs for application back ends.
- With API Gateway, you can launch new services faster and with reduced investment so you can focus on building your core business services.

When?
- You want to use a managed service to save the undifferentiated heavy lifting involved in securely and reliably running APIs.
- You want to save effort on API development and API management and generate client SDKs for a number of languages.

Where?
- Amazon API Gateway is a regional service.
- An API endpoint refers to the hostname of the API. For the REST APIs the API endpoint type can be edge-optimized, regional, or private, depending on where the majority of your API traffic originates from.

Who?
- Amazon API Gateway is a fully managed service that.
- It handles all of the tasks involved in accepting and processing concurrent API calls, including traffic management, authorization and access control, monitoring, and API version management.

How?
- You can get started by creating and publishing an API or by importing a supported API.
- Depending on the use case of your API, you can decide on a number of characteristics of your API. For example, you might want an API call to execute a Lambda function, make a database query, or call an application.

How Much?
- For HTTP and REST APIs, you pay only for the API calls you receive and the amount of data transferred out. For WebSocket APIs, you pay for messages sent and received and for the time a user/device is connected to the API.
- API Gateway caching is charged at an hourly rate based on the cache size.

Category: Networking and Content Delivery

Amazon CloudFront

What?
- Amazon CloudFront speeds up the distribution of your static and dynamic web content to your users.
- It reduces latency by delivering data through 310+ Points of Presence (300+ Edge locations and 13 regional mid-tier caches) with automated network mapping and intelligent routing.

Why?
- Compared to self-hosting, Amazon CloudFront spares you from the expense and complexity of operating a network of cache servers across multiple sites.
- It also eliminates the need to over-provision capacity in order to serve potential spikes in traffic.

When?
- You want to accelerate content delivery and APIs, stream live and on-demand video, reach viewers across the globe in milliseconds with built-in data compression, edge compute capabilities, and field-level encryption.
- You want to benefit from tight integration with other AWS Services.

Where?
- Amazon CloudFront is a global service. It serves content from an origin. An origin is the location where content is stored, and from which CloudFront gets content to serve to viewers.
- An origin can be Amazon S3 bucket, ELB, AWS Media Services or any HTTP host (including on-premises server).

Who?
- You can create a CloudFront distribution by specifying an origin and details about how to track and manage content delivery by configuring caching policy, security and logging.

How?
- When a user requests content that you are serving with CloudFront, the request is routed to the edge location that provides the lowest latency (time delay), so that content is delivered with the best possible performance. If the content is not in that edge location, CloudFront retrieves it from an origin that you have defined.

How Much?
- For on-demand pricing, CloudFront charges traffic served via data transfers out from edge locations, along with HTTP or HTTPS requests. There are no transfer fees for origin fetches from any AWS origin.
- For commitment based pricing use CloudFront Savings Bundle and Custom Pricing.

Category: Networking and Content Delivery

AWS Direct Connect

What?
- AWS Direct Connect (DX) establishes a dedicated network connection between your on-premises network and AWS. It links your internal network to a DX location over a standard Ethernet fiber-optic cable.
- With this connection in place, you can create virtual interfaces directly to the AWS Cloud, bypassing the public internet.

Why?
- The AWS Direct Connect service is the shortest path to your AWS resources.
- While in transit, your network traffic remains on the AWS global network and never touches the public internet. This reduces the chance of hitting bottlenecks or unexpected increases in latency.

When?
- You want to build hybrid applications that span AWS and on-premises networks.
- You want to ensure smooth and reliable data transfers at massive scale for large datasets and need predictable performance.

Where?
- AWS Direct Connect is a global service and available at locations worldwide.
- An AWS Direct Connect location provides access to AWS in the region with which it is associated.

Who?
- You need to make connections between the local service providers used at your on-premises locations, or work with an AWS Direct Connect Delivery Partner, to connect to AWS Direct Connect locations.
- AWS does not act as your "first mile" or "last mile" provider.

How?
- After deciding on an AWS Direct Connect location and connection size, create your connection request on the AWS management console. Download Letter of Authorization (LoA) and provide it to an APN partner and ask them to establish the connection on your behalf.

How Much?
- There are three factors that determine pricing: capacity (measured in Mbps/Gbps), port hours (measured in the time that a port is provisioned), and data transfer out (DTO) (charged per GB).
- AWS Direct Connect data transfer-in is free.

Category: Networking and Content Delivery

Amazon Route 53

What?
- Amazon Route 53 is a highly available and scalable cloud Domain Name System (DNS) web service.
- You can use Route 53 to perform four main functions in any combination: Domain registration, DNS service, Health checks, and DNS Resolver.

Why?
- The globally distributed nature of Route 53 service helps ensure a consistent ability to route your end users to your application by circumventing any internet or network-related issues.
- It is designed to automatically answer queries from the optimal location depending on network conditions.

When?
- You want to route traffic based on multiple criteria, such as endpoint health, geographic location, and latency.
- You want fine grained control for update of your DNS data using AWS IAM.
- You need to manage custom domain names for your internal AWS resources without exposing DNS data to the public Internet.

Where?
- Amazon Route 53 is a global service.
- Route 53 uses a global network of DNS servers at a series of world-wide locations to offer you high availability and increased performance.
- Route 53 can also be used with non-AWS resources.

Who?
- You can configure Hosted zones, Resource records, Health checks, Traffic Policies, Route 53 resources, and other settings for your resources.
- When you register a new domain with Route 53, AWS automatically makes Route 53 the DNS service for the domain. You can also migrate an existing domain to use Amazon Route 53 as the DNS service provider.

How?
- When Route 53 receives a DNS query for a resource in a hosted zone, it returns the IP address to the requester. For Amazon VPC, Route 53 Resolver automatically uses a Resolver on the VPC to answer DNS queries.
- It uses health checks to monitor the health and performance of your web applications, web servers, and other resources.

How Much?
- You pay a monthly charge for each hosted zone managed with Route 53.
- You incur charges for every DNS query answered by the Amazon Route 53 service.
- You pay an annual charge for each domain name registered via or transferred to Route 53.

Category: Networking and Content Delivery

Amazon VPC

What?
- Amazon Virtual Private Cloud (Amazon VPC) enables you to provision a logically isolated section of the AWS Cloud where you can launch AWS resources in a virtual network that you have defined.
- This virtual network closely resembles a traditional network that you would operate in your own data center.

Why?
- You can define your own network space, and control how your network and the resources inside your network are exposed to the Internet.
- You can also leverage more granular access to and from the Amazon EC2 instances in your virtual network.

When?
- You want to launch AWS resources in a logically isolated virtual network and spend less time setting up, managing, and validating your virtual network.
- You want to use multiple layers of security, including security groups and network access control lists.

Where?
- VPC is a regional entity and spans across all of the Availability Zones in the region.
- Each subnet must reside entirely within one Availability Zone and cannot span zones. You can launch AWS resources, such as EC2 instances, into a specific subnet.

Who?
- Your AWS resources are automatically provisioned in a ready-to-use default VPC or you can create additional VPCs.
- You can connect your VPC to other VPCs and on-premises networks.

How?
- When you create a VPC, you must specify an IPv4 CIDR block for the VPC.
- Afterwards, you can add subnets, route tables, security groups, network access control lists, an internet gateway, and other gateways as necessary.

How Much?
- There is no additional charge for using a VPC.
- There are charges for some VPC components, such as NAT gateways, Reachability Analyzer, and traffic mirroring. Usage charges for other services still apply at published rates, including data transfer charges.

Category: Networking and Content Delivery

Security, Identity, and Compliance

AWS Artifact
AWS compliance reports and agreements

AWS Certificate Manager
Provision, manage, and deploy SSL/TLS certificates

AWS CloudHSM
Managed hardware security modules in the cloud

Amazon Cognito
Federated identity management

Amazon Detective
Investigate and analyze potential security issues

Security, Identity, and Compliance

Amazon GuardDuty
Intelligent threat detection

AWS IAM
Identity and access management for AWS resources

Amazon Inspector
Automated vulnerability scanning service

AWS License Manager
Manage, discover, and report third-party license usage

Amazon Macie
Automatically discover, classify, and protect sensitive data in AWS

Security, Identity, and Compliance

AWS Shield

Managed DDoS Protection Service

AWS WAF

Web application firewall to protect web applications from attacks

AWS Artifact

What?
- AWS Artifact, is a compliance documents (also known as audit artifacts) retrieval portal for AWS' compliance documentation and AWS agreements.
- An audit artifact is a piece of evidence that demonstrates that an organization is following a documented process or meeting a specific requirement.

Why?
- You can provide the AWS audit artifacts to your auditors or regulators as evidence of AWS security controls.
- You can also use these documents as guidelines to evaluate your own cloud architecture and assess the effectiveness of your internal controls.

When?
- Use AWS Artifact Reports - to download AWS security and compliance documents, such as AWS ISO certifications, Payment Card Industry (PCI), and System and Organization Control (SOC) reports.
- Use AWS Artifact Agreements - to review and accept of AWS agreements such as the Business Associate Addendum (BAA).

Where?
- AWS Artifact is a global service.

Who?
- All AWS Accounts have access to AWS Artifact.
- Root users and IAM users with admin permissions can download all audit artifacts available to their account by agreeing to the associated terms and conditions.

How?
- AWS Artifact provides a self-service portal that provides customers with on-demand access to compliance documentation and agreements.
- You can review, accept, and manage agreements for individual accounts or for all accounts in your AWS Organizations.

How Much?
- There is no cost for using AWS Artifact.

Category: Security, Identity, and Compliance

AWS Certificate Manager (ACM)

What?
- AWS Certificate Manager (ACM) makes it easy to provision, manage, deploy, and renew SSL/TLS certificates for use with AWS services and your internal connected resources.
- SSL/TLS are industry standard protocols for encrypting network communications and establishing the identity of websites.

Why?
- AWS Certificate Manager can help you meet regulatory and compliance requirements for encryption of data in transit.
- It removes many of the time-consuming and error-prone steps to acquire an SSL/TLS certificate.

When?
- You need free public certificates for ACM-integrated services, such as Elastic Local Balancing (ELB), Amazon CloudFront, and API Gateway.
- You want to automate renewal and deployment of certificates.
- You need to create private certificates for your internal resources and manage the certificate lifecycle centrally.

Where?
- AWS Certificate Manager (ACM) is a regional service.
- Certificates generated by it can be used for ACM-integrated services which could be global such as Amazon CloudFront distribution.

Who?
- You can provide certificates for your integrated AWS services either by issuing them directly with ACM or by importing third-party certificates into the ACM management system.
- With ACM Private CA, you can create your own certificate authority (CA) hierarchy and issue certificates.

How?
- Step 1 - Request or import a TLS/SSL certificate.
- Step 2 - Validate domain ownership for your requested certificate using DNS or email validation to complete certificate issuance.
- Step 3 - Use your newly issued or imported certificates in supported AWS services.

How Much?
- Public and private certificates provisioned through ACM for use with ACM-integrated services are free.
- For AWS Certificate Manager Private Certificate Authority (CA), you pay monthly for the operation of the private CA and for the private certificates you issue.

Category: Security, Identity, and Compliance

AWS CloudHSM

What?
- AWS CloudHSM provides single-tenant, tamper-resistant hardware security modules (HSM) in your own Amazon VPC.
- An HSM is a special physical device that processes cryptographic operations and provides secure storage for cryptographic keys.

Why?
- AWS CloudHSM automates time-consuming HSM administrative tasks for you, such as hardware provisioning, software patching, high availability, and backups.
- You can scale your HSM capacity quickly by adding and removing HSMs from your cluster on-demand.

When?
- You need HSMs that comply with the U.S. Government's FIPS 140-2 Level 3 standard for cryptographic modules.
- You want to integrate with custom applications using industry-standard APIs, such as PKCS#11, Java Cryptography Extensions (JCE), and Microsoft CryptoNG (CNG) libraries.

Where?
- AWS CloudHSM is a regional service.
- It is recommended to use at least two HSMs across multiple AZs.
- You can also transfer your keys to other commercial HSM solutions to make it easy for you to migrate keys on or off of AWS.

Who?
- AWS CloudHSM is a fully managed service.
- The encryption keys that you generate and use with CloudHSM are accessible only by the HSM users that you specify. Separation of duties and role-based access control is inherent in the design of the service.

How?
- You start by creating a CloudHSM Cluster. Clusters can contain a single HSM or multiple HSMs.
- HSMs in a cluster are automatically synchronized and load-balanced. Each HSM appears as a network resource in your Amazon VPC.

How Much?
- You are charged an hourly fee for each hour (or partial hour) that an HSM is provisioned to a CloudHSM Cluster.
- A cluster with no HSMs in it is not billed; you are also not billed for automatic storage of encrypted backups.

Category: Security, Identity, and Compliance

Amazon Cognito

What?
- Amazon Cognito provides authentication, authorization, and user management for your web and mobile apps.
- Your users can sign in directly with a user name and password, or through a third party such as Facebook, Amazon, Google or Apple. The two main components of Amazon Cognito are user pools and identity pools.

Why?
- With Amazon Cognito, you can focus on creating great app experiences instead of worrying about building, securing, and scaling a solution to handle user management, authentication, and sync across devices.
- You can use Android, iOS, and JavaScript SDKs for Amazon Cognito to add user sign-up and sign-in pages to your apps.

When?
- Use User pools when you need a user directory that provides sign-up and sign-in options for your users.
- Use Identity pools when you want your users to obtain temporary AWS credentials to access AWS services, such as Amazon S3 and DynamoDB.
- You can use identity pools and user pools separately or together.

Where?
- Amazon Cognito is a regional service.
- Cognito works with external identity providers that support SAML or OpenID Connect, social identity providers (such as Facebook, Twitter, Amazon) and you can also integrate your own identity provider.

Who?
- Amazon Cognito is a fully managed service.
- Cognito exposes server-side APIs. You can create your own custom interface to Cognito by calling these APIs directly.

How?
- Once you have created a user pool for user management or an identity pool for federated identities or sync operations, you can download and integrate the AWS Mobile SDK with your app.
- Alternatively, you can call the Cognito server-side APIs directly, instead of using the SDK.

How Much?
- You pay based on your monthly active users (MAUs).
- If you have enabled advanced security features for Amazon Cognito, additional prices apply.
- Separate pricing applies for sending SMS messages for Multi-Factor Authentication (MFA) and phone number verification.

Category: Security, Identity, and Compliance

Amazon Detective

What?
- Amazon Detective automatically collects log data from your AWS resources and uses machine learning, statistical analysis, and graph theory to help you visualize and conduct faster and more efficient security investigations.
- It makes it easy to investigate, analyze, and quickly identify the root cause of potential security issues or suspicious activities.

Why?
- Amazon Detective presents a unified view of user and resource interactions over time, with all the context and details in one place to help you quickly analyze and get to the root cause of a security finding.
- Amazon Detective simplifies the investigation by consolidating disparate events into a graph model.

When?
- You want to triage security findings to decide whether the finding is a real security issue or a false positive.
- You want to investigate an incident to determine the extent of the malicious activity, its impact, and the underlying cause.

Where?
- Amazon Detective is a regional service.
- Amazon Detective is a multi-account service that aggregates data from monitored member accounts under a single master account within the same region.

Who?
- Amazon Detective automatically organizes data into a graph model and the model is continuously updated as new data becomes available.
- You don't have to organize any data or develop, configure, or tune your own queries and algorithms.
- There is no additional software to deploy or other feeds to subscribe to.

How?
- Amazon Detective collects and analyzes events from data sources, such as AWS CloudTrail, VPC Flow Logs, and Amazon GuardDuty findings, and maintains up to a year of aggregated data for analysis. From those events, it uses machine learning and visualization to create a unified, interactive view of your resource behaviors and the interactions between them.

How Much?
- Amazon Detective pricing is based on the volume of data ingested from AWS CloudTrail logs, Amazon VPC Flow Logs, and Amazon GuardDuty findings.
- You are charged per Gigabyte (GB) ingested per account/region/month.

Category: Security, Identity, and Compliance

Amazon GuardDuty

What?
- Amazon GuardDuty is a threat detection service that continuously monitors your AWS accounts and workloads for malicious activity and delivers detailed security findings for visibility and remediation.
- It analyzes your AWS account and workload event data found in AWS CloudTrail, VPC Flow Logs, and DNS Logs.

Why?
- Amazon GuardDuty delivers detailed and actionable alerts that are easy to integrate with existing event management and workflow systems with no additional software to deploy or threat intelligence feed to subscribe.
- It is fully managed with integrated threat intelligence, anomaly detection, and machine learning (ML) to identify threats.

When?
- You want to achieve organization-wide visibility into possible threats with only a few clicks and need to expose threats quickly with AWS threat intelligence, behavioural models, and third-party security feeds.
- You want access to built-in detection techniques developed, optimized and maintained for the cloud by AWS Security.

Where?
- Amazon GuardDuty is a regional service.
- Even when multiple accounts are enabled and multiple regions are used, the Amazon GuardDuty security findings remain in the same regions where the underlying data was generated.

Who?
- It supports associating and managing multiple AWS accounts from a single administrator account.
- GuardDuty findings are assigned a severity, and actions can be automated by integrating with AWS Security Hub, Amazon EventBridge, AWS Lambda, and AWS Step Functions.

How?
- GuardDuty analyzes continuous metadata streams generated from your account and network activity found in AWS CloudTrail Events, Amazon VPC Flow Logs, and DNS Logs. GuardDuty also uses integrated threat intelligence such as known malicious IP addresses, anomaly detection, and machine learning (ML) to more accurately identify threats.

How Much?
- Amazon GuardDuty charges are based on the quantity of AWS CloudTrail Events analysed (charged per one million events per month) and the volume of Amazon VPC Flow Log and DNS Log data analysed (charged per GB per month).

Category: Security, Identity, and Compliance

AWS Identity and Access Management (IAM)

What?
- AWS Identity and Access Management (IAM) provides fine-grained access control across all AWS Services. With IAM, you can specify who can access which services and resources, and under which conditions.
- With IAM policies, you manage permissions to your workforce and systems to ensure least-privilege permissions.

Why?
- You use IAM to control who is authenticated (signed in) and authorized (has permissions) to use resources.
- You can grant other people permission to administer and use resources in your AWS account without having to share your password or access key.

When?
- You want to grant different fine-grained permissions to different people for different resources.
- You need to use existing corporate identities to grant secure access to AWS resources using Identity Federation.

Where?
- IAM is a global service.
- You use IAM to control access to tasks that are performed using the AWS Management Console, the AWS Command Line Tools, or service API operations using the AWS SDKs.

Who?
- You manage access to AWS by creating policies and attaching them to IAM identities (users, groups of users, or roles) or AWS resources.
- You can create multiple IAM users under your AWS account or enable temporary access through identity federation. You can delegate access to users or AWS services to operate within your AWS account.

How?
- With IAM, you define who can access what by specifying fine-grained permissions. IAM then enforces those permissions for every request. Access is denied by default and access is granted only when permissions specify an "Allow".

How Much?
- There is no charge to use IAM.

Category: Security, Identity, and Compliance

Amazon Inspector

What?
- Amazon Inspector is an automated vulnerability management service that scans Amazon EC2 instances and container images residing in Amazon ECR for software vulnerabilities and unintended network exposure.
- It provides a highly contextualized and meaningful risk score for each finding to help you set more accurate response priorities.

Why?
- Amazon Inspector removes the operational overhead associated with deploying and configuring a vulnerability management solution.
- It includes a knowledge base of hundreds of rules mapped to common security standards and vulnerability definitions that are regularly updated by AWS security researchers.

When?
- You want to reduce mean time to remediate (MTTR) vulnerabilities and streamline workflows with Amazon EventBridge and AWS Security Hub integrations.
- You need an aggregated dashboard offering a high-level view of findings from across your environment.

Where?
- Amazon Inspector is a regional service.
- Amazon Inspector can be enabled for your entire organization.

Who?
- Amazon Inspector uses AWS Systems Manager (SSM) Agent to collect software inventory and configurations from your Amazon EC2 instances.
- Amazon Inspector automatically discovers and begins scanning your eligible resources.

How?
- After you enable Amazon Inspector scan type, Amazon Inspector immediately begins discovering and scanning all eligible resources.
- When a software vulnerability or network issue is discovered, Amazon Inspector creates a finding. A finding describes the vulnerability, the affected resource, rates the severity of it, and gives remediation guidance.

How Much?
- Monthly costs are determined by a combination of two dimensions: Amazon EC2 instances being scanned, and the total number of container images initially scanned when pushed to ECR and rescanned during a month.

Category: Security, Identity, and Compliance

AWS License Manager

What?
- AWS License Manager lets administrators create customized licensing rules that mirror the terms of their licensing agreements.
- License Manager supports tracking any software that is licensed based on virtual cores (vCPUs), physical cores, sockets, or number of machines.

Why?
- It reduces the risk of licensing overages and penalties with inventory tracking that is tied directly into AWS services.
- With rule-based controls on the consumption of licenses, administrators can set hard or soft limits on cloud deployments. Based on these limits, License Manager helps stop non-compliant server usage before it happens.

When?
- You need a built-in dashboard to provide ongoing visibility into license usage and assistance with vendor audits.
- You want to centrally distribute, activate, and track software licenses across accounts and throughout an organization.

Where?
- AWS License Manager is a regional service.
- AWS License Manager is integrated with Amazon EC2, AWS Systems Manager, AWS Organizations, AWS Service Catalog, and AWS Marketplace.

Who?
- You can manage your software licenses from software vendors centrally across AWS and your on-premises environments (using AWS Systems Manager Agent).
- Independent software vendors (ISVs) can also use AWS License Manager to easily distribute and track licenses.

How?
- You can get started by creating licensing rules. Afterwards, you attach the rules to the organization's specific AMIs, AWS CloudFormation templates, Amazon EC2 launch templates, or to applications in AWS Service Catalog.
- You can set hard or soft limits to control license usage and prevent the launch of a non-compliant instance.

How Much?
- There is no additional charge for AWS License Manager.
- You pay for AWS resources (e.g. EC2 instances) you create to run your application.

Category: Security, Identity, and Compliance

Amazon Macie

What?
- Amazon Macie is a fully managed data security and data privacy service that uses machine learning and pattern matching to help you discover, monitor, and protect sensitive data in your AWS environment.
- Amazon Macie gives you constant visibility of the data security and data privacy of your data stored in Amazon S3.

Why?
- Macie automates the discovery of sensitive data, such as personally identifiable information (PII) and financial data, to provide you with a better understanding of the data you store in Amazon S3.
- It also allows you to define your own custom sensitive data types using a regular expression (regex).

When?
- You want to automate discovery and reporting of sensitive data by creating and running sensitive data discovery jobs using different options for scheduling your data analysis, such as one-time, daily, weekly, or monthly.
- You want to get an inventory of your S3 buckets, and automatically evaluate and monitor those buckets for security and access control.

Where?
- Amazon Macie is a regional service and provides multi-account support.
- Macie also gives you the flexibility to identify sensitive data residing in other data stores by temporarily moving it to S3. For example, you can initiate Amazon RDS snapshots to Amazon S3 where it can be evaluated by Macie.

Who?
- Amazon Macie is a fully managed service.
- If Macie detects sensitive data or potential issues, it creates detailed findings for you to review and remediate as necessary.
- You can review and analyze these findings directly in Macie, or monitor and process them by using other services, applications, and systems.

How?
- Macie automatically provides an inventory of Amazon S3 buckets, including a list of unencrypted buckets, publicly accessible buckets, and buckets shared with AWS accounts outside those you have defined in AWS Organizations. Then, Macie applies ML and pattern matching techniques to the buckets you select to identify and alert you to sensitive data.

How Much?
- Cost is determined by two dimensions: You are charged based on the total number of buckets evaluated and data processed for a sensitive data discovery job (charged per GB per month).
- Apart from this, you will also incur the standard Amazon S3 charges for GET and LIST requests

Category: Security, Identity, and Compliance

AWS Shield

What?
- AWS Shield is a managed Distributed Denial of Service (DDoS) protection service that safeguards applications running on AWS.
- There are two tiers of AWS Shield - AWS Shield Standard (for protection against most common DDoS attacks) and AWS Shield Advanced (for additional protection against larger and more sophisticated attacks).

Why?
- AWS Shield provides dynamic detection and automatic inline mitigations that minimize application downtime and latency.
- You do not need any routing changes to enable protections offered by AWS Shield.

When?
- Use AWS Shield Standard for protection against common infrastructure (layer 3 and 4) attacks like SYN/UDP floods, reflection attacks.
- Use AWS Shield Advanced if you need to write customized rules with AWS WAF, get 24x7 access to the AWS Shield Response Team (SRT) for manual mitigation, and DDoS cost protection for scaling.

Where?
- AWS Shield is a global service.
- It can be used to protect your application hosted through global services (e.g. Amazon CloudFront, Amazon Route 53) and/or regional services (e.g. Amazon EC2, Elastic Load Balancing).

Who?
- AWS Shield is a managed service.
- For AWS Shield Advanced customers with Business or Enterprise support, the Shield Response Team (SRT) also applies manual mitigations for more complex and sophisticated DDoS attacks, and they can write rules for you to mitigate attacks.

How?
- AWS Shield Standard inspects incoming traffic to AWS services and applies a combination of traffic signatures, anomaly detection algorithms, and other analysis techniques to detect malicious traffic in real time.
- AWS Shield Advanced uses the health of your applications to improve responsiveness and accuracy in attack detection and mitigation.

How Much?
- AWS Shield Standard – No additional cost.
- AWS Shield Advanced – 1 year subscription commitment, $3,000 monthly fees and AWS Shield Advanced Data Transfer Out Usage Fees (per GB), in addition to standard fees on protected services (e.g. ELB, Amazon CloudFront, Amazon Route 53).

Category: Security, Identity, and Compliance

AWS WAF

What?
- AWS WAF is a web application firewall that protects web applications from attacks by allowing you to configure rules that allow, block, or monitor (count) web requests based on conditions that you define.
- These conditions include IP addresses, HTTP headers, HTTP body, URI strings, SQL injection, and cross-site scripting.

Why?
- AWS WAF protects your web applications or APIs against common web exploits and bots that may affect availability, compromise security, or consume excessive resources.
- You can quickly get started by using Managed Rules, which are managed and updated by AWS or AWS Marketplace Sellers as new issues emerge.

When?
- You want to support rules to block, or rate-limit, traffic and to inspect web requests with minimal latency impact to incoming traffic.
- You need near real-time visibility into your web traffic, which you can use to create new rules or alerts.

Where?
- When you use AWS WAF on Amazon CloudFront, your rules run in all AWS Edge Locations.
- When you use AWS WAF on regional services, such as Application Load Balancer, Amazon API Gateway, and AWS AppSync, your rules run in region.

Who?
- AWS WAF is a managed service.
- You can use Managed rules or customize rules to filter out specific traffic.

How?
- As the underlying service receives requests for your web sites, it forwards those requests to AWS WAF for inspection against your rules. Once a request meets a condition defined in your rules, AWS WAF instructs the underlying service to either block or allow the request based on the action you define.

How Much?
- AWS WAF charges are based on three dimensions: First - the number of web access control lists (web ACLs) that you create; second - the number of rules that you add per web ACL; and third - the number of web requests that you receive.

Category: Security, Identity, and Compliance

Storage

AWS Backup
Centrally manages and automates backups across AWS service

Amazon EBS
Block storage for use with EC2 instances

Amazon EFS
Managed file storage for EC2 instances

Amazon S3
Scalable object storage in the cloud

Amazon S3 Glacier
Archive storage in the cloud

Storage

AWS Snowball Edge
Edge computing, data migration, edge storage device

AWS Storage Gateway
Hybrid cloud storage service

AWS Backup

What?
- AWS Backup makes it easy to centralize and automate data protection across AWS services for compute, storage, and databases.
- Using AWS Backup, you can configure backup policies and monitor backup activities for your AWS resources in one place.

Why?
- AWS Backup removes the need for costly, custom solutions, custom scripts or manual processes by providing a fully managed, policy-based data protection solution.
- It allows you to automate and consolidate backup tasks that were previously performed service-by-service.

When?
- You need centralized console, automated backup scheduling, backup retention management, and backup monitoring and alerting.
- You want to apply Backup Plans to your AWS resources by simply tagging them.

Where?
- AWS Backup is a regional service.
- It stores backups in a backup vault - an encrypted storage location in your AWS account in a region.
- You can also configure Cross-Region and Cross-Account backups across your AWS accounts within your AWS organizations.

Who?
- AWS Backup is a fully managed service.
- You can create backup policies called Backup Plans that enable you to define your backup requirements and then apply them to the AWS resources you want backed up.

How?
- AWS Backup allows you to define a Backup Plan, a central data protection policy, and defines parameters like backup frequency and retention period.
- Once you define your data protection policies and assign AWS resources to the policies, AWS Backup automates the creation of backups and stores those backups in an encrypted backup vault.

How Much?
- Charges are calculated for: Backup storage pricing - amount of storage space your backup data consumes (GB-month)
- Restore pricing - amount of data restored for the month (per GB)
- Additional charges apply for Cross-Region data transfer and AWS Backup Audit Manager usage.

Category: Storage

Amazon Elastic Block Store (Amazon EBS)

What?
- Amazon Elastic Block Store (Amazon EBS) is a block-storage service designed for Amazon EC2.
- Once an Amazon EBS volume is attached to Amazon EC2 instance, you can create a file system on top of it, run a database, or use it for any other block storage need.

Why?
- Amazon EBS allows you to right-size your storage for performance and capacity by dynamically increasing capacity, tuning the performance, and changing the type of volumes with no downtime or performance impact.
- Data stored on an Amazon EBS volume can persist independently of the life of the instance.

When?
- Use Amazon EBS SSD-backed storage volume (io2, io2 Block Express, io1, gp3, gp2) for transactional workloads (performance depends primarily on IOPS, latency, and durability).
- Use HDD-backed storage volumes (st1 and sc1) for throughput-intensive workloads (performance depends primarily on throughput - MB/s).

Where?
- Amazon EBS volumes are placed in a specific Availability Zone (AZ) within a Region.
- Volume in an AZ can only be attached to an instance in the same AZ.
- Data stored on an Amazon EBS volume can persist independently of the life of the instance.

Who?
- Amazon EBS volumes are auto replicated within AZs. You can dynamically change the configuration of a volume attached to an instance.
- You can snapshot an Amazon EBS volume and then restore it to another AZ. Amazon EBS Snapshots (not volumes) can be copied across regions and can be shared publicly or with specific AWS accounts.

How?
- Create an Amazon EBS volume based on your application's needs and attach it to either a new or existing EC2 instance. Once attached, it will appear as a mounted device similar to any hard drive or other block device.
- Afterwards, the instance can interact with the volume as it would with a local drive, formatting it with a file system or installing applications on it.

How Much?
- Pricing for Amazon EBS Volumes is based on the amount of GB you provision, additional input/output operations per second (IOPS) and throughput beyond baseline performance.
- Amazon EBS snapshots charges are based on storage pricing (GB-month), restore pricing (GB of data retrieved) and API calls.

Category: Storage

Amazon Elastic File System (Amazon EFS)

What?
- Amazon Elastic File System (Amazon EFS) provides you with a shared file storage system without provisioning or managing storage.
- It provides highly durable and highly available shared filesystems for AWS compute services (Amazon EC2, AWS Lambda, Amazon container services - Amazon ECS, Amazon EKS, AWS Fargate) and on-premises resources.

Why?
- With Amazon EFS you don't have to worry about managing file servers or storage, updating hardware, configuring software, or performing backups.
- It supports the Network File System version 4 (NFSv4.1 and NFSv4.0) protocol, so the applications and tools that you use today work seamlessly with Amazon EFS.

When?
- You want to create a shared file system that can be accessed concurrently from multiple NFS clients.
- You want to scale your file system automatically as files are added, removed, and burst to higher throughput levels when necessary.

Where?
- Amazon EFS is a regional service.
- You can mount EFS file system to Amazon EC2 instances across region.
- You can also mount your Amazon EFS file systems on your on-premises data center servers when connected to your Amazon VPC with AWS Direct Connect or VPN.

Who?
- Amazon EFS is a fully managed service.
- You can decide to use any of the four classes offered by Amazon EFS - Amazon EFS - EFS Standard, EFS Standard–Infrequent Access (Standard-IA), EFS One Zone, and EFS One Zone–Infrequent Access (EFS One Zone-IA).

How?
- With Amazon EFS, you can create a file system, mount the file system using mount target (IP address for an NFSv4 endpoint) on supported services, and then read and write data to and from your file system.
- Once mounted, you can work with the files and directories in your file system just like you would with a local file system.

How Much?
- You pay for storage capacity, requests (read and write), and for any provisioned throughput.
- Data transfer charges are also applicable for EFS Replication.

Category: Storage

Amazon Simple Storage Service (Amazon S3)

What?
- Amazon Simple Storage Service (Amazon S3) is object storage built to store and retrieve virtually any amount of data from anywhere using a simple web service interface .
- It's a simple storage service that offers durability, availability, performance, security, and virtually unlimited scalability at very low costs.

Why?
- Amazon S3 offers scalable storage to meet fluctuating needs with 99.999999999% (11 9s) of data durability without an upfront investment.
- You want developers to build applications that make use of cloud-native storage and focus on innovation instead of figuring out how to store and manage their data.

When?
- You can use Amazon S3 for a range of use cases, such as data lakes, websites, mobile applications, backup and restore, archive, enterprise applications, IoT devices, and big data analytics.
- You need a storage that offers durability, availability, performance, security, and virtually unlimited scalability at very low costs.

Where?
- Amazon S3 stores data as objects within buckets. A bucket is created in an AWS Region and requires a globally unique name.
- With S3 Replication, you can replicate objects to one or more destination buckets across regions, across accounts.

Who?
- Upon creation, only you have access to Amazon S3 buckets that you create, and you have complete control over who has access to your data.
- You can optimize costs, organize data, and configure fine-tuned access controls to meet specific business, organizational, and compliance requirements.

How?
- You can get started by creating a bucket in a specific region and start storing objects in it. An object is composed of a file and any metadata that describes that file.
- When you store data, you assign a unique object key (to retrieve the data later), and can define access control and management options.

How Much?
- There are six Amazon S3 cost components to consider when storing and managing your data— storage pricing, request and data retrieval pricing, data transfer and transfer acceleration pricing, data management and analytics pricing, replication pricing, and the price to process your data with S3 Object Lambda.

Category: Storage

Amazon S3 Glacier

What?
- Amazon S3 Glacier is one of the many different storage classes for Amazon Simple Storage Service (Amazon S3), which is optimized for infrequently used data, or "cold data".
- S3 Glacier provides durable and extremely low-cost storage with security features for data archiving and long-term backup.

Why?
- Amazon S3 Glacier enables you to offload the administrative burdens of operating and scaling storage to AWS, so you don't have to worry about capacity planning, hardware provisioning, data replication, hardware failure detection and recovery, or time-consuming hardware migrations.

When?
- You want to store your data cost-effectively for months, years, or even decades.
- You need to use query-in-place functionality, allowing you to run powerful analytics directly on your archived data at rest.

Where?
- Amazon S3 Glacier is a regional service.
- Data is redundantly stored across multiple Availability Zones that are physically separated within an AWS Region.

Who?
- Data stored in S3 Glacier is automatically encrypted by AWS.
- For storing your data, you can choose from three storage classes optimized for different access patterns and storage duration - S3 Glacier Instant Retrieval, S3 Glacier Flexible Retrieval, S3 Glacier Deep Archive.

How?
- An archive is the base unit of storage in S3 Glacier. An archive is any object, such as a photo, video, or document that you want to store. Archives are stored in a Vault (a container for storing archives).
- After you create a vault, you can upload archives directly into the vault or use S3 lifecycle rules to transition data into it.

How Much?
- S3 Glacier charges are calculated based on monthly storage (GB-Month), number of requests (based on the request type), and data retrievals (per GB). Incoming transfers are free.
- Amazon S3 Glacier has minimum capacity charges for objects depending on the storage class you use.

Category: Storage

AWS Snowball Edge

What?
- AWS Snowball Edge is an edge computing and data transfer device with on-board storage and compute power for select AWS capabilities.
- Snowball Edge can do local processing and run edge-computing workloads in addition to transferring data between your local environment and the AWS Cloud.

Why?
- AWS Snowball Edge can operate in remote locations or harsh operating environments, such as factory floors, oil and gas rigs, mining sites, hospitals, and on moving vehicles.
- It does not have to be connected to the internet, so processing and data collection can take place within isolated operating environments.

When?
- You need to run computing in rugged, mobile, or disconnected (or intermittently connected) environments and physically transport data between your local environments and AWS without using the internet.

Where?
- AWS Snowball Edge devices are owned by AWS, and they reside at your on-premises location while they're in use.
- Snowball Edge devices are designed to be requested and used within a single AWS Region. The device may not be requested from one Region and returned to another.

Who?
- All logistics and shipping is done by Amazon.
- Once a device arrives, you connect it to your local network and unlock it for use.
- After data import job completion, an automated workflow cleans the returned device with a complete erasure.

How?
- In the AWS Snow Family console, select your preferred device, create a job with an Amazon S3 bucket, select Amazon SNS for tracking, and configure options like Amazon EC2 AMIs and a GPU.
- AWS prepares and ships the device to you, once the device arrives, use AWS OpsHub to manage the device.

How Much?
- Service fee per job - there is a one-time setup fee per job ordered.
- Per-day fee - The first ten days of onsite usage is free; you incur a fee for each additional day you keep the device.
- Committed upfront fee - If you plan to use a Snowball device for one to three years and want to pay the device fees up front.

AWS Storage Gateway

What?
- AWS Storage Gateway is a hybrid cloud storage service that connect on-premises applications to AWS storage services.
- AWS Storage Gateway consists of both cloud and on-premises components, which can be deployed in several methods based on your on-premises infrastructure needs.

Why?
- AWS Storage Gateway offers virtually unlimited cloud storage to users and applications without deploying new storage hardware.
- It provides low-latency performance by caching frequently accessed data on premises, while storing data securely and durably in AWS storage services.

When?
- You want to reduce your on-premises storage footprint and associated costs by leveraging AWS storage services.
- You want to local production or backup applications with NFS, SMB, iSCSI, or iSCSI-VTL, so you can adopt AWS Cloud storage without needing to modify your applications.

Where?
- AWS Storage Gateway is a regional service.
- The on-premises component (a virtual machine running storage gateway appliance software) can be deployed on supported platforms based on your on-premises infrastructure needs.

Who?
- AWS Storage Gateway is a fully managed service.
- You can download the on-premises component using AWS Management Console.

How?
- In the AWS Management console select the required gateway (Tape Gateway, File Gateway, Volume Gateway), download and setup the VM.
- Afterwards, activate it by connecting it to AWS Storage Gateway service and start using it for storage requirement of your applications.

How Much?
- Pricing is a combination of - Storage Pricing (capacity used in Amazon S3, Amazon FSx for Windows or Amazon EBS snapshots) and Request Pricing (data written/retrieval to AWS storage by your gateway).
- For Amazon FSx File Gateway you also pay a per hour Gateway Price.

Category: Storage

References

AWS Official Website

https://aws.amazon.com/

AWS Documentation

https://docs.aws.amazon.com/

AWS Pricing Calculator

https://calculator.aws/

AWS Management Console

https://aws.amazon.com/console/

AWS Architecture Icons

https://aws.amazon.com/architecture/icons/

Additional Resources

Check additional resources on Analogies Cloud Website

https://analogiescloud.com/

YouTube Channel	Udemy Trainings	Additional Books
Service Summary Cards in PDF Format		Drag & Drop activity to build AWS Architecture

BeSA
Become a Solutions Architect

This is a unique opportunity for you to be mentored by Amazonians to acquire skills to become a Solutions Architect.

In this free program, we will focus on technical and behavioural concepts for becoming a successful Solutions Architect, help you upskill for certifications, and provide interview coaching support for opportunities inside and outside AWS.

Check more details here:

https://become-a-solutions-architect.github.io/

A team of Amazonians will guide you to your next career step.

Printed in Great Britain
by Amazon

Upper Intermediate

Just Right

Jeremy Harmer
& Carol Lethaby

Workbook

Marshall Cavendish London • Singapore • New York

Text acknowledgements

p.6 Attitudes to Money based upon an article by Suze Orman; p.21 Surprise, based upon an article by Kathryn Flett, ©Guardian Newspapers Ltd 1997; p.31 Trainspotting based upon an article by Mark Oliver; p.35 Smiling and Frowning base upon an article from www.straightdope.com; p.46-47 Finding out about the Future, based upon information from various websites; p.52 Article based upon Six Thinking Hats by Sylvie Labelle; p.53 Based upon information from www.sixhats.com/edbio.htm; p.58 Articles based upon information from various websites; p.66 Northern Sky (Nick Drake) used by permission of Warlock Music Ltd. Available on the Nick Drake compilation A Treasury; p.69 Radio 2 website by Mick Fitzsimmons, reproduced kindly by BBC Radio 2; p.74-75 Climate Change more Dangerous than Terrorism, based upon an article by William S Kowinski; p.83 Radio Times article, reproduced kindly by The Radio Times; p.92 The Curious Incident of the Dog in the Night Time, by Mark Haddon. Used by permission of the Random House Group; p.93 Gladiator based upon original storyline from www.dreamworksfansite.com/gladiator/storyline/storyline.htm; p.101 Coughing for a Million, an article based upon various websites; p.105 Why Cat and Dog are no Longer Friends based upon an old Indian Folk Tale by Philip Sherlock.

Audio acknowledgements

p.113-114 Interview with Hag and Jeremy Harmer, reproduced kindly by Hag; p.120 Northern Sky, taken from the Nick Drake compilation A Treasury; p.122 Gladiator based upon original storyline from www.dreamworksfansite.com/gladiator/storyline/storyline.htm.

Photo acknowledgements

p.17 both ©Hag/Special Photographers Library; p.25 a ©John Foxx/Alamy, b ©Arco/WHJ Sator/Imagebroker/Alamy, c ©James Urbach/SuperStock/Alamy; p.28 top far left ©Tom Wagner/Corbis Saba, top left ©Jim McGuire/Index Stock/Alamy, centre ©Royalty Free/Corbis, top right ©gkphotography/Alamy, top far right ©Kelly Redinger/Design Pics Inc/Alamy, bottom far left ©Aflo Foto Agency/Alamy, bottom left ©ICIMAGE/Alamy, bottom centre ©Royalty Free/Corbis, bottom right ©Yavuz Arslan/Black Star/Alamy, bottom far right ©Scott Hortop/Alamy; p.31 ©Sami Sarkis/Sarkis Images/Alamy; p.41 top ©John Foxx/Alamy, centre ©Comstock Production Department/Comstock Images/Alamy, bottom ©John Foxx/Alamy; p.44 ©Bill Ross/Corbis; p.51 ©Herbie Knott/Rex Features; p.58 top to bottom ©Joe Partridge/Rex Features, ©Associated Press/Atkins Centre, ©Bobbie Bush, used with kind permission of HarperCollins, USA, ©Wilfredo Lee/Associated Press; p.61 left ©Justin Kerr/Maya Museum, centre ©C/B Productions/Corbis, right ©Joff Lee/Anthony Blake Picture Library; p.66 ©Island Records, used with kind permission of Nick Drake's estate; p.74 both ©TM & Copyright 20th Century Fox/Rex Features; p.90 1 ©Jack Hollingsworth/Alamy, 2 ©Hulton-Deutsch Collection/Corbis, 3 ©ImageSource/Alamy, 4 ©Don Hammond/Design Pics Inc./Alamy, 5 ©Royalty Free/Corbis, 6 ©MAPS.com/Corbis, 7 ©Bettmann/Corbis, 8 ©Steve Allen/Brand X Pictures/Alamy, 9 John Foxx/Alamy, 10 ©Gerhard Steiner/Corbis, 11 ©Forrest J. Ackermann Collection/Corbis; p.93 a ©Corbis Sygma, b ©Corbis Sygma, c ©Rex Features; p.101 all ©Rex Features; p.107 both ©Van Gogh Museum, used with kind permission.

© 2005 Marshall Cavendish Ltd

First published 2005 by Marshall Cavendish Ltd

Marshall Cavendish is a member of the Times Publishing Group

All rights reserved; no part of this publication may be reproduced, stored in a retrieval system, transmitted in any form, or by any means, electronic, mechanical, photocopying, recording, or otherwise, without the prior written permission of the publishers.

Marshall Cavendish ELT
119 Wardour Street
London W1F 0UW

Designed by Hart McLeod, Cambridge
Editorial development by Ocelot Publishing, Oxford, with Geneviève Talon
Illustrations by Yane Christiansen, Francis Fung

Printed and bound by Edelvives, Zaragoza, Spain

Contents

Unit 1 — 5
Winning, hoping, giving

Unit 2 — 13
Photographs

Unit 3 — 21
Wolf

Unit 4 — 28
Just for fun

Unit 5 — 35
Getting angry

Unit 6 — 44
Looking forward

Unit 7 — 51
Out of the blue

Unit 8 — 58
Food for thought

Unit 9 — 66
First impressions

Unit 10 — 74
Heavy weather

Unit 11 — 82
Famous for 15 minutes?

Unit 12 — 90
Writing and writers

Unit 13 — 98
Crime and punishment

Unit 14 — 105
Stories from the heart

Audioscript — 113

Table of phonemic symbols — 125

UNIT 1 Winning, hoping, giving

Vocabulary: money words and sayings

1 Complete this table with the appropriate words associated with money.

Verb	Noun or gerund	Person who does it
a borrow		
b	donation	
c invest		
d		lender
e loan		XXXXX
f gamble		
g	spending	
h withdraw		XXXXX
i lose		
j	winnings	
k earn		
l waste		
m		saver
n	deposit	

2 Use a word from the table in Activity 1 to replace the words in italics so that the sentences mean the same. The first one is done for you.

a I asked if *she would lend* me some money until pay day.

I asked if <u>I could borrow</u> some money <u>from her</u> until pay day.

b After winning a lot of money in the lottery, she decided to *give some away* to her favourite charity.

c He had a big family, so he needed to *put some money away* for a rainy day.

d If you *put money into* this restaurant, you won't regret it.

e Why did you *throw away* your money on that car? It's always breaking down.

f She went into the bank and *put* the cheque into her account.

g The Las Vegas casinos are full of *people betting money on their luck*. I saw one woman who won $100 on a slot machine and then put *the money she won* back into the same machine.

h She *took out* £200 from the cash machine. She immediately *blew* it on a new pair of shoes.

Reading: attitudes to money

3 Look up these expressions in the dictionary and write your own definition for each one.

a penny-pincher

b spendthrift

c on the right track

d daredevil

You can now do the quiz on page 6.

What's your attitude to money? Are you a penny-pincher, a spendthrift, a daredevil, or on the right track? Take this quiz and find out.

Circle the letter corresponding to the answer which best applies to you.

1 Saving
A When you receive a gift of money, you don't even consider saving it. Instead, you buy something extravagant.
B Every month you save as much money as you can, even when it means doing without 'luxuries' such as some new clothes, a new CD or a movie.
C You have no money in savings, you owe people money and you have no savings account.
D You save a manageable amount of money every month, and you have specific ideas about what you are going to do with it.

2 Spending
A You buy what you want, when you want it – on credit if necessary – because you just know that you'll earn the money to pay for it.
B You often put off buying the essential things you need, although you can easily afford to buy them.
C Shopping is a competitive sport for you. If a friend buys the latest watch, jacket or trainers, you have to have them, too. Your wardrobe is full of clothes you've hardly ever worn.
D You buy what you need, you aren't often tempted by what you don't need, and most importantly you understand the difference between 'need' and 'want'.

3 Bills and records
A You can't be bothered to look at records of what you spend and don't spend. Shouldn't the banks keep track of your money?
B You check all your account statements frequently, either by phone or online, to make sure your records match exactly. You keep your cash point receipts, credit card vouchers and cancelled cheques for years.
C Because you don't pay your bills on time, you often owe a late fee, and sometimes you can't even find your bills amid the clutter on your desk. You pay the minimum amount due on your credit cards.
D Your accounts are balanced and your bills are paid as soon as they come in.

4 Giving
A When it comes to giving things to people, you tend to be impulsive and you're likely to give more than you can afford.
B You give things to people but you give relatively small amounts compared to what you can afford to give.
C You repeatedly give away large amounts of money, especially for social events and raffles, even though you don't have any savings.
D Every month, you donate the same affordable amount to the causes of your choice. You've carefully budgeted your money and your time to support the causes that are important to you.

Count how many of each letter you have circled and record the number below. The biggest number will reveal your attitude to money.

A .... B .... C .... D ....

Interpreting the results

A DAREDEVIL
You are generous, true, but you are too often reckless. You identify yourself more by what you do with money than by who you are, which means that somewhere along the way you've lost a sense of your own identity.

B PENNY-PINCHER
You are a penny-pincher. You have more than enough money, but you won't spend your money. You are afraid of never having enough.

C SPENDTHRIFT
Your spending is way out of control. Sooner, rather than later, financial reality will catch up with you – with huge credit card interest or, in the worst case, bankruptcy. Wouldn't you rather put a stop to it before that happens?

D ON THE RIGHT TRACK
Congratulations! You are creating a life where people come first, then money, then things. You have learned to value who you are over what you have. You are on the right road.

4 Now look at *Interpreting the results*, upside down on page 6. What kind of attitude to money do you have, according to the quiz?

....

5 Read these pieces of advice and match them to the descriptions of the different money personalities.

a You have to start spending money to make money. Why deprive yourself of fun and friends? Learn to enjoy money more.

   Personality ....

b Continue to budget carefully and set yourself clear financial goals. This is the best way to deal with money.

   Personality ....

c If you think about the things that are really important to you, you'll find that they are not the things you bought, but the things that money can't buy. You need to be honest with yourself and who you are. Ask your friends and family to help you.

   Personality ....

d You're in a dangerous situation and now is the time to stop and think about the future. You need to think about who you are and what you want in life and start to save money.

   Personality ....

Now check your answers.

6 Use one of the words or expressions in blue from the quiz or results of the quiz to complete these sentences.

a My brother is a very .... driver. He's always having accidents.

b John .... get cash from the machine so he pays for his shopping using his credit card, even though his parents have told him only to use it in emergencies.

c She went to the .... , took out her new dress and slipped it over her head. It had been worth every penny!

d The designer shoes were .... and she couldn't afford them, so she left the store without even trying them on.

e She couldn't find her Discman .... in her bedroom.

f He bought a couple of tickets for the .... hoping that he would win a prize for his family.

g He knew he couldn't finish all his homework that night, but doing his English and mathematics was .... and he could get up early to finish the rest.

h Looking at her .... from the bank, she saw that she had been spending too much in the last month.

i Why did he find it so hard to .... what he was spending? Maybe he should start writing it all down.

j She was .... the little black dress, but it was really too expensive.

Grammar: question forms

7 The conversation on page 8 is an interview for a job in a bank. Look at these questions and write them in the right place in the interview. The first one is done for you.

a What kind of qualifications do you have?
b Now, why do you want to work at this bank?
c So, how would you feel if we offered you a job in a different branch in a different city?
d That was in the West Morley Journal, was it?
e Now, who told you about this job?
f It's not exactly a big city, is it?
g Good morning. Are you Ms Crane?
h When would you be available to start?
i And do you have any experience working in an office?
j Did you enjoy that?
k What kind of work experience do you have?

unit one 7

LINDA: (1) *Good morning. Are you Ms Crane?* ?

JENNIFER: Yes, I'm Jennifer Crane.

LINDA: Nice to meet you Jennifer. I'm Linda Ross.

JENNIFER: Nice to meet you too, Linda.

LINDA: Now first of all, can you tell me a little about your background?
(2) .... ?

JENNIFER: Well, I have eight GCSEs and three A levels.

LINDA: OK, that's good. (3) .... ?

JENNIFER: I saw the advertisement in the paper.

LINDA: Oh, yes. (4) .... ?

JENNIFER: Yes, that's right. I always read the paper.

LINDA: That's good. It's important to keep up with what's going on.
(5) .... ?

JENNIFER: Well, I've always been interested in working in finance and I'd like to stay in this town.

LINDA: I see and why do like this town so much? (6) .... ?

JENNIFER: No, it's not very big, but I think it's a very interesting place and there's a great sense of community – people really care about the town and the people who live here.

LINDA: (7) .... ?

JENNIFER: Well, I'd be very happy with that, too, but I would like to move back here and live here at some point.

LINDA: OK, that's fair enough, I think. Now, what about your experience?
(8) .... ?

JENNIFER: I've had holiday jobs as a waitress in a restaurant and I spent one summer in France on a work camp.

LINDA: Oh really? (9) .... ?

JENNIFER: Oh yes, it was great. I really felt that I was doing something worthwhile.

LINDA: (10) .... ?

JENNIFER: Well, no, not really. I help my parents with their filing, they're both self-employed.

LINDA: I'm sure they're very happy about that. (11) .... ?

JENNIFER: Right away – I can start immediately.

LINDA: That's good news for us, because we need someone right away. OK, well, we'll call you in a couple of days when we've finished interviewing. Thanks for coming in.

JENNIFER: Thank you. It was nice to meet you.

8 Look at the questions in Activity 7 and say whether they are 'yes / no', open-ended, subject questions or tag questions. Write the letter of the question in these columns.

Yes / No	Open-ended	Subject	Tag

8 unit one

Pronunciation: intonation

9 Listen to these questions on Track 1. Does the intonation rise or fall at the end? Circle your answer. The first one is done for you.

a Where have you been? — rise / (fall)
b Would you like some cake? — rise / fall
c Who told you about it? — rise / fall
d He's French, isn't he? — rise / fall
e It's a beautiful day, isn't it? — rise / fall
f Did Susan tell you she was coming over? — rise / fall
g What's the matter with her? — rise / fall
h Do you know who painted that picture? — rise / fall
i He's pretty famous, isn't he? — rise / fall
j It hasn't started raining, has it? — rise / fall

Functional language: expressing sympathy

10 Match the two parts of the dialogues.

a I just had a big argument with my boss. ....
b Jane's son has been missing lessons at school and she doesn't know what to do about it. ....
c The day before she was supposed to go on holiday, my sister broke her leg. ....
d I wanted to listen to some music last night, but our stereo's broken. ....
e Remember that Internet company we invested in? It's gone bankrupt! ....
f I was really hoping to get that job, but they gave it to someone else, who's not even as qualified as I am. ....

1 What a shame. I'm so sorry that things didn't work out for you. I know you really wanted it.
2 That's awful. I'm sorry to hear that. I know you don't like him.
3 Oh no! I'm so sorry to hear that. I hope you didn't lose a lot.
4 That's worrying. How did she find out? How is she going to persuade him to go back?
5 What a shame! Did she decide to go anyway?
6 That's a shame. What did you do instead?

Listening: a lateral joke

11 Look at the picture and choose the best interpretation of it.

a The man is a doctor and he's trying to help the woman.
b The woman is trying to ignore someone who is talking too much.
c The man is trying to persuade the woman to marry him.
d The woman is so bored that she has fallen asleep.
e Something else.

Listen to Track 2 and check your answer.

12 Listen to Track 3 and circle the correct answer.

a The man pays the woman   £5   £10   £20
b The woman pays the man   £2   £5   £20

13 Listen to Track 3 again. Are these statements *True* or *False*, according to what you hear? Write *T* or *F* in the brackets.

a The man wants to sleep. [ ]
b The woman is not interested in the game. [ ]
c The man tells her the rules of the game. [ ]
d The man makes the game more tempting for her so that she will play. [ ]
e The woman thinks that if she plays the game the man will leave her alone. [ ]
f She does not know the answer to the question he asks. [ ]
g The question she asks is more difficult than the man expected. [ ]
h The man tries to find the answer in more than one place. [ ]
i The woman knows the answer to the question she asks. [ ]

14 Complete the sentences below with words and expressions from Tracks 2 and 3.

a He just won't ....
b The guy keeps asking her questions and then, to ...., he turns to her and ...
c ... and closes her eyes to go to sleep hoping that he'll ....
d Even though she ...., he tells her the rules.
e The woman analyses the situation and .... that the only way to get some sleep is to ...
f The man is .... when he asks the first question.
g He thought this was going to be .... for him.
h 'I don't know the answer!' he whispers, ... with despair.
i The man is completely ....
j 'Please ....,' he pleads.

Writing: mind maps

15 Make a mind map of your ideas for the answer to this question:

Is it better to be a spendthrift or a penny-pincher?

Use these ideas and others that you have to help you make a mind map.

spendthrift

penny-pincher

spending money is fun
it is good to be careful with money
you don't enjoy your life if you are always counting your pennies
people who are generous have more friends
it's better to spend money wisely
penny-pinchers can become very rich
spendthrifts can get into debt easily

16 Now write your answer to this question using the outline to help you.

Introduction
Say what the topic of the discussion is.
Paragraph 2
Discuss the advantages and disadvantages of being a spendthrift.
Paragraph 3
Discuss the advantages and disadvantages of being a penny-pincher.
Conclusion
Give your opinion and conclusion based on your arguments.

Culture and language

17 Re-write the following sentences so that they reflect your own reality, views or language. Who is 'we' in each case?

a We use this gesture to indicate money.
....
....

b The name of the currency we use is 'pounds'.
....
....

c If two friends go out to dinner together they usually pay their own share.
....
....

d We don't usually ask people how much they earn as it is considered impolite.
....
....

e We have to spend a high percentage of our income on housing.
....
....

f We can change the meaning of questions depending on the intonation we use.
....
....

g We use a different structure in English for subject / agent and 'open' questions.
....
....

h In English we have special expressions to express sympathy.
....
....

Self-check

18 Put 1 to 10 in the brackets to show how difficult the following abilities are for you in English.
1 = 'I feel confident about this / I can do it', but 10 = 'I am not at all confident about this / I'm not sure I can do it'.

a Using money words and sayings [ ]
b Understanding and identifying different types of money personality [ ]
c Understanding and using different question forms [ ]
d Hearing and making the difference between rising and falling intonation in tag questions [ ]
e Expressing sympathy [ ]
f Identifying sentence stress in sentences using *so* and *such* [ ]
g Identifying and using ellipsis in spoken English [ ]
h Understanding a joke which is being told [ ]
i Discussing the best ways to spend money [ ]
j Using mind maps to help with writing [ ]

Take the items you scored from 6 to 10 and look back at the appropriate place in Unit 1 of the Student's Book.

unit one 11

Test your knowledge

19 Translate the following sentences and questions.

a I asked if she could lend me some money.

b My best friend asked to borrow some money.

c He's not stingy, is he?

d They aren't coming, are they?

e Do you know what time it is?

f Could you tell me where the bank is?

g It's such a shame that you lost your job.

h I'm so sorry that you lost your cat.

Did you have problems? If you did, go back to the relevant activity in the Student's Book to check on meaning and use.

The phonemic alphabet

20 Consult the table of phonemic symbols on page 125 and then write these words in ordinary spelling.

a /ˈpeniːˌpɪntʃə/

b /wɪðˈdrɔːəl/

c /ˈspenθrɪft/

d /ɪkˈstrævəgənt/

e /ˈrekləs/

f /ˈstɪndʒiː/

g /ˈbænˌkrʌpt/

Check your answers by listening to Track 4.

UNIT 2 Photographs

Reading: what cameras are used for

1 Read the text and write the names or numbers in the space provided.

   a   He invented speed cameras. ....

   b   He was punished for going too fast. ....

   c   the speed at which accidents are often fatal ....

   d   the percentage by which accidents fell in a UK study ....

The Big Brother Site
The place where civil liberties are put to the test

- HOME
- BIG BROTHER IS WATCHING YOU
- THE GATSOMETER: FRIEND OR FOE
- SMILE! YOU'RE ON CAMERA
- ID CARDS – WHO IS BEING PROTECTED FROM WHOM
- BBS MESSAGE BOARD
- CONTACT US

Thank you Maurice Gatsonides?

Although most people do not know who Maurice Gatsonides was, almost all of us know about his most famous invention. It is used in over 35 countries worldwide. In Britain it is sometimes called the 'Gatsometer'.

Gatsonides was a Belgian rally driver who invented the speed cameras which you can see on motorways all over Europe, the Gulf region, North and South America and the Far East. The cameras are activated either by sensors on the surface of the road or by a radar device which picks up cars as they pass. Pictures of vehicles are taken less than half a second apart, and this tells the machine exactly how fast they are travelling.

Speeding – and attempts to control it – is not a modern phenomenon. For example, when the first 'horseless carriages' were introduced in Britain in the 19th century, they were not allowed to go faster than a walking pace. A man had to walk in front of these new vehicles with a red flag in order to protect the public. But all that changed in 1896 when the maximum speed limit was increased to 14 miles per hour (22.5 kph). That was too late for Londoner Walter Arnold, however. A few months before the new law came into effect, he had been fined a shilling (five pence) for driving at 8 miles an hour (nearly 13 kph), in a 2 mph speed limit area. He was caught by a policeman on a bicycle who chased him and brought him to justice.

Speed limits are faster now, from 50 mph (80 kph) on most US freeways to 70 mph (112 kph) on British motorways. Other countries set their own limits. In Germany, for example, the top autobahn speed limit is 130 kph. Yet people still die as a result of speeding, especially in built-up areas where the difference between being hit by a car at 20 mph and 30 mph is often the difference between injury and death. Speed cameras, in towns and on the open road, are designed to stop the big toll of injury and death on our roads. As such they are, surely, uncontroversial.

Or are they?

For and against

There are people who hate speed cameras. Some go even further and set cameras on fire or cover their lenses with black paint so that they do not work.

Among the arguments against speed cameras are that:
- Motorways are safe. Speed isn't the main cause of accidents.
- When speed cameras are visible – because they are painted in bright colours – drivers slow down. But many speed cameras are nearly invisible or hidden so their only function must be to make money for the police.
- People say that speed cameras have lowered the accident rate, but this could be due instead to better road surfaces, advances in vehicle design and better security measures (which means that not so many cars are stolen by young 'joyriders').

Yet, police forces around the world reply by saying that the results of experiments are quite clear. In Britain, for example, the first UK trial of a brightly painted 'Gatso' camera at a notorious black spot saw an 80 per cent reduction in injury and accidents. In towns, speeds have been cut and anyway, they point out, anything that saves even one life must be worth the effort.

What's your view? Do you love your Gatsometers or would you like to see them all torn up and thrown away? Contact us and join the debate.

2 Match the sentence halves. The first one is done for you.

a A man with a red flag — 9
b A policeman on a bicycle
c Police authorities around the world
d Some people believe that
e Some people think that improved road safety
f Some protesters
g Speed cameras
h Speed cameras work because
i The Gatsometer
j Walter Arnold
k When a highly-visible speed camera
l You can drive faster

1 believe that speed cameras make the roads safer.
2 caught Walter Arnold driving too fast.
3 is a British 'nickname' for speed cameras.
4 is the result of better car design and road surfacing rather than speed cameras.
5 of radars or road-based sensors.
6 on German autobahns than on American freeways.
7 speed cameras which you can't see are just a way of getting money from drivers.
8 try to stop speed cameras working.
9 used to walk in front of the first cars.
10 was put at a black spot, the accident rate fell.
11 was travelling 6 mph too fast.
12 were invented by the Belgian rally driver Maurice Gatsonides.

3 Complete each blank with one word or phrase from the text. Do not change it in any way.

a The alarm was .... when the thief walked through a radar beam by mistake.

b .... were placed on the patient's skin to measure temperature and heart rate.

c When oil spills out of a ship, it remains on the .... of the water.

d A biometric scanner is a .... for checking someone's identity

e The increase in the world's temperature is a .... that cannot be denied.

f We call an area .... if there are many houses and shops there.

g Years of playing American football have taken a heavy .... on his health, which is now poor.

h We call something .... when we think that people are not likely to argue about it.

i We call young people who steal cars and then drive them very fast just for fun ....

j A .... is a place where more accidents happen than in many other places.

Functional language: asking for help

4 Put the following words in order to make up sentences and questions. Put in the correct punctuation (full stops, questions marks, capital letters). The first one is started for you.

a a / back / bit / could / couldn't / further / go / you / you
....You couldn't go
....

b a / come / it'll / minute / oh / on / only / take /
....

c a / could / do / favour / me / you
....

d a / could / do / of / photo / take / think / us / you / you /
....

e a / background / in / me / mind / mountain / of / photo / taking / the / the / with / would / you
....

f far / not / too
....

g help / just / once / out / please / this / us
....

h me / excuse
....

5 Now write the questions and sentences from Activity 4 in the correct blanks.

1 ....
....
- Yes?

2 ....
....
- That depends on what it is.

3 ....
....
- Sorry, but …

4 ....
....
- Well …

5 ....
....
- Just this once? Oh all right.

6 ....
....
- Of course, I'll just walk back a bit.

7 ....
....
- Is this OK?

8 ....
....
- I'd rather not. But OK …

Vocabulary: photography (compound nouns)

6 Complete the following sentences with the appropriate compound noun.

a When you take a photograph you look through a ....

b Most cameras have a .... which allows you to take photographs of things that are far away.

c At weddings people sometimes give their guests .... to take photos of the wedding. The guests then leave them behind so the bride and groom can have the photos printed.

d When people need passport photos, they usually go to a ....

e Politicians like being photographed with children, film stars, etc. They're always looking for a good ....

f It's difficult to talk to Joe. He's always in the .... developing his pictures.

g No one could decide which horse had won the race. It was a ...., but they gave the race to Dublin Boy.

h She's got a picture of her son in a .... by her bedside.

i I've bought a .... because I'm fed up with using film.

7 Use these words as the first part of compound nouns. Write the compound nouns in the correct blanks. The first one is started for you.

alarm ◆ birthday ◆ contact ◆ credit ◆ front ◆ greenhouse ◆ heart ◆ human ◆ race ◆ shopping ◆ steering ◆ washing ◆ windscreen

The (a) *alarm* .... that you gave me as a (b) .... nearly gave me a (c) .... last night when it woke me up. I had been watching some depressing programmes on TV. The first was about the (d) .... and how the world is literally warming up and the second was about how (e) .... were denied to many people in a country where (f) .... between black, white and Asian people were really terrible. I was really depressed. I put a fresh load of dirty clothes into the (g) .... and then went up to bed and fell asleep. I dreamt that I had gone out without putting in my (h) .... and so I couldn't see anything. For some reason I was carrying a (i) .... – the kind I normally take to the supermarket – and I got in the car. But it was raining and the (j) .... weren't working. And when I turned the (k) .... nothing happened. At that moment your present suddenly made the most frightening noise. In my dream I thought it was a police car. I woke up. For a minute I didn't know where I was. I jumped out of bed, took my (l) .... from my pocket in case I needed to buy something, and ran downstairs. By the time I opened the (m) .... I was completely awake, and feeling very foolish!

unit two 15

Grammar: the past (tenses and habits)

8 Put the correct form of the verbs in the brackets. Use *used to* or *would* when you can. The first one is done for you.

Where did we go on holiday when I was a child? Well that's easy. We (**a.** go) *used to go* on holiday to Cornwall every summer. Cornwall is in the south-west of England but we (**b.** live) .... right in the middle of the country, so it (**c.** be) .... quite a long journey. We (**d.** start) .... off at the crack of dawn, because there (**e.** not be) .... any motorways in those days. My father (**f.** drive) .... one car and my mother the other, and we (**g.** drive) .... in convoy, one car after the other. I (**h.** love) .... those journeys. There was always a sense of adventure, and you never (**i.** know) .... how long it (**j.** take) .... , nor whether one of the cars would suddenly boil over, or something else (**k.** go) .... wrong. After a few hours we (**l.** stop) .... on Dartmoor, a beautiful desolate area in the south of England. My mother (**m.** spread) .... rugs on the ground and we (**n.** have) .... a picnic – sandwiches and lettuce and bottles of ginger beer. The dogs (**o.** run around) .... and everyone (**p.** worry) .... about whether there were going to chase sheep or something. After lunch we (**q.** set off) .... again, and our cars would rattle towards the coast. Sometimes we (**r.** get) .... stuck in horrible traffic jams, but it never (**s.** seem) .... to matter. And then, as we got into Cornwall, the excitement (**t.** increase) .... Who (**u.** be) .... the first to see the sea? And although we always (**v.** see) .... it at exactly the same time from exactly the same place on the road, we (**w.** start) .... to shout and cheer when it appeared, and my father (**x.** sound) .... the horn of his car – usually the one in front – and we were there. You know I'm glad you asked me about that. I (**y.** almost forget) .... all about it.

9 Re-write the following sentences using the exact words in blue.

a Did you play football when you were young? use

....

b Did you switch off the iron? remember

....

c I didn't listen to anything my mother said. would

....

d I didn't play football when I was a kid. remember

....

e I enjoy listening to folk music. used

....

f I took a picture of my cat to school. forgot

....

g We didn't do much music in primary school. use

....

h We went round to my friend's house in the evening. would

....

i You didn't tell me to lock the back door. remind

....

j You must bring your homework tomorrow. forget

....

16 unit two

Listening: combination pictures

10 Listen to Track 5 and circle the best answer.
  a 'Hag' is short for Ian.
  b Most people call Ian James Hargreaves 'Hag'.
  c Everyone calls Ian James Hargreaves 'Hag'.
  d 'Hag' was the name Ian James Hargreaves chose for himself when he was six or seven.

11 Look at the pictures (*1* and *2*) and listen to Track 6. Write *1*, *2*, or both *1* and *2* next to the statements below.

  a Hag doesn't really like it. ....
  b It earned Hag a lot of money. ....
  c It is 'exactly what it says it is'. ....
  d It is a combination picture. ....
  e It is made by exposing the same piece of photographic paper to a number of different enlargers. ....
  f It is made out of more than one original photograph. ....
  g Many people have bought it. ....
  h People like it. ....
  i You can find it on pillowcases. ....
  j You have to be patient to make it. ....
  k You make it by printing bits of different negatives onto the same piece of paper. ....

12 Match the words and phrases with their definitions. Write the numbers in the spaces provided.

  a a storm in a teacup ....
  b abstract ....
  c blended ....
  d duvet ....
  e elements ....
  f enlargers ....
  g flattering ....
  h image ....
  i negative ....

  1 an image on film that shows dark areas as light and vice versa
  2 another word for 'picture'
  3 bits
  4 showing shapes and colours, but not real objects
  5 mixed together
  6 photographic machines to make an image bigger
  7 pleasing because people have a high opinion of you or your work
  8 something like a blanket to cover you in bed
  9 a completely exaggerated situation (like an unnecessary row)

13 Complete the following extracts with one word for each blank.
  • I have to have a (a) .... Doesn't matter whether I use it or not but it has to be there. I don't feel (b) .... without it.
  • And there we are, still sitting around a table eating meals with (c) .... because it's nice because they have a certain quality that you cannot get anywhere else except by a (d) .... (e) .... and that live (f) .... on the table has a certain essence that you do not get from a (g) ....
  • Now people will pay for that rather than buying a (h) .... file that's been created on a (i) .... and then (j) .... , no matter how well. It's not the same thing, it's a (k) .... of a (l) .... file.

  Listen to Track 7. Were you correct?

Writing: headlines (précis)

14 Complete the sentences a–j with words and phrases from the box to make headlines.

> applauds Jamaican reggae star
> by community leaders
> film cameras in latest survey
> from photofit picture
> hit by angry pop star
> into Sydney harbour
> old pictures
> statistics show sharp increase
> to avert war
> washing machine

a Careless photographer falls ....

b Cat trapped in ....

c Darkroom discovery saves ....

d Digital photography replaces ....

e Festival crowd ....

f Heart attack ....

g Murder suspect identified ....

h Photographer ....

i President in talks ....

j Race relations report attacked ....

15 Read the following stories and then complete the headlines using the words in italics (and any other words from the stories as you need). Remember, headlines should be short. The first one is done for you.

a A *cat* was *found* by his anxious owner in the *washing machine*. 'We thought we'd *lost* him,' said Mrs Halibend, 'but then we saw his face at the washing machine glass. When we opened the door he was frightened and wet but he was still alive.'

> **Lost cat found in washing machine**

b A *man* was *saved from drowning* when he fell into a freezing river. His *dog* jumped in after him and pulled him to safety.

c A *photographer* was *invited* by the president to the *White House* in Washington after he took the photograph which many people believed helped the president win the election.

d James Maudsley, the *fashion photographer*, was today *arrested* for *theft* after he allegedly stole a Ferrari *car* from one of his subjects.

e A *motorist* was *caught* by a speed camera on the M1 *motorway* doing *120 miles an hour*. Police said she must have been *mad* to be driving so fast.

f According to the local police, this year's *folk festival* was the *most peaceful* yet with *only 10 arrests*.

g 'Candlelight *is here to stay*. It's *romantic* and gives a completely different feel to everything,' he says.

18 unit two

Pronunciation: intonation clues

16 Read the following phrases and sentences and say them to yourself. Think carefully where the stress goes and what the intonation might be. Then listen to Track 8 and number the phrases and sentences in the order of the stress and intonation patterns you hear. The first one is done for you.

a I'd rather not.
b You couldn't open the window, could you?
c It's not a patch on the real thing.   [ ]
d It changed the course of history.   [ ]
e It depends what it is.   [ ]
f Did you use to play football?   [ ]
g Could you give me a hand?   [1]
h Turn off that alarm clock!   [ ]
i They used to live on a farm.   [ ]
j Of course I could.   [ ]

Culture and language

17 Are things the same or different in your country? Circle *S* or *D*.

a In British and American English, headlines in newspapers usually miss out 'small' words like *a*, *the*, *of*, etc., and they are often written in the present simple.   S / D
b In Britain and America, photographs like the one of black students at Little Rock, Arkansas in 1957 can change history.   S / D
c In British English, we often refuse to help someone by using 'polite' phrases (like *I'm afraid I can't* and *I'd rather not*) instead of just saying *no!*   S / D
d In British and American English, we use intonation to show our mood and our enthusiasm (or lack of it) when talking to people.   S / D
e More and more people in Britain now have digital cameras.   S / D
f In Britain, people used to put all their photographs in albums, but now many keep them on their computer hard disks.   S / D

Self-check

18 Read the following statements and put a tick in the correct column.

As a result of studying Unit 2 …	Yes, definitely	More or less	Not sure
I can agree to help people in English when they ask for it. I can ask people for help in English in a number of different ways.			
I can hear the difference between people sounding enthusiastic and unenthusiastic.			
I can refuse to help people in English when they ask for it.			
I can summarise a piece of writing by making headlines about it.			
I can talk about the qualities of a good photograph and choose a winner.			
I have listened to people talking about their favourite photographs and understood them.			
I have read and understood the story about William Counts' photographs at Little Rock in 1957.			
I know how to use *used to* and *would*.			
I know what a compound noun is and can use a wide variety of them.			
I know when *would* can not be used.			
I understand the difference between *forget*, *remember* and *remind* and can use them successfully.			

If you have ticked 'more or less' or 'not sure', go back to the appropriate place in the unit so that you can tick the 'yes, definitely' column.

Test your knowledge

19 Which of the following sentences are written in correct English? Put a tick (✓) or a cross (✗) in the brackets. If there is an error, correct it.

a When I was a kid I used to like listening to my father's records. [ ]
b We would live in Seattle when I was a child. [ ]
c Could you give me a favour with the washing up? [ ]
d This photograph dates back to the 1920s. [ ]
e You couldn't lend me ten pounds, could you? [ ]
f I hadn't seen the photofit picture when I met him. [ ]
g Did you remind to turn off the iron when you left home? [ ]
h I was sleeping soundly when the alarm clock woke me up. [ ]
i I didn't use to own a digital camera, but I do now. [ ]
j If you do that, there'll be trouble. [ ]

The phonemic alphabet

20 Consult the table of phonemic symbols on page 125 and then write these words in ordinary spelling.

a /ˈnjuːsˌpeɪpə/

b /ˌmʌðəˈtʌŋ/

c /ˌθrəʊəweɪ ˈkæmrə/

d /ˈwɪnskriːn ˌwaɪpə/

e /ɪtsə ˈfæktəv ˈlaɪf/

f /nɒtə ˈpætʃɒn ðəˈrɪəl ˈθɪŋ/

g /ˈmɔː ðənə ˈməʊmənt/

Check your answers by listening to Track 9.

20 unit two

UNIT 3 Wolf

Reading: surprise

1 Match the creatures with the pictures.

alien • bat • cow • crocodile • dog • galah • goat • kangaroo • koala bear • ostrich • sheep • snake • stallion • wolf • wombat

a .... [ ] b .... [ ] c .... [ ]

d .... [ ] e .... [ ] f .... [ ]

g .... [ ] h .... [ ] i .... [ ]

j .... [ ] k .... [ ] l .... [ ]

m .... [ ] n .... [ ] o .... [ ]

2 Read the text. Put a tick in the square brackets under the pictures if the creatures are mentioned.

Kathryn Flett, a journalist living and working in London, describes going home to Australia unexpectedly.

I crept up to the back door, dodging some of the animals that might give me away: Eric the goat; Wylie, Trousers and Bo, the sheep; Murdoch, Pugsley, Benny and Nellie, the dogs; and Foster, the galah; while Don Carlos, the Arab stallion, snickered and eyed me warily as I eased open the door. At the end of the corridor my mother was sitting in the kitchen with a cup of coffee. She turned and stared. And stared. And carried on staring. Then her jaw really did drop. And after that there was some running and hugging and tears, and I thought: the 13,000 miles to Australia is a very long way to go to surprise your mother, but worth it.

My 16-year-old brother tried to be cool when we collected him from school (a 30-mile drive, half on dirt roads) but I've never seen him lost for words before. Last time I saw him at my wedding, he had a pudding-basin haircut and was the same height as me. Now an achingly handsome young guy with expensive tastes in go-faster footwear, he is 5ft 11 and growing. My runaway husband wouldn't stand a chance. Indeed when Johnny threatened to kneecap him, I was touched.

One night I helped Johnny with his homework, then, armed with a torch and camera, we went wombat-hunting. The stars were so bright it was like walking underneath a floodlit colander. We disturbed kangaroos and cows (which I mistook for aliens; easily done) but wombats remained elusive. After about an hour of my brother helping me over fences and saying things like, 'if you see a snake, keep perfectly still,' we sat on a boulder for a rest. There was a rustling noise a few feet away. I aimed the lens vaguely in the right direction and shot.

'Betcha goddit!' said Johnny. While I betted that I hadn't, we ambled back to the house via the dam, where tiny wombat footprints could be seen in the mud.

'Find any?' asked my mother.

'No. But we did get abducted by cows,' I said. Johnny giggled as we both slumped in front of the television and our mother cooked us dinner, which I love because it happens so rarely.

I was in Australia for nine days and it wasn't long enough. Most of the time I mooched around looking miserable about my divorce and then apologising for it. I didn't want to talk about it. I just wanted my dinner cooked and my washing done and to stay up late watching bad telly.

While I was waiting for the 8.15 from Golburn station to take me to Sydney to catch a plane to Bali, to catch a plane to Kuala Lumpur, to catch a plane to London, our friend took a picture of Mummy, Johnny and I beneath the station clock. At Sydney airport I had time to kill so I got the film processed. The group shot under the clock was delightful. God knows when we'll have another one done, but I know that Johnny will be even taller.

Incidentally, there was no wombat, just aliens.

unit three 21

3 Answer the following questions with 'yes' or 'no', and say how you know.

a Was Kathryn's mother surprised to see her? How do you know?

b Was Kathryn's brother surprised to see her? How do you know?

c Was Kathryn's husband with her? How do you know?

d Had Kathryn's brother changed since she had last seen him? How do you know?

e Was it a dark night when they went out wombat-hunting? How do you know?

f Did Kathryn and her brother take a gun? How do you know?

g Did Kathryn take any successful photographs? How do you know?

h Was Kathryn pleased to be at home? How do you know?

i Did Kathryn get a direct flight back to London? How do you know?

4 Read the sentences (a–n) and then write the number of the correct definition (1–17) of the words in blue at the end of each sentence. The first one is done for you.

a I crept up to the back door, dodging some animals that might give me away.   8
b Then her jaw really did drop.
c And after that there was some running and hugging and tears.
d I've never seen him lost for words before.
e He had a pudding-basin haircut.
f My runaway husband wouldn't stand a chance.
g Indeed when Johnny threatened to kneecap him, I was touched.
h It was like walking underneath a (1) floodlit (2) colander.
i Wombats remained elusive.
j I aimed the lens vaguely in the right direction and shot.
k We did get abducted by cows.
l Johnny giggled as we both slumped in front of the television.
m I mooched around looking miserable.
n I had time to kill.

1 a metal bowl with a lot of holes used for drying salad, spaghetti, etc.
2 difficult to find
3 embracing
4 half lay, half sat
5 her mouth opened in surprise
6 laughed quickly in a high voice
7 moved around with no real purpose
8 moved in a 'secret' quiet way
9 nothing much to do for a period
10 old-fashioned like an upside-down cooking dish
11 shoot someone in the knees as a punishment
12 survive / be successful
13 taken away, kidnapped
14 tell someone that I was there even though it was a secret
15 took a photograph
16 unable to speak because of surprise
17 with a bright light shone on it

Vocabulary: animal metaphors

5 Find words or phrases associated with animals in the word chain. The first one is done for you.

```
barkbleatcluckfromthehorse'smouthhisshowl
purrroarsmellaratsqueal
```

6 Replace the words and phrases in blue with words and phrases which are based on the animals in the box. The first one is done for you.

bird ◆ cat ◆ cock ◆ dog ◆ fish ◆ mouse ◆
pig ◆ rat ◆ sheep ◆ turkey

a Don't be so unpleasant! *Don't be so catty!*

b Everyone admires the way he is so determined.

c I've made a mess of this.

d OK, OK, there's no need to get so irritated and angry with me.

e Look at her. She's such a frightened little creature.

f The new play we saw last night was a complete disaster.

g This whole situation is very suspicious.

h Tidy this place up. It's a real mess.

i What have you done to this book you borrowed from me? It's all messed up.

j If we're going to visit your mother, we might as well see your aunt as well. It's always worth doing two things at the same time if that's possible.

k Why did you tell that secret? Now I'm in real trouble.

l There's no need to use that guilty smile. We know how you won the competition!

m Stop asking me to say how wonderful you are. You might not like what you hear!

Grammar: adverbs and adverbial phrases

7 Read the sentences. Are the words in blue adjectives or adverbs? Put *Adj* (adjective) or *Adv* (adverb) in the brackets.

a I've just bought a very fast [ ] car. It runs beautifully [ ].
b It is possible [ ] that wolves will come back to Britain. That would be fantastic [ ].
c It was a rough [ ] crossing but our little [ ] boat survived it well [ ].
d People think that wolves are dangerous [ ], but in fact it's the wolves themselves that are in deadly [ ] danger.
e When I met him he was walking tall [ ], proud [ ] of what he had achieved.
f Wolves can run incredibly fast [ ].
g You haven't been around much lately [ ]. That's been hard [ ] for me.
h Your decision is just plain wrong [ ] as far as I am concerned.

8 Put the adverbs and adverbial phrases from the box in the blanks. Use each of them once only.

always ◆ badly ◆ dangerously ◆ for a few months
happily ◆ hard ◆ long and hard ◆ loudly ◆
purposefully ◆ sadistically ◆ sometimes ◆ tidily ◆
vertically ◆ very much

My friend likes living (a) .... After working (b) .... in a bank (c) .... – it was his first job – he decided he wanted to do something else, so he thought (d) .... and came up with the idea of Cybil the snake – a puppet he made, and which he does theatre shows with. He holds Cybil up (e) .... and (f) .... treats 'her' very (g) .... in 'their' performances. The audience (h) .... reacts very (i) .... and starts shouting (j) .... They seem to almost (k) .... forget that Cybil is made of material and isn't really alive at all! But it doesn't worry him (l) .... He puts his things away (m) .... at the end of each show and goes home (n) .... to plan the next stage of his life.

unit three 23

Functional language: warnings and threats

9 Put the following words and punctuation in order to make warnings and threats. Put the number of the correct picture in the brackets. The first one is started for you.

a cables / : / Danger / electrical / . / overhead

   Danger: overhead electrical cables. [6]

b again / and / angry / Do / ! / get / I'll / really / that

   Do that again and I'll get really angry! [1]

c asking / again / borrow / Don't / ever / . / laptop / me / my / without

   Don't ever borrow my laptop again without asking me. [8]

d again / and / book / Do / Drive / . / ? / fast / I'll / that / understand / you / you

   Drive that fast again and I'll book you, do you understand? [4]

e get / I / . / I / if / on / that / was / wouldn't / you

   I wouldn't get on that if I was you. [2]

f again / come / . / here / I'm / in / not / to / warning / you

   I'm warning you, not to come in here again. [5]

g don't / finish / getting / going / you / If / . / , / I'm / immediately / leave / ready / to / without / you

   If you don't finish getting ready immediately, I'm going to leave without you. [3]

h a / , / above / ! / head / out / right / snake / there's / Watch / your

   Watch out, there's a snake right above your head! [7]

Listening: animals in danger

10 Look at the pictures. What are these animals and where are they found in the world?

a   b   c

11 Listen to Track 10 and answer these questions.

a What does the World Conservation Monitoring Centre do?

1 ....
2 ....
3 ....
4 ....

b What are the three categories of endangered animals?

.... [ ]
.... [ ]
.... [ ]

c Which category is in most danger? Which is in least danger? Write *1*, *2* and *3* in the brackets above.

12 Listen to Track 11 and write *E* (elephant), *R* (rhino) or *O* (orang-utan) on the line next to the places where the animals are found.

Africa
....
Kenya ....
Zimbabwe ....
Namibia ....
South Africa ....
Borneo ....
Sumatra ....

13 Listen to Track 11 again and complete the interviewer's notes.

14 Complete the sentences below with words and expressions from Tracks 10 and 11.

a Well scientifically we consider three things: the .... of mature animals that exist, the .... in the species over the last ten years, and the .... reductions in numbers for the next ten years.

b Sadly, it is mostly because of human beings .... these animals that they are in danger. In the case of the black rhinoceros, for example, it has been .... for its horn, which is used in a lot of traditional medicines as well as for ....

c As for the African elephant, this species is endangered because of .... , as more and more of their territory is being taken over by humans who are .... for more land to .... the increasing populations.

d There is .... an international .... on killing elephants, but it still goes on illegally.

e Huge areas of forest are being cleared and consequently these .... animals have nowhere to live.

Name of animal	Category	Number left	Reasons it is in danger

unit three 25

Writing: linking words and phrases

15 Complete the following text with words and phrases from the box.

> as a result ◆ and furthermore ◆
> however ◆ in conclusion ◆
> in contrast ◆ moreover ◆
> not only that, but ◆
> on the other hand

A neighbour of mine has a considerable fear of spiders, and (a) .... she doesn't like travelling, in case she suddenly finds herself face to face with one.
(b) .... , her arachnophobia is so bad that she asks other people to check the bath before she goes into the bathroom.
Such phobias are not that uncommon, (c) .... they can be very debilitating, causing people a lot of inconvenience – and serious panic attacks. (d) .... people who have such panic attacks can suffer a big loss of self-esteem.
(e) .... , help is at hand in the form of various forms of counselling and discussion. (f) .... some therapists make sufferers confront their fears head on. If they can survive controlled exposure to the animals they have phobias about, their theory goes, they will be cured.
(g) .... , they may be scarred for life!
(h) .... , many people have phobias about animals, but they can be helped to overcome them.

Pronunciation

16 Listen to the sentences on Track 12. Are they more like warnings or threats? Write *W* or *T* in the brackets.

a Be careful. [ ]
b I would think very carefully before I did that again. [ ]
c I wouldn't touch that computer if I was you. [ ]
d I'm telling you not to do that. [ ]
e If you don't get ready soon you'll miss the film. [ ]
f If you shout at my dog you'll live to regret it. [ ]
g Stop that right now. [ ]
h Treat him properly or else you'll be in trouble. [ ]

What helped you decide in each case?

Culture and language

17 Re-write the following sentences so that they reflect your own reality, views or language. Who is 'we' in each case?

a We have a lot of stories about the people who 'built' or 'formed' our country.
....

b We have a wide literature of books written especially for children.
....

c We modify nouns by using adjectives.
....

d We modify verbs by using adverbs of manner, time, place, etc.
....

e We often read aloud to children at school and at home before they go to bed.
....

f We often use imperatives ('Be careful!' 'Don't shout!') when we want to warn somebody or threaten them with something.
....

g We use *wolf* in a lot of sayings / metaphors. *Wolf* always refers to something bad.
....

h We use a lot of animal metaphors.
....

i We use stress to emphasise different parts of sentences so that they have different meanings.
....

j We used to have a lot of wolves, but we destroyed most of them so there aren't many left now.
....

Self-check

18 Put 1 to 10 in the brackets to show how difficult the following abilities are for you in English. 1 = 'I feel confident about this / I can do it', but 10 = 'I am not at all confident about this / I'm not sure I can do it'.

- a Changing adjectives into adverbs and vice versa. [ ]
- b Following a story when it is read out loud in English. [ ]
- c Understanding a writer's point of view (in this case in the text about wolves). [ ]
- d Understanding the difference between *hear*, *listen* and *listen to* and being able to use them effectively. [ ]
- e Using a variety of adverbs (time, manner, place, etc.) to modify verbs. [ ]
- f Using different adverbs in the right places in sentences. [ ]
- g Using different constructions (imperatives, conditional sentences, etc.) to make threats. [ ]
- h Using idiom and metaphor in English, especially concerned with animals. [ ]
- i Using linking words like *moreover* and *therefore* in written English. [ ]
- j Warning people in English in a variety of situations. [ ]

Take the items you scored from 6 to 10 and look back at the appropriate place in Unit 3 of the Student's Book.

Test your knowledge

19 Translate the following sentences and questions.

a A man with an extremely loud voice was shouting at me.

b You should be ashamed of yourself!

c If you behave like that you'll be in serious trouble.

d Watch out! There's a wolf behind you.

e I like looking at animals in the zoo and as a result some people are very critical of me.

f I wouldn't say that again if I was you.

g They're fantastically funny.

h I'm earning enough to keep the wolf from the door anyway.

Did you have problems? If you did, go back to the relevant activity in the Student's Book to check on meaning and use.

The phonemic alphabet

20 Consult the table of phonemic symbols on page 125 and then write these words in ordinary spelling.

a /sə'dɪstɪkliː/

b /'dɒgɪəd/

c /'səʊʃəbəl/

d /ə'wʊlf ɪn ʃiːps 'kləʊðɪŋ/

e /ðeɪə 'fɪʃɪŋ fə 'kɒmplɪmənts/

f /aɪ 'smelə'ræt/

g /'həʊldʒə 'hɔːsɪz/

Check your answers by listening to Track 13.

unit three 27

UNIT 4 Just for fun

Listening: leisure centre

1 Look at these pictures of leisure centre activities and tick the ones that you would expect to see at a leisure centre.

ballet □ □   aerobics □ □   gym □ □   swimming pool □ □   tennis □ □

judo □ □   indoor soccer □ □   basketball □ □   indoor climbing wall □ □   ice-skating □ □

Now listen to Track 14 and tick the activities which are mentioned.

2 Listen to Track 14 again. Match the sentence halves. Write the correct numbers in the spaces provided.

a To become a member of High Park Leisure Centre, you should ....
b The High Park Leisure Centre is open ....
c If you are under 13 ....
d If you pay £5 for the day, you can ....
e You can play tennis any time ....
f A ballet class lasts ....
g If you go online, you can ....
h By pressing 1, you will ....

1 every day of the week.
2 for ten weeks.
3 hear the information again.
4 push the number 2 button on the phone.
5 see what classes are available.
6 there is a free court available.
7 use the swimming pool and the gym.
8 you may not skate alone.

28 unit four

3 Match these words (*a–h*) from the listening passage with a synonym or definition (*1–8*).

a leisure ....
b facilities ....
c take advantage of ....
d concludes ....
e accompanied by ....
f courts ....
g matches ....
h consult ....

1 rooms, equipment, etc. that you can use
2 competitions, games
3 with
4 places to play tennis, badminton or squash
5 look at
6 free time
7 ends, finishes
8 use

4 Now use one of the words or expressions in the sentences below.

a I'm going to .... the dictionary to find the meaning of this word.
b We need to .... this good weather and finish painting the outside of the house, before it starts to rain.
c This piece .... our concert for tonight. We hope you enjoyed it and look forward to seeing you again.
d The players came out onto the .... and the crowd started to cheer. They took out their rackets and began to warm up.
e The famous actor was seen at the party .... an unknown woman and their photo was on the front page of the tabloid newspapers the next day.
f She doesn't know what to do with her life – I think she has too much .... time on her hands and she needs to get a job.
g The new school has state-of-the-art .... including a new science lab and a huge computer room.
h I just play tennis for fun now, I don't take part in .... any more.

Vocabulary: hobbies and activities

5 Re-arrange the letters to make the names of hobbies and people who do them.

a e-f-l-o-r-w   a-a-g-g-i-n-n-r-r
....
b a-m-i-n-n-o-u-t   b-c-g-i-i-l-m-n
....
c a-m-p-s-t   c-c-e-l-l-o-o-r-t
....
d d-e-i-k-r-s-v-y
....
e a-e-g-l-n-r
....
f e-h-l-o-o-p-r-t
....
g b-e-e   e-e-e-k-p-r
....
h d-e-l-m-o   a-e-k-m-r
....
i a-e-r-t-w   e-i-k-r-s
....
j a-i-n-r-t   e-o-p-r-s-t-t
....
k a-b-c-s-u   d-e-i-r-v
....
l a-a-b-d-e-e-k-o-r-r-s-t
....
m a-b-d-e-n-o-o-r-r-s-w
....
n b-d-i-r   a-c-e-h-r-t-w
....

6 Complete the following sentences with one word for each blank.

a Sometimes I think I'm addicted .... chocolate.
b I'm really keen .... mountaineering.
c I'm absolutely mad .... swimming.
d I'm not too crazy .... listening to his music, to be honest.
e I'm extremely interested .... the history of modern China.
f I am completely obsessed .... that novel I read on holiday last year.
g I'm really .... bowling at the new bowling alley near our house.
h I get a kick .... going to the gym.
i Jazz doesn't do much ....
j Reality TV doesn't really turn ....

unit four 29

Grammar: present perfect continuous (and simple)

7 What have these people been doing? Read the descriptions and write what you think has been happening. The first one is done for you.

a Two boys are climbing out of a pool. They are dripping with water.

The boys have been swimming.

b Mark is holding a cloth and a can of window cleaner and standing back from a shiny window.

....

c The ground is covered with snow. The sun is shining and the sky is clear.

....

d Tom has just come off the dance floor. He's absolutely exhausted.

....

e Jane is wearing oven gloves and carrying a steaming dish in each hand to the table. Her friends are sitting at the table talking and waiting to eat.

....

f Mr and Mrs Thomas are walking into their home carrying carrier bags and boxes of things that they have bought at department stores.

....

g Megan is standing in front of a painting – she is holding a paintbrush, and her clothes are covered in paint.

....

h My dog is covered in mud and he's standing in a hole in the garden. There's mud all around him.

....

8 Choose the correct word or phrase from the box to complete the following dialogue.

> noticed ◆ lost ◆ haven't done ◆ been working ◆ ever tried ◆ used ◆ ever been ◆ haven't ◆ n't had ◆ have found

IAIN: Have you (a) .... karate?

DENNIS: No, I'm afraid I (b) ....

IAIN: What about kick boxing?

DENNIS: No, I'm afraid I (c) .... that either.

IAIN: There is a martial arts centre round the corner. Have you (d) .... there? My girlfriend and I have (e) .... it lots of times.

DENNIS: No I haven't (f) .... it. Anyway, recently I have (g) .... enough time to do that kind of thing. I've (h) .... very hard.

IAIN: Yes, I know what you mean. Our jobs are very stressful, too, but we (i) .... it relaxing. You really should come too.

DENNIS: No thanks. I seem to have (j) .... my shorts. And actually I prefer to watch a video to relax.

30 unit four

Reading: train-spotting

9 Match the best heading (*a–g*) to the paragraph (*1–7*) that it describes.

a The necessary equipment ....
b Finding a hobby that you love ....
c Famous train-spotters ....
d Train-spotting in the USA ....
e What is train-spotting? ....
f The book, the film and the pastime ....
g The origins of the hobby ....

Train-spotting – *the hobby*

Looking at the practice that has NOTHING to do with the movie.

1
Many people around the world have seen Danny Boyle's movie *Trainspotting** based on Irvine Welsh's novel of the same name and starring Ewan McGregor, but how many of us can really claim to know what train-spotting is all about? Now this is not considered the coolest hobby in town and the word 'train-spotter' in Britain has become synonymous with 'geek' or 'nerd', but is this reputation really deserved?

2
First of all, let's define train-spotting. There are said to be some 100,000 train-spotters in the UK. What do they do? Well, exactly as the title suggests, they spot trains, that is, they stand in train stations, look at the serial numbers of the trains that leave and arrive and write them down. The ultimate aim is to have seen every train in the country.

3
Being obsessed with railways and trains is not a modern hobby and dates back to 1804 when Richard Trevithick built the first steam locomotive, which hauled a load of ten tons of iron, 70 men and five wagons along a nine-mile stretch of track in two hours. As the number of trains grew and they got faster and faster, so did the interest in them grow. Is this any stranger than people who love cars?

4
So, what do you need to be a train-spotter? Well, it's a wonderfully inexpensive pastime – all you really need is a pen or pencil and a notebook to write down the train numbers. Other optional equipment includes hot tea in a thermos flask, a camera and some sandwiches for those long afternoons spent on train platforms when you don't want to risk the delights of railway station food. The modern train-spotter may also carry binoculars and a video camera, but for the purists these are unnecessary.

5
It's interesting to note that despite the stigma of train-spotting, there have been famous railway enthusiasts in history, such as the poet WH Auden, the comedian Michael Palin and, of course, Alfred Hitchcock, who was obsessed with trains and featured them regularly in his films, especially *The 39 Steps*. There is evidence, too, that being a train-spotter is not necessarily a peculiarly British hobby.

6
One glance at the array of US train sites should be enough to convince you that transatlantic train-spotters are alive and well. In America, they try to call rail enthusiasts 'trainfans' and talk of 'trainfanning'. Don't let this fool you – these people are train-spotters and there are a lot of them. Each month, two million pages are visited on the website TrainWeb.org. And you may also be interested in the distant, more athletic relative of the trainfanner – those daredevil types who inhabit the illegal world of freight train-hopping.

7
So call them 'nerds' or 'geeks', but they are here to stay and this is certainly not a hobby that is violent or dangerous in any way, nor does it cause any kind of damage to the environment. What do you think is healthier – sitting in front of a TV screen and criticising those who do something that doesn't interest you? Or going out and finding and following your passion whatever that happens to be? I know what I think.

*Train-spotting can be written with or without a hyphen.

10 Are these statements *True* or *False* according to the text? Write *T* or *F* in the brackets.

a There is a famous movie which is about the hobby. [ ]
b Train-spotting is a very cool hobby. [ ]
c The objective of train-spotting is to see as many trains as possible. [ ]
d The author thinks it is strange to be interested in cars. [ ]
e It does not cost a lot of money to be a train-spotter. [ ]
f All train-spotters use binoculars. [ ]
g There are no images of trains in the movie *The 39 Steps*. [ ]
h In the USA, train-spotters have a different name. [ ]
i It is against the law to get on and ride a goods train. [ ]
j The author thinks train-spotting is a worthless hobby. [ ]

11 Look at the way the following words and phrases are used in the text and then write them in the correct gaps.

> daredevil ◆ freight ◆ obsessed with ◆ stigma ◆ synonymous with ◆ thermos flask ◆ transatlantic ◆ ultimate

a He takes a lot of risks in his car. He's a .... when it comes to driving.
b She took some coffee with her in a .... and it was still hot when she drank it at lunchtime.
c In some situations, 'light' is .... 'not heavy', but sometimes it can mean the opposite of 'dark'.
d He doesn't know whether he can re-sit his exam: he is waiting for the school's .... decision.
e She watches movies all the time and talks about them. She is .... cinema.
f There are no passengers allowed on that ship. It's for .... only.
g There is a .... attached to being an ex-convict even though that person has been punished and has paid their debt to society.
h I have a meeting in New York next week so I'm taking a .... flight on Sunday.

Functional language: asking for clarification / buying 'thinking time'

12 Complete the dialogue with the words and phrases in the box. The first one is done for you.

> Could you repeat that? (x 2) ◆
> Do you know what I mean? ◆ Look ◆ Mmm ◆
> Sorry ◆ sorry to interrupt ◆ what-do-you-call-it ◆
> you know

A: Did you see that?
B: (a) *Sorry?*
A: The 4.16 from Liverpool.
B: (b) .... I don't know what you're talking about.
A: The 4.16 from Liverpool. It's a class 6J Swindon diesel.
B: What so special about that?
A: What's so special … (c) .... , where do I start?
B: I don't know. I can't see anything special about the (d) .... …
A: Swindon 6J diesel. There were only 26 built seven years ago, before the company stopped making them, and we don't get much of a chance to see them so it's really exciting when one of them suddenly …
B: Look, (e) .... but I'm not remotely interested in diesel engines, where they were made, who made them or anything. It bores me to death, frankly.
A: I didn't quite understand what you were saying. Sorry … (f) ....
B: You didn't quite … I was just trying to, (g) .... , tell you I wasn't interested in this conversation. I'm not the kind of person you want to be talking to. (h) ....
A: (i) .... … Only I don't believe I'm hearing you right.
B: You heard me all right. Now if you don't mind I have a train to catch.
A: I didn't quite catch that. Would you like to know what kind of engine is pulling your train?
B: !!!

Writing: email interview

13 Match the email questions and answers. The first one is done for you.

QUESTIONS
a >>What's your most vivid childhood memory? [6]
b >>What living person would you most like to meet? [   ]
c >>What language do you use most often? [   ]
d >>What's your idea of perfect happiness? [   ]
e >>What is your greatest fear? [   ]
f >>Who or what is the greatest love of your life? [   ]
g >>What is your greatest regret? [   ]
h >>How do you relax? [   ]
i >>What is the most important lesson life has taught you? [   ]

ANSWERS
1 Falling asleep when I'm driving.
2 Your family is the most important thing in your life.
3 My Mum and Dad.
4 Reading books and listening to good music.
5 The president of my country. I've got lots to tell him.
6 The first time I went in an aeroplane.
7 Spanish at home, but at work I always speak English.
8 Sitting on a beautiful beach in the sunshine surrounded by my family.
9 I didn't learn a musical instrument when I was a kid.

14 Now answer the email questions about you.

a ....
b ....
c ....
d ....
e ....
f ....
g ....
h ....
i ....

Pronunciation: same or different?

15 Listen to the pairs of sentences on Track 15. Are they the same or different? Put *S* or *D* in the brackets.

a [   ]
b [   ]
c [   ]
d [   ]
e [   ]
f [   ]
g [   ]
h [   ]

Culture and language

16 Are things the same or different in your country? Circle *S* or *D*.

a English words often group together to make phrases that people use and learn as a unit (e.g. *to lose your grip*, *to name but a few*) rather than as lists of individual words. S / D
b In English, we can express the difference between things that happened in the past (*I lived*) and things which happened in the past but still have a present 'feel' to them (*I have lived*). S / D
c In England and the USA, train-spotting (or trainfanning) is quite a popular hobby. S / D
d In English, we often show that we are interested in what people are saying by raising the pitch of our voice and exaggerating the intonation patterns we use. S / D
e In English, we use different phrases to mean the same thing depending on whether we are speaking or writing. S / D
f In English, in conversation, we use a lot of words and phrases to 'buy time' while we try and think what to say. S / D
g In Britain, more than 57% of the population are connected to the Internet and write emails. S / D

unit four 33

Self-check

17 Read the following statements and put a tick in the correct column.

As a result of studying Unit 4 …	Yes, definitely	More or less	Not sure
I can plan a presentation, and using my plan, give a short talk in English.			
I can understand the difference between the present perfect simple (*I've played football*) and the present perfect continuous (*I've been playing football*). I can use both of them.			
I can use a variety of compound nouns to describe different hobbies.			
I can use a variety of expressions to show that I like or don't like certain hobbies.			
I can usually understand the difference between spoken and written language.			
I could write questions and send them to someone via email in order to 'interview' them in English.			
I have been able to understand and make the difference in intonation between showing genuine interest and just using polite words when not really interested.			
I have been able to listen to different people talking about their hobbies and understand what they do and why they do it.			
I read texts about people with dangerous hobbies, understood the information and was able to share it with my classmates.			
In conversation, I can use a variety of words and phrases to 'buy time', check that I have understood and show that I'm interested.			

If you have ticked 'more or less' or 'not sure', go back to the appropriate place in the unit so that you can tick the 'yes, definitely' column.

Test your knowledge

18 Which of the following sentences are written in correct English? Put a tick (✓) or a cross (✗) in the brackets. If there is an error, correct it.

- a I've never had many trouble. [ ]
- b I am addicted about mountain-climbing. [ ]
- c Flower arranging doesn't really turn me on. [ ]
- d She has been living here for six years. [ ]
- e I have heard the singer Jimmy Cliff in concert last weekend. [ ]
- f I have never broken any world records. [ ]
- g Sorry, I didn't quite catch what you said. [ ]
- h I have been thinking of taking up skydiving. [ ]
- i Train-spotter is a boring hobby. [ ]
- j You haven't been here before, haven't you? [ ]

The phonemic alphabet

19 Consult the table of phonemic symbols on page 125 and then write these words in ordinary spelling.

a /bɪˈnɒkjuːləz/

b /ˈpɒtˌhəʊlə/

c /ˈskuːbə ˌdaɪvɪŋ/

d /ˈdaʊnt luːz jɔː ˈgrɪp/

e /ˈnɒnʃələntliː/

f /ʃiː ˈgetsə ˈkɪk ˈaʊtəvɪt/

g /ɪt dʌzə duː ˈmʌtʃ fəˈmiː/

Check your answers by listening to Track 16.

UNIT 5 Getting angry

Reading: smiling and frowning

1 Look at the text and answer the following questions in your own words.

  a Where does the text come from?

  ....

  ....

  b How serious are the answers that people offer?

  ....

  ....

  ....

  c Tick the following opinions if you find them in *Notes & Queries*.

  1 We frown more than we smile. [ ]
  2 We smile more than we frown. [ ]
  3 Frowning must be a good form of exercise. [ ]
  4 Laughter lines are good. [ ]
  5 Laughter lines are bad. [ ]
  6 When you smile nobody smiles back. [ ]
  7 No one can tell if your smile is genuine. [ ]

Notes & Queries

I have heard that it takes many more muscles to frown than to smile. Is it true, and does that mean that smiling is easier?
Phil Discarson, Preston, England

It's only easier if you have something to smile about. Otherwise it's almost impossible!
Katie Davis, Canterbury, UK

I read on a website (www.straightdope.com) that the opposite is true. According to someone called Doctor Song, a plastic surgeon, you use 12 main muscles for a genuine 'zygomatic' smile, but only 11 for a frown. But he says that even though we use more muscles to smile, it's actually easier because, since we smile more often than we frown, our smiling muscles are in better condition.
Carl Preston, San Francisco, USA

If scientists have been studying how many muscles it takes to smile and frown, it shows they have way too much free time on their hands, but since they've told us, we'd better all do a lot of frowning since it burns more calories.
Bob Cartwright, Johannesburg, South Africa

It depends what you mean by smiling. Remember that line from Shakespeare, 'a man may smile and smile and be a villain' – I think it's from his play *Hamlet*. Anyone can look as if they are smiling by using the *zygomaticus major* and *minor* (they pull up the corners of the mouth), the *levator labii superioris* (which pull up the mouth and the corners of the nose) and the *risorius* (which pulls the corner of the mouth to one side). But that's not a real smile. A real smile uses the *orbicularis oculi* which encircle each eye and so when you smile like this, these muscles tighten the skin round the eye to give that 'crinkling' effect which creates 'laughter' lines. That's a REAL smile!
Sarah Green (Dr), Birmingham, UK

Smiling or frowning, who cares?! They both give you lines when you're older so my advice is to avoid doing them completely. Especially when you're young.
Miriam Sterling, Aberdeen, Scotland

Counting the muscles it takes to smile and frown isn't the issue, for me. I am more interested in the fact that you can find examples of the saying that 'it takes less effort to smile than to frown' as far back as the 19th century. That's because it's a piece of advice, not a scientific fact. 'Smile, and the world smiles with you' is another saying like that. Others say that if you smile, you will almost always feel happier. So which comes first, the smile or the happiness?

   Well I just read some research which said that when we smile (or frown), our bodies get the message, even if we are only pretending. Apparently they got some people to pretend to be angry, sad, disgusted, etc., and use the appropriate facial expressions, and measured what happened to their bodies. And the incredible thing was that even though the test subjects knew they were acting, their bodies didn't. Their heart rates increased, their skin temperature got hotter and there were signs of sweating – all physical manifestations of real anger, etc.
Felicity Poole, Amsterdam, Holland

Home

Recent queries

Send a query

Any answers?

I don't know about smiling and frowning, but when I tell jokes, nobody laughs. What's the scientific explanation for that?
Danuta Ross, Penzance, UK

It may be easier, but whether it is nicer depends on your dentist!
Bud Karlowski, Portland, USA

QUERIES

Why don't cats like dogs?
Hugh Foster, London, UK

Why do football teams have 11 players?
Caroline Hartley, Melbourne, Australia

Why is English spelling so confusing?
Sergio Cardenas, Barranquilla, Colombia

What will happen when all the traffic in the country grinds to a halt?
Martin Goodman, Cambridge, UK

How did early humans decide which plants were OK to eat?
Petra Weiss, Basel, Switzerland

2 Who:

a ... doesn't know how people discovered poisonous foods?
....
b ... has a question about animals? ....
c ... makes a comment about white teeth? ....
d ... suggests that smiling actually makes you happier?
....
e ... is worried about how they are going to look later on?
....
f ... says that you have to smile with your eyes if you want it to be genuine? ....
g ... makes a joke about scientists? ....
h ... suggests that smiling is easier because we get a lot of smiling practice? ....
i ... thinks that smiling is sometimes difficult?
....
j ... wants to know whether smiling is easier than frowning?
....
k ... is depressed about the reaction of other people?
....
l ... has a question about sports? ....

3 Complete the sentences with the following words and phrases from the text *Notes & Queries*.

appropriate facial expressions ◆ as far back as ◆ burn calories ◆ depends on ◆ free time ◆ get the message ◆ in better condition ◆ laughter lines ◆ physical manifestations ◆ pretending ◆ tell jokes ◆ villain

a If someone is fitter than they were, we can say that they are ....
b If the teacher is the person who can decide if you can go to the next class, we say that it .... the teacher.
c If we say that something took place a long time in the past (say in the 17th century), we can say that it happened .... 1657.
d If you are trying to make people believe that something which is untrue is true, you are .... that it is true.
e If you change the look of your face to show the kind of emotion you are trying to convey, you use ....
f If you understand what someone is trying to say to you, you ....
g Raised heart rate and sweating are .... of fear.
h The lines at the sides of people's eyes are often called ....
i The main bad character in a story is often called the ....
j The time when we are not working or doing some other obligatory activity is ....
k When we transfer the food we have eaten into energy by taking exercise, we ....
l When you .... , you try and make people laugh.

36 unit five

Grammar: the third conditional

4 Match the sentence beginnings (*a–h*) with their completions (*1–8*). Write the numbers in the spaces provided.

a Even if I had studied harder, ……………
b If it hadn't rained so hard, ……………
c If only I'd studied a bit harder, ……………
d If she hadn't tripped over at the airport in Delhi, ……………
e If you hadn't lost your temper, ……………
f If you lose your temper, ……………
g She would have won the race ……………
h You are most unlikely to be attacked by a shark ……………

1 I might have passed my medical exams.
2 I probably wouldn't have passed my medical exams.
3 I wouldn't have got so wet.
4 I'll never speak to you again.
5 if she hadn't tripped over another runner.
6 if you stay in a designated swimming area.
7 she wouldn't still have a swollen ankle.
8 we might still be friends.

5 Read the story and then complete the sentences *a–l* on page 38 about it. Use different modals apart from *would* if you can, and remember that if the consequence clause refers to the present or future you can use different tenses. The first one is done for you.

Quite by chance, Martin wandered into a café on his way back from work the other day and ordered a coffee. He decided to drink the coffee there but all the tables were full except for a couple outside on the pavement, so he went and sat there. He stretched out his legs and another person of about his age tripped over them and fell over. When he got up, he was very angry and so Martin apologised and offered to do anything the man wanted.

The man (called Patrick) calmed down and said that he needed someone to help him with repairs to his house at the weekend, and so Martin agreed.

The next weekend, Martin went to Patrick's house and while he was painting the kitchen, Patrick's sister Caroline came in. They started talking and Caroline told Martin she was a skydiving instructor. She invited him to try skydiving the next weekend. Martin agreed.

The next weekend, Martin had his first skydiving experience strapped to Patrick's sister. He loved it and soon became addicted to the sport. Over the years, he got better and better, and last month he became the world champion skydiver. And in the meantime he and Caroline fell in love and got married, and now they have two children!

a If Patrick hadn't asked Martin to help him, Martin ....
   ...would never have met his future wife..........................

b If Martin hadn't wandered into the café on his way back from work, ...

c If Martin .... ,
   he might not have any children now.

d If .... ,
   Martin might not have sat outside.

e If Martin hadn't stretched out his legs, ...

f Patrick ....
   if he hadn't tripped over Martin's legs.

g If Caroline ...., she probably ....

h If Martin .... ,
   .... skydiving champion.

i If .... ,
   Martin wouldn't have got addicted to the sport.

j If Martin hadn't gone to Patrick's house, ...

k If .... ,
   Martin wouldn't have gone to Patrick's house.

l If .... ,
   they probably wouldn't have fallen in love.

Vocabulary: being angry

6 Use the word fragments in the box to complete the words and phrases.

a a...
b an...
c ba...
d c...
e cau...
f cr...
g fe...
h fu...
i g...
j gr...
k hac...
l irr...
m ke...
n m...
o mo...
p s...
q si...
r ta...

> ad
> alm down
> ck and tired of
> d up with
> d-tempered
> ep your cool
> ght off balance
> itable
> ke it easy
> ked off
> ngry
> noyed
> ody
> oss
> rious
> rouchy
> ulky
> umpy

38 unit five

7 Re-write the following sentences using exactly the words in blue, and starting with the word in brackets. The first one is done for you.

a She makes me angry. cross (I)

I am really cross with her.

b His brother made him angry. hacked off (He)

....

c John's behaviour made me very angry. at (I)

....

d Losing her job has not made her happy. bad mood (She)

....

e Telling him about the shark attack made him very angry. lost (He)

....

f The fact that he had made a mess of her car made her very cross. absolutely furious (She)

....

g The political situation makes me cross. annoyed (I)

....

h Working is no fun anymore for me. fed up (I)

....

i Your bad behaviour is too much for me. sick and tired (I)

....

Listening: the radio lecture

8 Here are some of the words you will hear in the lecture. What do they mean? What is the talk going to be about, do you think? Write your prediction in the space provided.

bell ◆ experiment ◆ fur coat ◆ press a bar ◆ rabbit ◆ rat ◆ ring ◆ salivate ◆ theory

....
....
....

Listen to Track 17. Were you correct?

9 Listen to Track 17 again and put the following summary sentences in the appropriate order.

a A modern view of Watson and Raynor's experiment is that it wasn't very ethical. [ ]
b An example of behaviourist research is the work of Watson and Raynor. [ ]
c Behaviourism involves habit formation. [ ]
d Experiments with dogs and rats have shown behaviourism at work. [ ]
e The theory of behaviourism has had a big impact on learning. [ ]
f There are different theories of learning. [ ]
g Conditioning is not the only way of learning. [ ]
h Watson and Raynor wanted to reverse their experiment. [ ]

unit five 39

10 Answer the questions.

a What do you understand by 'habit formation'?

b What did Pavlov's dogs think when they heard the bell?

c What did the rats learn to do in the end?

d Who was Albert?

e Why did Albert become frightened of his pet rabbit?

f What was the effect of other animals and fur on Albert?

g What was the response of Albert's parents to the researchers' desire to reverse the experiment?

Functional language: wishes and regrets

11 Complete the following conversation with the correct form of the verb in brackets. The first one is done for you.

A: I wish I (a. come) 'd come here earlier.
B: Why?
A: Well Jimmy Cliff was singing on Stage 2 and I missed him.
B: Well why didn't you come earlier?
A: Because I don't have a programme. I wish I (b. have) .... a programme.
B: Well buy one.
A: There aren't any left. If only I (c. buy) .... one yesterday!
B: Stop complaining! You can always buy one of his CDs at the record store.
A: They've closed it down because people are buying all their music on the internet.
B: That's progress for you!
A: I wish they (d. not stop) .... going to the store.
B: Why? Times change, things move forward.
A: I wish things (e. not move) .... so fast.
B: Well they do. Anyway you have a computer, don't you?
A: Don't talk to me about computers.
B: Why not?
A: I lost four hours' work yesterday. If only I (f. save) .... it before that power cut happened.
B: You worked for four hours and didn't save what you were working on? I don't believe it.
A: I wish it (g. not be) .... true. But it is.
B: Oh stop being so miserable. Let's go and listen to Gillian Welch. She's about to start singing on Stage 1.
A: I can't. I'm meant to be meeting Kenny. If only I (h. bring) .... my mobile phone, I could find out where he is.
B: Here – use mine.
A: Thanks, but I don't know his number. I wish we (i. arrange) .... to meet somewhere special.
B: Well, who's he likely to be listening to?
A: I don't know. If only I (j. ask) .... him …
B: Right, that's it. No more 'I wish', no more 'if only'. Let's go and enjoy some music.
A: Oh all right.

40 unit five

Writing: designing leaflets

12 Match the text with the spaces on the leaflet. Put the correct numbers from the leaflet plan in the brackets.

a Ballroom dancing [ ]
b Celia Barcell, LLD, artistic co-ordinator [ ]
c Classical ballet / modern dance [ ]
d Courses in [ ]
e Dance and rhythm classes for all styles and ages [ ]
f 'Dancing is a way of life, not a hobby' (Paul Szwzinckkopptki) [ ]
g Fast Feet [ ]
h info@ff.tecno.celsius.co.uk [ ]
i Marvin Hartnell, LLD, director [ ]
j Music and rhythm [ ]
k Sarah Mitchell, administrator [ ]
l The Dance Centre
   3A The Close
   Copperbridge
   Somerset SR3 8TW [ ]
m 09773 5647381 [ ]
n www.tecno.celsius.co.uk/ff [ ]

FAST FEET

Fast Feet staff:

1 ....

2 ....

3 ....

Contact *Fast Feet* at:

4 ....

Tel: 5 ....
Email: 6 ....
Website: 7 ....

8 ....
9 ....
10 ....

11 ....
* Hearing the rhythm in different pieces of music
* Moving to different rhythms
* Using musical rhythm for fitness training

12 ....
* Glide around the dance floor with a partner of your choice
* Monthly full-dress events for an evening of old-fashioned glamour
* All the best tunes from the dance halls of the past

13 ....
* Study great dancers of the past on film and video
* Learn the moves from the classics
* Study movement that has revolutionised the art of dance performance

14 ....

unit five 41

Pronunciation

13 Circle the stressed syllables in the following utterances. Underline the syllable that you think has the main stress. The first one is done for you.

a Don't be so bad-tempered.
b I wish I'd been more careful.
c If only I'd got here earlier.
d Take it easy.
e Use your imagination.
f He's absolutely out of control.
g She drives me absolutely crazy.
h Why should I tidy my room?
i I wish I was a bit taller.

Listen to Track 18 and check your answers.

Culture and language

14 Re-write the following sentences so that they reflect your own reality, views or language. Who is 'we' in each case?

a If we are questioned by the police we have the right to have a lawyer with us to protect us.

b If we are under 18 when we are questioned by the police, one of our parents is usually allowed to be with us.

c We are keen on going to places which make us feel 'better' by helping us to relax in different ways.

d We design cheap leaflets and put them through people's letterboxes if we want to promote a small business.

e We have many words that are only different from each other because of one sound (e.g. *wash* and *watch*).

f We normally go to school from 9 am to 3 or 4 pm.

g We often describe sudden anger as 'losing' something (like control, your head, your temper, etc.).

h We often use anger as a way of covering up or responding to some other emotion like shock, fear or sadness.

i We use words like *mad* and *crazy* to mean not only mentally unstable, but also angry.

j When things go wrong, we often talk about our regrets and say *If only* ... in an attempt to 're-write history'. Other people often say 'There's not point in saying *if only*. You can't turn back the clock. It happened.'

Self-check

15 Put 1 to 10 in the brackets to show how difficult the following abilities are for you in English.
1 = 'I feel confident about this / I can do it', but 10 = 'I am not at all confident about this / I'm not sure I can do it'.

a Being able to use conditional sentences, especially the third conditional when referring to hypothetical events in the past. [ ]
b Expressing regrets about the past. [ ]
c Hearing the difference between two sounds (and so choosing the right word). [ ]
d Role-playing a police interview situation. [ ]
e Talking about things you wish you could do. [ ]
f Understanding a text about anger and how to handle it, and sharing information with classmates. [ ]
g Understanding an interview with an anger 'expert', including how to control anger. [ ]
h Understanding issues of leaflet design. [ ]
i Using a variety of words to describe anger and other moods. [ ]
j Writing a leaflet to promote an organisation. [ ]

Take the items you scored from 6 to 10 and look back at the appropriate place in Unit 5 of the Student's Book.

Test your knowledge

16 Translate the following sentences.

a Calm down! There's no need to go over the top.

....

....

b If the shark hadn't been hungry, he wouldn't have attacked the boy.

....

....

c He drives me crazy.

....

....

d That was when I lost my temper.

....

....

e I wish I could speak Arabic, but I can't.

....

....

f If only I hadn't fallen asleep, I wouldn't have missed the lecture.

....

....

g If you don't know the answer, use your imagination.

....

....

h I wish she hadn't been so bad-tempered.

....

....

Did you have problems? If you did, go back to the relevant activity in the Student's Book to check on meaning and use.

The phonemic alphabet

17 Consult the table of phonemic symbols on page 125 and then write these words in ordinary spelling.

a /ˌbæd'tempəd/

....

b /'grʌmpiː/

....

c /'ɪrɪtəbəl/

....

d /ˌrɪəliː fed'ʌp/

....

e /'kaːm 'daʊn/

....

f /aɪ 'fiːl 'træpt/

....

g /hiː 'getsɒn maɪ 'nɜːvz/

....

Check your answers by listening to Track 19.

unit five 43

UNIT 6 Looking forward

Vocabulary: seeing and believing (multiple meanings in words and phrases)

1 Complete these sentences with the correct form of the verb *see* or *believe*. The first one is done for you.

a What are you saying? I don't ......*see*...... what that has to do with it!

b I'm going to be 40 on Friday, ... it or not.

c Did you .... the game on TV last night?

d I wouldn't have .... it if I hadn't .... it with my own eyes.

e I .... he lives in London, but I may be wrong.

f I .... the Australians won the game yesterday. There's a report on it in the newspaper.

g Do you .... what I mean? Or do I need to explain again?

h When are you .... your friend again? On Friday?

i Do you .... in magic? Or do you think it's all trickery?

j The robber is .... to be about six feet tall and was wearing a black sweater and jeans.

2 Read these sentences (*a–i*) and match the meaning of the word *head* in each one with a definition (*1–9*). Write the letters in the spaces provided.

a He headed into the woods.
b The footballer headed the ball into the net.
c She shook her head vigorously to indicate that no, she did not want a piece of cake.
d She had been head at the school for 20 years and now was the time to retire.
e The manager asked whether she would like to head the committee on market research.
f It's too high here! I don't have much of a head for heights.
g I'd like a head of lettuce and some tomatoes, please.
h Matters came to a head and they had a huge row.
i When I arrived, he was sitting at the head of the table looking very pleased with himself.

1 to hit with the head   ....
2 top end   ....
3 part of the body   ....
4 leader   ....
5 climax or turning point   ....
6 unit of a mass of leaves   ....
7 to take charge of   ....
8 to go towards   ....
9 capacity for, ability to withstand   ....

Listening: space tourism

3 Read these sentences. Do you think they are *True* or *False*? Write *T* or *F* in the brackets.

a Most people in industrialised countries would like to travel to space.   [ ]
b At the beginning, space travel will be very cheap.   [ ]
c A holiday in space will cost just a few thousand dollars in the future.   [ ]
d There will be millions of space tourists per year in the future.   [ ]
e Governments will continue to fund space travel in the future.   [ ]
f There have already been some space tourists.   [ ]

Now listen to Track 20 and check your answers.

44 unit six

4 Listen to Track 20 again. Who:
   a ... is from Texas?
   b ... would like to travel to space?
   c ... is from Kent?
   d ... will the early tourists be?
   e ... will be able to travel to space in the third phase?
   f ... wants to know how space travel is funded?
   g ... used to pay for all space travel?
   h ... will pay for the space tourism industry?
   i ... was the first space tourist?

5 Look at these words and expressions from the interview and write them in the right place to complete these extracts.

   average person in the street • the whole idea •
   futuristic • equivalent • pretty basic • stepping in •
   improve greatly • the general public •
   bring down • in the first place

   a Dr Kenney, how .... is this?
   b ... it's becoming increasingly clear that this is something .... wants.
   c Will space tourism be available to the .... ?
   d ... but .... of space travel is that it will generate a lot of money.
   e Accommodation in space orbit will be .... and prices will be very high.
   f ... and the facilities in orbit will ....
   g ... the price will be the .... of a few thousand dollars.
   h ... the money generated from space travel helping to .... prices.
   i ... but where is the money to start these programmes going to come from .... ?
   j ... private industry is now .... to fund these space tourism programs.

   Now listen to Track 20 again and check your answers.

Functional language: speculating

6 Match the two parts of the conversations. Write the numbers in the brackets. The first one is done for you.
   a Do you think it'll rain tomorrow?   [3]
   b What are the chances of your son helping me move house at the weekend?   [ ]
   c What do you reckon it would cost me to get my house painted?   [ ]
   d I wouldn't be surprised if Jimmy is out when we get home.   [ ]
   e Do you suppose the boss would give me the day off tomorrow?   [ ]
   f If you ask me, prices seem to be going up and up.   [ ]
   g Do you reckon Rangers will win the big game on Saturday?   [ ]
   h It's hard to say for sure, but I'm confident that she'll pass the exam easily. [ ]
   i Any idea what time Jenny will be home?   [ ]

   1 Well, she's certainly studied very hard over the last couple of weeks.
   2 Yes, Friday night he often goes clubbing.
   3 Not a chance! Look at that beautiful blue sky.
   4 I'm not sure. Their best player is injured.
   5 Hmm. It's a big job – you'd better get some experts to make an estimate.
   6 I don't see why not. We're not very busy and you did overtime last week.
   7 No, not really. She said she'd be back in an hour and that was three hours ago.
   8 I agree. I can't believe how much a week's shopping costs.
   9 Pretty good, I'd say. He's not doing anything, so he's free.

Pronunciation: assimilation of /d/ and /j/ (/dʒ/)

7 Listen to these sentences on Track 21. Underline all the examples of /d/ and /j/ being pronounced together.
   a Do you reckon it'll rain tomorrow?
   b Do you suppose he'll win?
   c What do you think will be the score?
   d Did you see the game on Saturday?
   e What do you reckon she'll do?
   f Do you think they'll get there before we do?
   g Who do you suppose will be there?
   h Did you know they were going to be here?

   What do you notice about the sounds /d/ and /j/ when they are said together?

8 Practise saying the sentences with the same pronunciation.

Reading: finding out about the future

9 Match the name of the text type to the US website extract (*1–6*).

a an advertisement for a book   [ ]
b a weather forecast   [ ]
c an advertisement for a fortune-teller [ ]
d a horoscope   [ ]
e part of a city guide to events   [ ]
f an advertisement for a science exhibition [ ]

① Event Overview

See how information technology is rapidly transforming enterprise operations, the e-entertainment industry and business e-marketing strategies around the world. This event brings IT professionals together in a forum of knowledge exchange and networking to advance the IT industry. International experts will speak about the direction of the IT industry and share practical knowledge on the latest technological innovations and current business and management issues. Technology vendors will showcase the newest innovations of the industry. IT decision-makers will find that perfect business and technology solution for their enterprise. The **IT WorldExpo** is where the IT community converges.

②

Fri 11 **Takes and Out-takes from the Andy Warhol Museum** *Ronald Feldman Fine Arts*
Tue–Sat 10am–6pm; Mon by appointment.
The gallery hosts an exhibit of art and archival material from the Prince of Pop to celebrate the Andy Warhol Museum's tenth anniversary. Thu 10–Jul 30.

Sun 13 **60 contemporary Chinese artists** *Asia Society* and *International Center of Photography*
Tue–Sun 11am–6pm; Fri 11am–9pm. $7, students and seniors $5, children under 16 accompanied by an adult and members free; Fri 6–9pm free.
An avant-garde community began brewing in China at the end of the Cultural Revolution in 1976, and things really got cooking in the 1990s, when a new generation dealing with issues of identity, modernity and tradition turned to photography and video. The work of 60 contemporary Chinese artists is now on view at the Asia Society and ICP. Zhang Dali, Liu Zheng and Lin Tianmiao are among those exhibited.
Fri 11–Sept 5.

③

'Hi, my name is Wayne. As a clairvoyant and master Tarot reader, I can help you in matters of the heart as well as questions about your life path. The journey to peace and love is right in front of you.'

Read more about Wayne
'It's all about finding your way. I've dedicated myself to making connections with each of my clients to ensure they get the best possible reading every time. And I'm proud to be able to prove to my clients time and again that my readings are fact-based, accurate and inspirational.'
**Find out more. 10-minute psychic reading for only $10.
Call 1-800-PSYCHIC**

④

Capricorn (22nd December – 21st January) – the month ahead

Your sense of purpose is strong all month, thanks in part to the feeling of optimism that keeps you going from 1st through 10th. On the 3rd you find that all the seeds you have sown are beginning to flower, while on the 5th and 6th you realise that you are in control of your destiny. By the 11th you should be keeping a record of all that you've done, because time has a way of changing our memories. Do practical things on the weekend of the 12th instead of letting the desire for adventure take over. The 14th and 15th of the month will be very social, although you should keep an eye on your spending. If you're not careful, the 17th will find you broke and with a bunch of freeloaders. Be kind to these people at least through the 22nd. They're not trying to be mean and they really like hanging out with you. On the 24th you're ready for some real action. You'll step right into it without even noticing. Resist the impulse that you might feel on the weekend of the 26th to make big changes. You're back in control on the 28th, and that's where you'll stay.

5

Nostradamus, His Works and Prophecies
by Michel Nostradamus, Theodore Garencieres

EDITORIAL REVIEWS

About the author
Nostradamus (1503-1566) was a medieval physician who became an astrologer and prophet. His renown has grown immensely in recent years as we have witnessed the passing of his predictions. He wrote his prognostications in poetic form and they have challenged and inspired readers for over 400 years.

Book description
Has Nostradamus predicted the coming Apocalypse along with a thousand other great events? His believers claim that in the 1500s he predicted historic milestones that have or will alter the course of human history, such as the rise of Napoleon and Hitler. Published here are the hard-to-find original English translations from 1672 to help you answer that question. Finally, you can look through the actual work of Nostradamus to see if you can solve his riddles. Study of his work can be a fascinating hobby or intellectual exercise that can be quite enjoyable. What great event will be discovered next in this cryptic text?

6

Detailed Local Forecast for London, ENG

Tonight: Mostly cloudy. Low near 60F. Winds WSW at 5 to 10 mph.

Tomorrow: Partly to mostly cloudy. High 73F. Winds SW at 10 to 15 mph.

Tomorrow night: Clear to partly cloudy. Low 58F. Winds WSW at 10 to 15 mph.

Friday: Times of sun and clouds. Highs in the low 70s and lows in the mid 50s.

Saturday: Showers. Highs in the upper 60s and lows in the mid 50s.

Sunday: Mostly cloudy. Highs in the mid 70s and lows in the mid 50s.

---

10 Which one of these sources might you consult if:
- a ... you were going on holiday to London? [ ]
- b ... you were a fan of art looking for something to do on a rainy day? [ ]
- c ... your birthday was in late December? [ ]
- d ... you were interested in the connection between history and the future? [ ]
- e ... you wanted to find out about the newest computer developments? [ ]
- f ... you wanted to find out about what is going to happen in your future? [ ]

11 Who or what is:
- a ... WorldExpo?
- b ... Andy Warhol?
- c ... Liu Zheng?
- d ... a tarot reader?
- e ... a psychic reading?
- f ... a freeloader?
- g ... Nostradamus?
- h ... the Apocalypse?
- i ... in the upper 60s?

12 What do these words and abbreviations from the texts mean?
- a IT
- b e-entertainment, e-marketing
- c Tue–Sun
- d avant-garde
- e clairvoyant
- f hanging out with you
- g prognostications
- h WSW
- i mph
- j 73F

Grammar: future perfect and continuous

13 Read the following sentences. Which describe (1) something that (we guess) is happening now, (2) plans for the future which are fixed and decided, (3) something that is going to be completed in the future and (4) something that will be in progress at a particular moment in the future? Write *1–4* in the brackets.

a Don't phone them now. They'll be having dinner. [ ]
b Jane will have finished the cake by 4 this afternoon. We can pick it up then. [ ]
c This time on Friday, we'll be flying over the Atlantic on our way to New York. [ ]
d I'll be working here for another three months and then I'm going on a trip around the world. [ ]

14 Complete these two conversations with the appropriate form of the verb in brackets. The first one is done for you.

SUSAN: This time next week, I (a. garden) .will be gardening. instead of working. I can hardly wait for my retirement. By Friday, I (b. work) .... there for 30 years and six months.
JAKE: That's a long time. What (c. do) .... with yourself when you retire?
SUSAN: Well, I' (d. enjoy) .... my garden for a few months, then my husband and I (e. take) .... a trip to Japan in July.
JAKE: That sounds great. You certainly (f. not think) .... about work, I'm sure!

RECEPTIONIST: Can I help you?
JOHN: Yes, I'm calling to say that I (g. arrive) .... late for my appointment.
RECEPTIONIST: What time was your appointment?
JOHN: At 9 o'clock, but we (h. get) .... there around 9.30, because the traffic's so bad.
RECEPTIONIST: I'm afraid Dr Legend (i. see) .... another patient at that time.
JOHN: (j. finish) .... he .... by 10?
RECEPTIONIST: Yes, but he (k. leave) .... the office if you get here any later than 10.15.
JOHN: Not a problem. We (l. arrive) .... by 10. Thanks.

Writing: planning compositions

15 Read these titles, notes and compositions and write the letter of the parts that go together.

Title	Notes	Composition
....	....	....
....	....	....

Titles

a Talk about the last trip you took and what you did during your trip.
b Where would you like to go for your next holiday? Why would you like to go there and what would you like to do there?

Notes

c

Where? When?	• New York • summer holiday
Why?	• Empire State Building • typical landmarks • art museums • theatre productions
What to do?	• Met Museum of Art

d

Where? When?	• New York • last weekend
What we did before	Checked online: • weather • Time Out
What we did	• art exhibitions

Compositions

e Last week, we went to New York for the weekend. First we checked online to see what the weather was going to be like and then I looked at Time Out to see what was going on in the city. I'm really interested in art so I wanted to go and see an exhibition and fortunately for me there were two shows that really interested me and I got to see both of them. The first one was a show featuring the work of Andy Warhol and the second one was an exhibition of Chinese art, which was very interesting.

f During the summer holiday, I'd like to visit New York with my friend Jin. We want to go to the art exhibitions and we'd especially like to visit the Metropolitan Museum of Art. New York is a great city and it has many great things to offer a tourist. First there is the Empire State Building and all the typical landmarks of the city and then there are the wonderful cultural events like the art museums and the theatre productions. Hopefully, by the middle of July we'll be flying to New York ready to enjoy two weeks in this great city.

16 Now read these notes and add ideas of your own to answer this question:

Would you like to travel to space and what do you think space tourism will be like?

Living

basic, live on a spaceship, not much room to move or to exercise

Food and entertainment

dehydrated food, DVDs, music, read, no real entertainment

Would I like to go? Why / Why not?

Now write a composition from your notes.

Culture and language

17 Are things the same or different in your country? Circle *S* or *D*.

a In English, there are many different structures and ways to talk about the future. S / D

b In English, the same word can have a lot of different meanings. S / D

c In the UK, people like to speculate about the weather and sports games. S / D

d In the USA and in Britain, there are a lot of advertisements for clairvoyants and psychics. S / D

e In Britain and the USA, it is common for young people to start planning very early on for their retirement by investing in a pension fund. S / D

f In Britain and the USA, technology has become very important and people use computers a lot in everyday life. S / D

g Many people are concerned about the future and what will happen. S / D

h Many people believe in paranormal phenomena and many people don't. S / D

unit six 49

Self-check

18 Read the following statements and put a tick in the correct column.

As a result of studying Unit 6 …	Yes, definitely	More or less	Not sure
I can understand the difference between the verbs *see* and *believe* and the different ways they are used.			
I can use the future perfect and the future continuous tenses appropriately.			
I can use a variety of expressions to speculate about the future.			
I was able to identify different text types and what the texts can be used for.			
I could plan a composition by writing notes and write a composition based on those notes.			
I was able to complete a summary of a listening text.			
I can hear the difference between stressed and weak forms of *have*.			
I'm able to use a variety of future forms to make predictions and talk about the future.			
I can talk about belief and disbelief and use a variety of phrases to express these concepts.			
I can hear and make the sound /dʒ/ .			

If you have ticked 'more or less' or 'not sure', go back to the appropriate place in the unit so that you can tick the 'yes, definitely' column.

Test your knowledge

19 Which of the following sentences are written in correct English? Put a tick (✓) or a cross (✗) in the brackets. If there is an error, correct it.

a I'm reckoning we'll be living on the moon in about 50 years. [ ]
b What are the chances of life on other planets? [ ]
c Do you believe what I mean? [ ]
d I couldn't believe my eyes when I saw him! [ ]
e The winner of the lottery believes to live in London. [ ]
f What will you be doing at 6 tomorrow? [ ]
g I'll have finishing reading this book by Friday. [ ]
h She'll be lie on a beach somewhere, I bet. [ ]
i I believe she's a TI expert. [ ]
j Highs will be in the mid-60s and lows in the mid-50s. [ ]

The phonemic alphabet

20 Consult the table of phonemic symbols on page 125 and then write these words in ordinary spelling.

a /ˌəʊvəpɒpjuːˈleɪʃən/

b /ˈrəʊˌbɒt/

c /kleəˈvɔɪənt /

d /əˈstrɒlədʒiː/

e /ˈspeɪs ˌtɔːrɪzm/

f /ðə ˈdʒenrəl ˈpʌblɪk/

g /ɪn ðə ˈfɜːst pleɪs/

Check your answers by listening to Track 22.

UNIT 7 Out of the blue

Vocabulary: colours

1 Complete these sentences with the correct colour word.

a When I saw her new car, I was .... with envy.

b She was so embarrassed at what she had said that she turned bright ....

c 'What's the matter?', I said when I saw him. 'You're as .... as a sheet.'

d The surveillance camera in the store meant that the security guards caught the thief ....-handed. He was captured on video for all to see.

e 'We've worked hard all week, let's go out and dance. Get changed and we'll go and paint the town ....'

f 'I'm fed up with this. I've told you again and again until I'm .... in the face – tidy up your bedroom!'

g So I was at home and then, out of the ...., Dave shows up. I hadn't seen him for about two years.

h When he told her that everything she had done was wrong and she had to re-do it, she saw .... She was so angry.

i We're still waiting for the .... light to open our restaurant. We still don't have the permit that we need.

j 'Come inside – you're .... with cold. Come and sit by the fire.'

2 Write what these people are wearing as accurately as possible.

Reading: six thinking hats

3 Do you know this man and anything about why he is famous? Read the introduction and find out.

Edward de Bono is regarded as the leading international authority in conceptual and creative thinking and in the teaching of thinking as a skill. He originated the term 'lateral thinking', which now has an entry in the Oxford English Dictionary, and is well known for the deliberate creative techniques associated with it and for the powerful 'six thinking hats' method.

4 Read the first part of the passage on page 52 quickly and answer these questions.

a What do the six hats represent?

b Why do people use the technique?

Can you predict what the six different ways of thinking about a problem might be?

unit seven 51

MAKING DISCUSSIONS AND MEETINGS MORE EFFECTIVE

Do you find meetings boring? Here's a technique that may help you.

In the 1980s, Dr Edward de Bono, a world-famous professor from Malta, invented a technique for group problem-solving called the 'six thinking hats'. Many large companies around the world, including IBM, Federal Express, British Airways and PepsiCo, have used this method to help them. But it would be just as useful for a school meeting or any other kind of group session.

The idea is that the whole group wears six different 'hats' when considering a problem. Each of these hats is given a different colour and represents a different way of talking and thinking about something.

There are three main reasons to use this technique.

- It focuses on the topic or problem, not on individual people.
- It allows people to look at the problem in many different ways.
- It allows people to all think effectively about a problem at the same time.

Below is a summary of the different 'hats', what they signify and how the technique can be used. It is important that everyone in the group is thinking with the same hat at the same time. Imagine you are in a group trying to decide where to go on vacation together – here's how the six hats can help you.

When the group is thinking about facts and information, this is 'white hat thinking'. Here, you would think about how much money and time you have available, for example.

The red hat covers intuition, feelings and emotions. It allows the thinker to put forward an intuition without any need to justify it. 'Putting on my red hat, I think this is a terrible proposal.' Feelings and intuition can only be introduced into a discussion if they are supported by logic. Usually the feeling is genuine but the logic is spurious. The red hat gives full permission to a thinker to put forward his or her feelings on the subject at the moment. Red hat thinking is about emotions, thoughts and feelings. When the group puts on this hat, they respond to ideas emotionally, not logically. Here, people would discuss how they *feel* about the different places proposed.

The logical thinking hat, which calls for caution and careful analysis, is the black hat. This is the hat of judgement and caution. It is a most valuable hat. It is not in any sense an inferior or negative hat. The black hat is used to point out why a suggestion does not fit the facts, the available experience, the system in use, or the policy that is being followed. The black hat must always be logical. If someone suggests staying in a luxury hotel and there is not enough money, when you are wearing the black hat, you can discuss this. This is the logical positive hat and is used when discussing why something will work and why it will offer benefits. It can be used in looking forward to the results of some proposed action, but can also be used to find something of value in what has already happened.

The yellow thinking hat is the voice of positive reason. The group is looking for the benefits of suggestions and proposals. This is when the group would look at the advantages of the different places suggested.

The green hat is the hat of creativity, alternatives, proposals, things that are interesting and exciting changes. Creativity is called for when the group is wearing the green hat. Here, people would generate ideas for different places to go, combining ideas and thinking creatively.

The blue hat is the 'overview' or process control hat. It looks not at the subject itself but at the 'thinking' about the subject. 'Putting on my blue hat, I feel we should do some more green hat thinking at this point.' In technical terms, the blue hat is concerned with metacognition. The blue hat is the hat that makes an evaluation of the whole process of thinking. For example, if all the suggestions are in other countries and not everyone has a passport, someone might say, 'We need some more black hat thinking here'. If there is only one suggestion, you may need more green hat thinking.

Would you like your meetings and decision-making to be more creative, more positive and more logical? Would you like to have the opportunity to express your emotions without worrying? Why not give the 'six hats' idea of Edward de Bono a try? At the very least, it should make your meetings more fun!

5 Read the second part of the passage on page 52 (starting 'Below in a summary …'). Complete the table about the six thinking hats.

Colour of hat	What are you thinking about when you wear this hat?
(white hat)	
(red hat)	
(black hat)	
(yellow hat)	
(green hat)	
(blue hat)	

6 Can you guess the meaning from the context? Match these words from the text with their definitions.

a intuition ……..
b spurious ……..
c caution ……..
d logical ……..
e policy ……..
f overview ……..
g inferior ……..
h metacognition ……..

1 careful consideration of dangers
2 knowledge of how you think
3 false, not real
4 broad, comprehensive investigation
5 using rational thinking
6 plan or system of action
7 something you feel to be true, without knowing why
8 not as good as others

Listening: the driving lesson

7 Match the words with the pictures.

a accelerator ………………
b brake ………………
c clutch ………………
d gear stick ………………
e radiator ………………
f rear-view mirror ………………
g steering-wheel ………………
h wing mirror ………………

8 Listen to Track 23. Are these statements *True* or *False*? Write *T* or *F* in the brackets.

a Mr Radinski has not driven before. [ ]
b Mr Radinski's father is a farmer. [ ]
c Mr Radinkski has never had any problems driving before this lesson. [ ]
d Mr Radinski hits a pedestrian at a roundabout. [ ]
e The pedestrian is a woman. [ ]
f Mr Radinski hits a lorry at a roundabout. [ ]
g Mr Radinski is a good driver. [ ]

9 Complete the map showing where the impact took place. Use the following symbol for the car which Mr Radinski was driving.

unit seven 53

10 Complete these two extracts with the words Mr Radinski spoke (but which we don't hear on Track 23). The first one is done for you.

1

INSTRUCTOR: Well now, Mr Radinski, have you ever driven a car before?

RADINSKI: (a) Yes, I have.

RADINSKI: (b) ......

RADINSKI: (c) ......

RADINSKI: (d) ......

INSTRUCTOR: ... and your father is buying some new wing mirrors because you drove too close to the fence ...

2

INSTRUCTOR: Yes, yes, Mr Radinski ... the truck driver was very rude ...

RADINSKI: (a) ......

RADINSKI: (b) ......

RADINSKI: (c) ......

RADINSKI: (d) ......

RADINSKI: (e) ......

RADINSKI: (f) ......

INSTRUCTOR: Yes, yes, Mr Radinski. That is the end of this lesson.

Pronunciation: word stress

11 Look at these words and underline which syllable carries the main stress.

a accelerator
b gear stick
c radiator
d rear-view mirror
e steering-wheel
f wing mirror
g pedestrian
h roundabout
i engine
j neutral
k handbrake
l mirror

Now listen to Track 24 and check your answers.

12 Practise saying the words with the correct syllable stress.

Grammar: needs doing / have something done

13 Match the two parts of the conversation.

a The washing machine is not working well again.
b Your hair is too long.
c You have a flat tyre, you know.
d There's a button off your shirt.
e The boiler is broken. It's not heating the water.
f I love the colour of your hair.
g Is your printer working? Mine's broken.

1 It needs repairing. I'll phone the gas company.
2 Use mine if you want. Have you got your disc with you?
3 Thanks. I had it done this morning.
4 I know. I'm having it cut this afternoon.
5 Yes. I have to get it changed.
6 I'll have it mended when I take it to the cleaners.
7 Well, you need to have it serviced every year.

14 Change these sentences using the structures *to have something done* or *something needs doing* so that the meaning stays the same.

a The cleaning company cleaned our whole house in just three hours.
We had ......

b They resprayed the car at Gerry's garage.
I had ......

c We need to get the bumper replaced.
The bumper ......

d Someone stole my bicycle today.
I had ......

e They painted our house while we were on holiday.
We ......

f We have to get the roof mended, because there's a hole in it.
The roof ......

g The dentist says that I need to clean my teeth more thoroughly in future.
My teeth ......

h The computer store said the hard drive on my computer had a serious problem and I should replace it.
The hard drive on my computer ......

i A photographer took five photos of the entire family.
They ......

54 unit seven

Functional language: taking something to be fixed

15 Solve the puzzle. Find two conversations here and put them in order. The first few answers are done for you.

a Well, it's making a funny noise from the engine.
b What seems to be the problem with it?
c I've brought my car to be serviced.
d Well, it all started when it mysteriously erased my email.
e Hmm. All right, we'll investigate that rattle.
f Could you have a look at my laptop?
g Yes, it's also rattling when I change gear.
h Well, then I couldn't get it to start up.
i You'll have to leave it for a few days, because we're really busy.
j Five o'clock sounds great.
k Certainly. I'll call you as soon as I know what's wrong with it.
l Thanks. When will it be ready?
m Thanks. I'll be expecting your call then.
n That's fine, but can you phone me to tell me when it will be ready?
o Then what happened?
p OK. Let me fill out a service order. Is there anything wrong with it?
q From the engine? OK. I'll make a note of that. Anything else?
r Tonight by 5 if all's well.

Conversation 1:

c   p ....

Conversation 2:

f   ....

16 Match the conversation to the correct picture.

Sophie: ....   Patrick: ....

Writing: instructions

17 Make computer instructions by joining clauses in columns A, B and C. Use the meaning, but look at the grammar to help you too. Two of the answers are done for you.

A
a1 Connect the power supply to the ABS drive,
a2 To add the picture to
a3 To move a file or folder,
a4 To increase or decrease the volume for any music, speech, or other sounds
a5 To be able to control the volume
a6 To use a different date format,

B
b1 click the 'Date' tab,
b2 drag its icon
b3 every slide in your presentation,
b4 of your computer from the menu bar,
b5 plug it into an outlet,
b6 that play through your computer's speakers,

C
c1 add it to the slide master.
c2 and then select the options you want.
c3 and turn it on.
c4 drag the 'output volume' slider at the bottom of the window left or right.
c5 select the 'show volume in menu bar' checkbox.
c6 to the new folder.

a1 ......b5......

a2 ....

a3 ....
   ......c6......

a4 ....

a5 ....

a6 ....

18 Write sentences a1–a6 from Activity 17 under the correct picture.

A

B

C

D

E

F

Culture and language

19 Re-write the following sentences so that they reflect your own reality, views or language. Who is 'we' in each case?

a We often use the colour red to indicate a warning or danger.

b Traditionally pink is a colour we use for baby girls and blue is a colour for baby boys.

c We tend to use the colour black with negative connotations and the colour white with positive connotations.

d We use the structure *to have something done* to talk about things that we do not do ourselves.

e We say that *something needs doing* to indicate that something is necessary, without saying who is going to do it.

f When we deal with service providers (in shops, garages, etc.), they are usually polite to customers.

g We use imperative verbs (*connect*, *click*, *select*) to give instructions and explanations.

h When we say multi-syllable words, there is always one syllable that is stressed more than others.

i We use *to* + verb to mean *If you want to do something* (e.g. *To add a picture to every slide in your presentation, add it to the slide master*).

Self-check

20 Put 1 to 10 in the brackets to show how difficult the following abilities are for you in English. 1 = 'I feel confident about this / I can do it', but 10 = 'I am not at all confident about this / I'm not sure I can do it'.

a Using colour vocabulary [ ]
b Understanding the 'six hats' thinking technique [ ]
c Recognising word stress in English words [ ]
d Using verbs and complements in car vocabulary [ ]
e Using the structure *something needs doing* [ ]
f Using the structure *to have something done* [ ]
g Asking to get something fixed [ ]
h Hearing and making the difference between the sounds /s/, /z/ and /tʃ/ [ ]
i Writing step-by-step instructions for doing something [ ]

Take the items you scored from 6 to 10 and look back at the appropriate place in Unit 7 of the Student's Book.

Test your knowledge

21 Translate the following sentences and questions.

a She's wearing a coffee-coloured shirt.

b Why don't you sit down and chill out?

c The colour red elicits a strong psychological response from many people.

d I haven't the slightest idea what you're talking about.

e Our house needs painting.

f She's going to have her hair dyed blue.

g The brakes don't seem to be working.

h Logical thinking solves problems using facts and evidence while lateral thinking asks you to look for original solutions.

Did you have problems? If you did, go back to the relevant activity in the Student's Book to check on meaning and use.

The phonemic alphabet

22 Consult the table of phonemic symbols on page 125 and then write these words in ordinary spelling.

a /ɪt 'niːdz 'mendɪŋ/

b /pə'destriːən/

c /ˌmetəkɒg'nɪʃən/

d /aɪ 'hæd maɪ 'kɑː 'wɒʃt/

e /'laɪmgriːn 'tiːʃət/

f /'keəfʊl ə'nælɪsɪs/

Check your answers by listening to Track 25.

UNIT 8 Food for thought

Reading: the battle of the diets

1 Read these four descriptions of different weight-loss systems and write the name of the system each person invented under the picture.

Bernice Weston

Dr Robert Atkins

Dr Barry Sears

Dr Arthur Agatson

Named one of People magazine's '25 most intriguing people' at the end of the 20th century and one of Time magazine's 'people who mattered' at the end of 2003, Dr Atkins was a cardiologist with a pioneering perspective on nutrition and health. The Atkins Diet suggests that conventional medicine's low-fat approach to dieting just isn't working. Instead, Dr Atkins and his followers advocate a high-protein, low-carbohydrate (low-carb) approach to losing weight. What makes the Atkins Diet so controversial is its two-week induction phase, which is the first stage of the programme. Dieters eat virtually no carbohydrates (only 20g per day from vegetables are permitted), but can eat fatty foods freely. This means absolutely NO bread, pasta, rice or fruit, but liberal amounts of meats (including red meat and bacon) and full-fat cheese.

The South Beach Diet is designed not only to help you lose weight but also to improve your health. It was developed by Dr Arthur Agatson. Agatson's idea is not that all carbs and fat are bad, but that we have to learn to eat only 'good' carbs such as those found in fruits and vegetables, and eliminate 'bad' carbs (those found in processed foods like breads, snacks and soft drinks). According to Agatson, our bodies cannot process these foods adequately and, as a result, the body stores more fat than it should, especially in the midsection. The diet also allows plenty of healthy monounsaturated fats such as olive and canola oils as well as meats and seafood. These are the 'good' fats. In addition to actually reducing the risk of heart attack and stroke, they taste good and make food palatable. They're filling too.

In 1976, Brooklyn-born Bernice Weston founded Weight Watchers of Great Britain on a budget of £1500. In ten years, the organisation had grown to 800 clubs and 1.5 million members. Her story is an inspiration for the weight-loss system that she started. From being just a 'fat girl', she has become one of the most successful businesswomen of her generation.

Weight Watchers works by assigning points to foods according to how many calories they contain and allowing members to eat a certain amount of 'points' per day. The most important part of the Weight Watchers system is the weekly meetings where members go for their weigh-in and meet with other members as a kind of support group to encourage each other to continue with the diet in order to reach each individual's 'weight-loss goal'. The leaders of the meetings are all people who have lost weight themselves as members of Weight Watchers.

Dr Sears began the research that led to the development of the Zone Diet for a very selfish reason: he wanted to do what he could to support his heart. All the males on his father's side of the family had died of heart disease in their early 50s and he didn't want to be one of them.

Dr Sears thinks that Mother Nature has designed our digestive system to operate correctly when eating just two food groups: (1) lean protein like boneless, skinless chicken and (2) natural carbohydrates like fruits and fibre-rich vegetables. Sears feels that our bodies are not able to deal adequately with grains, bread and pasta as the digestive system was not designed to process these.

The Zone Diet works on the idea that every meal that we eat should contain 40 per cent of its calories from carbs, 30 per cent from protein and 30 per cent from fat (fat is found in meats, seafood, dairy products, nuts and even some fruits like avocados). Each person eats the amount of food she or he needs according to a chart based on weight and how active she or he is. Seven grams is known as one 'block' in this diet.

2 Now read the passages again and answer these questions. Who or what:

a ... are bad carbs? ....
b ... was overweight as a child? ....
c ... believes in healthy eating? ....
d ... wanted to improve his own health? ....
e ... is only allowed to eat 20g of carbs a day? ....
f ... are natural carbohydrates? ....
g ... gets weighed every week? ....
h ... is or was a cardiologist? ....
i ... are good fats? ....
j ... called Dr Atkins 'an intriguing person'? ....
k ... thinks it's important to diet with other people? ....
l ... believes in a low-carb diet? ....

3 Read these lists of ingredients (*a–d*) and match them with the directions for making the recipe (*1–4*).

a
- 3 ounces of boneless, skinless chicken breast, raw
- 1/4 cup of black bean sauce
- 2 teaspoons of olive oil, extra light flavour
- 2 cups of broccoli, flower clusters, raw
- 1 cup of orange segments

b
- 4 tablespoons extra virgin olive oil
- 1 garlic clove, crushed
- 3 boneless skinless chicken breast halves, cut into strips
- 1/8 teaspoon salt
- 1/4 teaspoon coarsely ground black pepper
- 1/2 cup dry white wine
- 3 medium tomatoes, sliced

c
- medium chicken breast (2.5)
- pureed tomatoes (0.5)
- medium portion of pasta (2)
- broccoli (0)
- 10g half fat cheese, grated (0.5)
 (5.5 points per serving)

d
- 2 tablespoons olive oil, divided
- 1 small onion, chopped
- 1/2 small carrot, chopped
- 1 celery stalk, chopped
- 2 garlic cloves, sliced
- 2 ounces baked ham, diced
- 2 pounds boneless, skinless chicken thighs
- 1/2 cup red wine
- 1/2 cup reduced-sodium chicken broth
- 1/2 bay leaf
- 2 tablespoons chopped fresh parsley

1 Burgundy chicken ....

1. Heat 1 tablespoon oil in a large, heavy skillet over medium heat. Add onion, carrot and celery. Cook 5 minutes, until vegetables soften. Add garlic and ham and cook 2 minutes more. Transfer mixture to a bowl.
2. Heat remaining oil and brown chicken thighs. Add wine, broth and bay leaf to skillet. Reduce heat to medium-low and cook 35 minutes, until chicken is cooked through and most of the liquid is reduced. Return vegetables and ham to skillet. Mix well, heat through 5 minutes. Sprinkle with parsley before serving.

2 Broccoli chicken with Chinese black bean sauce ....

Cut broccoli into bite-sized pieces. Cut chicken into bite-sized pieces. Heat oil in nonstick pan and toss in broccoli. Cook about one minute and add chicken pieces. Cook chicken and broccoli until chicken is done and broccoli is bright green. Add black bean sauce, stir and remove from heat.

Enjoy orange sections for dessert.
The recipe is 3.3 blocks, balanced, and only 315 calories!

3 Chicken in white wine ....
- In a medium skillet, heat the oil and garlic over medium heat. Sprinkle the chicken with the salt and pepper, then add to the skillet and cook for 7 to 10 minutes. Add the white wine and cook for an additional 2 minutes.
- Remove the chicken to a platter. Sauté the tomatoes in the skillet for 2–3 minutes. Place the tomatoes over the chicken and cover with the pan drippings.

4 Chicken, tomato and broccoli pasta ....
- Dice and dry-fry chicken breast until cooked thoroughly.
- Cook pasta and broccoli as normal.
- Slowly heat the tomatoes in a pan for a few minutes or heat in microwave.
- Mix chicken and drained broccoli into tomatoes and serve on a bed of pasta, topped with cheese.

4 Match the definitions *1–8* to the words *a–h*, taken from the lists of ingredients on page 59.

a stalk ....
b clove ....
c chopped ....
d crushed ....
e ground ....
f boneless ....
g skinless ....
h pureed ....

1 with the skin removed
2 made into a powder
3 stick
4 made into a liquid or paste
5 cut into small pieces
6 small section of a bulb of garlic
7 pressed until broken
8 with the bones removed

5 Read the recipes on page 59 again and match the type of diet (see page 58) with the recipe.

a Burgundy chicken ....
b chicken in white wine ....
c chicken, tomato and broccoli pasta ....
d broccoli chicken with Chinese black bean sauce ....

1 Weight Watchers
2 the Zone Diet
3 the Atkins Diet
4 the South Beach Diet

Vocabulary: food and drink (idioms)

6 Complete these expressions with one of these food words and phrases. You will have to use one word twice.

hot potato ◆ fruit cake ◆ two peas in a pod ◆ cucumber ◆
beetroot ◆ mustard ◆ pancake ◆ pie ◆ candy

a She's great in a crisis. She's so calm – she stays as cool as a ....
b The car ran over the ball and left it as flat as a ....
c The exam was as easy as .... and everyone got the answers right.
d Whenever he saw Julie, he turned as red as a .... She made him so nervous.
e Jeff couldn't understand why Sally didn't get on with her mother. She was always as nice as .... when he was at their house.
f The trainer liked Scott. He was as keen as .... and always volunteered.
g People said the old man was nutty as a .... , but no one really knew if he was crazy or not, because no one ever spoke to him.
h The boss told the gang the crime would be easy – like taking .... from a baby.
i As soon as she found out he had another girlfriend, Wendy dropped Jake like a ....
j The twins are as alike as .... It's hard to tell them apart.

7 Complete these sentences with one of the expressions in the box.

piece of cake ◆ the apple of my eye ◆ full of beans ◆ cup of tea ◆
the big cheese ◆ bread and butter ◆ cream of the crop ◆
breadwinner ◆ a bad egg ◆ piece of the pie

a I don't want to see that action movie. It's not really my ....
b They took me to see the big boss, the person in charge. He was really ....
c That exam was so easy – it was a ....
d My granddaughter is .... She's such a sweet little girl and I give her everything she wants.
e I'm a plumber, so fixing leaky pipes and dripping taps is my ....
f They're the best students by far. They're the ....
g My husband is out of work, but I have a good job at the bank, so I'm the sole .... for the family at the moment.
h When the family found out that the old lady had left a lot of money in her will, they all wanted a ....
i She has always been .... She's dishonest and never tells the truth.
j My grandson always leaves me exhausted. He's three and he's .... – he never stops for one minute.

Listening: delicious and good for you too?

8 Read these statements about chocolate. Do you think they are *True* or *False*? Write *T* or *F* in the brackets.

a People think that eating chocolate causes skin problems. [ ]
b Cacao is another word for chocolate. [ ]
c Chocolate has never had any medicinal value. [ ]
d The Aztecs ate bars of chocolate. [ ]
e Before the 19th century, chocolate was a luxury item. [ ]
f Chocolate can be good for the heart. [ ]
g Chocolate may help prevent cancer. [ ]
h Milk chocolate is healthier than dark chocolate. [ ]
i There are 300 chemicals in chocolate. [ ]
j Chocolate is addictive. [ ]
k Eating chocolate can make you feel good. [ ]
l In Mexico, chocolate is eaten with chicken. [ ]

Now listen to Track 26 and check your answers.

9 Listen again and complete these notes about chocolate from what you hear.

Good effects

a Flavonoids are good for your ....
b Antioxidants .... damage to the body's cells and tissues.
c Serotonin levels in the .... go up because of the .... and this makes us feel ....

Harmful effects

a Chocolate contains .... and saturated ....
b .... chocolate is more harmful than .... chocolate.
c The sugar in chocolate can cause ....
d Large quantities of .... and .... can lead to ....

10 Match the words from Track 26 with their definition.

a decay ....
b acne ....
c chocoholic ....
d decadent ....
e emaciated ....
f stimulate ....
g crushed ....
h mass-produce ....
i craving ....

1 make in large quantities
2 pressed into very small pieces
3 dangerously thin
4 very strong desire
5 spots, pimples on the skin
6 someone who likes chocolate a lot
7 increase activity
8 immoral, sinful
9 decomposition, destruction

Pronunciation: stress and rhythm

11 Read this paragraph containing the words from Activity 10, making sure that you use appropriate word stress, sentence stress and rhythm.

I often have a craving for chocolate. I know that it's decadent, but I love to bite into a rich creamy bar of chocolate, the kind that are mass-produced for people like me who must have chocolate to give them a boost and stimulate them to get through the rest of the day. I don't care what they say about acne and tooth decay, but I do worry about my weight. Do those emaciated-looking models in magazines never eat chocolate bars?

Listen to Track 27 to check your reading.

Which parts of the paragraph do you agree and disagree with?

Make notes below.

_____
_____
_____
_____
_____
_____

Functional language: making a complaint

12 Which picture goes with which complaint? Write the letter of the picture in the appropriate sentences (1–6).

1 Excuse me. I hate to complain, but my room has not been cleaned and this is the second time it has happened. ....

2 Good morning. I'd like to complain. The heel broke off the first time I wore them. ....

3 Excuse me, but there's something in my soup. ....

4 I have a complaint to make. I made a reservation last week and there are no tables available. ....

5 It doesn't seem to be working. Would it be possible to change rooms? ....

6 Hello, may I speak to the manager please? I bought this last week and it has a hole in it. ....

13 Now match the reply to the complaint. Write the correct number from Activity 12 in the blanks.

a I'm afraid the manager is busy, but I can exchange that for you, if you'd like. ....

b I'm so sorry about that. Would you like your money back or would you like us to fix them? ....

c The hotel is rather full tonight, but I think there are one or two rooms free, so that should be fine. ....

d I don't know how that happened. We always honour our reservations – I'll find a table for you as soon as I can. ....

e Let me check with the cleaning staff and I'll send someone up immediately. ....

f I'll take that back to the kitchen. What can I get you instead? ....

62 unit eight

Grammar: using articles

14 Complete these sentences with the definite or indefinite article, or with no article. The first one is done for you.

a ...X... shopping can be very boring, especially when you go to .... supermarket that you are not familiar with.
b There are many different kinds of .... music and of course .... musicians.
c Do you prefer to eat .... food that is low in .... carbohydrates or low in .... fat?
d This is .... restaurant where we came on our anniversary. It's .... French restaurant where they serve .... best crêpes in .... world.
e Do you read .... labels on the side of .... packets? This is where you will find .... ingredients and .... number of calories.
f Would you like .... piece of cake? We have .... apple cake or .... lemon cake.
g What did you think of .... meal? I thought it was very good, but .... beans were a little undercooked.

15 Read these sentences and give a reason (*a–f*) why the article is used or not used with the nouns in blue.

The noun is:
a ... a non-specific, singular countable noun.
b ... a noun which has already been mentioned and refers to something specific.
c ... a unique noun, something which there is only one of.
d ... a general, non-specific plural noun.
e ... a defined noun or one that is understood to refer to something specific.
f ... an uncountable noun referring to something in general.

1 One day I'd like to travel around the world. ....
2 I'd like to buy a new computer. ....
3 Can you show me the one in the shop window? ....
4 Do you like apricots? ....
5 Would you like a piece of cake? ....
6 Lucy decided to go to a club. When she got to the club, she found that her friend, Marie, had already arrived. ....
7 The sun was burning down on them. ....
8 If you see a pair of trousers you want, you can buy the trousers with the money you got for your birthday. ....
9 Life has a way of helping you out sometimes. ....
10 Did you see those children playing in the water? ....

Writing: describing graphs and tables

Why Do We Fail?
Reasons why Americans are not successful at losing their desired weight
(% of adult Americans reporting that they need to lose weight who...)

Reason	%
Don't exercise enough	60%
Feel metabolism is slowing down	59%
Too often splurge on favorite foods	45%
Don't have enough self-discipline	44%
Snack too much	41%
Often over eat at mealtimes	33%
Often eat for emotional reasons	31%
Eat too many high fat foods	30%
Have trouble eating properly at restaurants	28%
Only watch fat, not calories	19%
Only watch calories, not fat	14%

Source: Calorie Control Council National Consumer Survey, 2004.

16 Read these sentences. Are they *True* or *False* according to the table? Write *T* or *F* in the brackets.

a The graph shows the reasons why Americans go on a diet. [ ]
b The graph shows the reasons why Americans do not achieve the weight they wish to achieve on a diet. [ ]
c More than 50% of people in the survey feel that they do not exercise enough. [ ]
d Less than 50% of the people surveyed think that they don't have enough self-discipline. [ ]
e People are more likely to fail on a diet if they watch their fat intake rather than their calorie intake. [ ]
f More than a third of the people surveyed said they eat for emotional reasons. [ ]
g Less than half the people surveyed said they snack too much. [ ]
h 28% of the people surveyed mentioned eating in restaurants as a reason why they failed while dieting. [ ]
i Almost 60% of the people who fail when dieting say that they feel their metabolism is slowing down. [ ]
j Over 50% of the people surveyed said that eating too much of their favourite foods caused them to fail in their goal. [ ]

Correct the sentences that are false so that they are true.

unit eight 63

17 Use the sentences from Activity 16 on page 63 to write a paragraph about what the graph shows.

This graph shows

....

....

....

It shows that most people

....

....

....

Another main reason why

....

....

....

Other reasons why

....

....

....

Only .... of people interviewed said

....

....

....

Culture and language

18 Are things the same or different in your country? Circle *S* or *D*.

a In Britain, people usually eat food with a knife and fork.	S / D
b There are programmes on the TV about cooking and how to make recipes.	S / D
c In English, we have many words and expressions connected with food.	S / D
d People are usually polite and formal when a complaint is made in a restaurant or store.	S / D
e There are many jokes about waiters, restaurants and food.	
f We don't use articles when we refer to things in general.	S / D
g People are very interested in diets and other ways of losing weight.	S / D
h Chocolate is a very popular sweet snack and can be bought in most food and sweet shops (as well as supermarkets).	S / D
i There are special restaurants for vegetarians and vegans.	S / D

Self-check

19 Read the following statements and put a tick in the correct column.

As a result of studying Unit 8 …	Yes, definitely	More or less	Not sure
I can understand and use food idioms and vocabulary.			
I can read a dictionary entry and tell when the word is used in spoken or written English.			
I can listen to different people speak and identify the main point of what each person says.			
I can use language to make a polite complaint about services.			
I can understand some jokes in English.			
I can use the definite and indefinite article appropriately.			
I can understand and explain what charts and graphs show in English.			
I can understand recipes and different ways of cooking foods.			
I was able to read extracts from different websites and use the information to discuss topics related to food.			
I was able to listen to different people talking about restaurants and use the information to talk about opening a restaurant.			

If you have ticked 'more or less' or 'not sure', go back to the appropriate place in the unit so that you can tick the 'yes, definitely' column.

Test your knowledge

20 Which of the following sentences are written in correct English? Put a tick (✓) or a cross (✗) in the brackets. If there is an error, correct it.

a Put the no skin chicken into a skillet. [ ]
b The exam was a piece of cake. [ ]
c Who wins the bread in your family? [ ]
d This TV doesn't seems to be working. [ ]
e I have a complain to make. [ ]
f This hamburger is overcooked. [ ]
g The results show that 26% of people asked eat junk food regularly. [ ]
h Some doctors say the animal fat is important to the diet. [ ]
i Sun rises at 6 am at this time of year. [ ]
j These chocolates taste stale. [ ]

The phonemic alphabet

21 Consult the table of phonemic symbols on page 125 and then write these words in ordinary spelling.

a /kɑːdiːˈplədʒɪst/

　..

b /ˈkuːl əzə ˈkjuːkʌmbə/

　..

c /hiː ˈseɪvd maɪ ˈbeɪkən/

　..

d /ˈtʃɒklət/

　..

e /ɪˈmeɪsɪeɪtɪd/

　..

f /aɪd ˈlaɪk tə ˈmeɪk ə kəmˈpleɪnt/

　..

g /ˈmænədʒə/

　..

Check your answers by listening to Track 28.

UNIT 9 First impressions

Listening: *Northern Sky*

1 Read the two Internet comments about the song 'Northern Sky' from the album *Bryter Layter* by British singer-songwriter Nick Drake, and answer the questions which follow.

Arlene
It's almost impossible to pick my favorite Nick song, but if I absolutely had to choose I guess I'd go with the one that many Nick fans pick, 'Northern Sky', one of the most stunningly-beautiful songs ever written.

Jake
When all is said and done, this is as good a love song as any ever written; Drake's delicate vocals play against an effortless folk-rock arrangement to create yet another first-rate masterpiece.

Find:

a ... two words or expressions which mean the same as 'choose'. ....
b ... a word which means 'definitely'. ....
c ... an expression which means 'my considered opinion is that …' ....
d ... a word which means 'fine, pleasant, but not strong'. ....
e ... a phrase that means 'very high quality'. ....

2 Listen to Track 29 ('Northern Sky'). What is your first reaction? Choose a number between 0 and 5 from the line below.

I completely agree with the statements in Activity 1.	5 .... 4 .... 3 .... 2 .... 1 0	I completely disagree with the statements in Activity 1.

3 Read the lines *a–i* from the song. Listen to Track 29 again. Put the pairs of lines in the right order in the table (some lines occur more than once).

Northern Sky

a But now you're here
   Brighten my northern sky.
b I never held emotion in the palm of my hand
   Or felt sweet breezes in the top of a tree.
c Would you love me for my money?
   Would you love me for my head?
d I've been a long time that I've wandered
   Through the people I have known.
e I never felt magic crazy as this;
   I never saw moons knew the meaning of the sea.
f Oh, if you would and you could
   Come blow your horn on high.
g Oh, if you would and you could
   Straighten my new mind's eye.
h I've been a long time that I'm waiting.
   Been a long time that I'm blown.
i Would you love me through the winter?
   Would you love me 'til I'm dead?

1 ....
2 ....
3 ....
4 ....
5 ....
6 ....
7 ....
8 ....
9 ....
10 ....
11 ....

66 unit nine

Vocabulary: physical description (connotation)

4 Use phrases from the box to complete the sentences under the pictures.

bald ◆ bright ◆ chin (x 2) ◆ curly ◆ eyes ◆ generous ◆ gorgeous ◆ nose ◆
protruding ◆ slim and elegant ◆ small dark ◆ straight ◆ straight nose ◆ strong ◆
thick wavy ◆ thinning ◆ wavy

a He has deep-set .... under .... hair, a long .... and a square ....

b She's got .... eyes, a turned-up .... and a .... mouth.

c He's got .... hair, in fact he's nearly ....

d She's absolutely .... She's .... with long thick .... hair.

e He has .... hair, ... eyes, and a .... chin.

f She's got .... hair, a weak .... and .... eyes.

5 Write the following words and phrases from the box in the correct rows in the table.
Write P (= positive), NT (= neutral), or NG (= negative) in the brackets. The first one is done for you.

a bit of a mess [NG]
a little bit pudgy [ ]
a little overweight [ ]
a little plump [ ]
absolutely gorgeous [ ]
absolutely puny [ ]
absolutely voluptuous [ ]
emaciated [ ]
extremely beautiful [ ]
extremely flabby [ ]
extremely well-built [ ]
fantastically hideous [ ]
fantastically muscular [ ]
incredibly cute [ ]
incredibly handsome [ ]
incredibly obese [ ]
incredibly ugly [ ]
incredibly untidy [ ]
kind of skinny [ ]
rather attractive [ ]
rather elegant [ ]
rather plain [ ]
rather scruffy [ ]
rather slim [ ]
rather stout [ ]
rather ugly [ ]
very underweight [ ]

Thin
Not thin
General description of looks and appearance

unit nine 67

Reading: beauty and sadness

6 Read the biographical note and complete the table.

Nick Drake (see page 66), a British singer-songwriter, was born in 1948 and died in 1974. He made three records that everyone said were fantastic, but hardly anybody bought. But, since his death, his fame has grown, so that more than 30 years later, his songs have been included on the soundtrack of at least three Hollywood movies, and documentaries about him and his music have been aired repeatedly on American and British radio and television. The latest of these was a radio programme narrated by the Hollywood star Brad Pitt, a committed fan. Many 21st-century musicians (Coldplay, Beth Orton, Norah Jones, for example) say his music influenced theirs and there are countless websites devoted to his memory and his music.

Name	a
Dates	b
Number of records	c
Admirers of his music	d 1 2 3 4

7 Read the comments which were sent to a recent BBC website about Nick Drake. Who:

a ... desperately wanted to find a CD of Nick Drake's music?

b ... first heard Nick Drake's music in a documentary on American radio?

c ... first heard Nick Drake's music in a television commercial?

d ... first heard Nick Drake's music because of a friend from Scotland?

e ... first heard Nick Drake's music when her boyfriend played it to her?

f ... found the music of Nick Drake by searching on the world wide web?

g ... liked Nick Drake's music the moment he first heard it?

h ... once went through a stage in her life when she was rather unhappy and didn't know who or where she was?

i ... still listens to Nick Drake's music at the age of 30?

j ... thinks Nick Drake's music means different things at different times?

k ... wants to tell everyone about Nick Drake's music?

l ... got very involved with Nick Drake's music after listening to 'Cello Song'?

8 Match the words in blue with the following definitions.

a a noun meaning the opposite of 'foreground'

b a verb meaning 'to be attracted very strongly by something when it is drawn to your attention'

c a verb meaning 'to be caught in something as if by ropes or a net'

d a verb meaning 'charmed as if by magic'

e an adjective meaning 'not belonging to any particular period of history'

f an adjective describing something that gives you great pleasure or joy

g an adjective meaning 'sad'

h an adjective meaning 'sad and impossible to forget'

i an adjective describing something that gives you ideas about how to make your life better

j an adjective describing something that makes you feel happier and more positive about the future

k a noun which means 'aims'

l an adjective which means 'young and without much experience'

I was introduced to Nick Drake's music by a Scottish pen-friend some 14 years ago at the tender age of 16. I don't think there is much else that I listened to and loved back then that I still listen to on a regular basis. Nick Drake's music is timeless and beautiful, melancholic yet uplifting – I always return to it.

Sarah Beatrice, Bristol

I first heard of Nick Drake on 'E' Network, which is a local cable station in my area. A documentary was aired a few years ago. It captured my attention instantly. There was this lovely, haunting beauty in his words and melodies that just sucked me into another dimension. I was obsessed with finding a CD. It was so different from anything I'd ever heard. It was like finding a lost treasure. I rarely hear of any fans mentioning how charming he looked as a man. I just can't find the words to describe how much Nick's music has captivated and enchanted me since the discovery and I never tire of listening.

Tonya Swift, Little Rock, Arkansas

I was introduced to Nick Drake's music just over a year ago and I was instantly captivated by it. His music is so incredibly beautiful and the words are so poignant. I particularly love 'Man in a shed' and 'Time of no reply' but I don't have one favourite song as they're all truly unique. His songs have inspired my music so much. I am glad his music is getting recognition as he deserves it. If only he could be here today to see the recognition he is now getting.

Bentley, Derbyshire

Nick's music was introduced to me by a now ex-boyfriend. I am extremely fortunate to have encountered his work, which I find is sometimes inspirational, sometimes haunting; it just hits the spot for 'mood music'.

Usha Jain, London

I'm almost embarrassed to say I found Nick Drake through a commercial for the Volkswagen Cabrio. 'Pink Moon' was the background music; it haunted me. I searched the Internet for mentions of the song and finally found Nick Drake. What a revelation!

Jesse, Glendale, California

My dad first introduced me to Nick Drake's work at a time in my life when I had lost my way a bit. The first song I heard was 'Way to blue' and ever since then, I've bought every one of his albums. At first, his music made me feel sad, but now I see his work as an inspiration to us all. I believe Nick's music helped me to recover from my problems and, although I am only 17, I have played his music to all my friends and they agree that there is something to be said about music that is not necessarily from our era but is still truly great. It is one of my missions in life to spread the word and keep the memory of Nick Drake alive.

Lucy Sparrow, Bath

'Most people think his music is as sad as his life was, but I think there is a glimpse of beauty in that sadness.' These were the words of a friend of mine who introduced me to Nick Drake's music just last summer. The first song I ever listened to was 'Cello song', and I became completely entangled in his music. I do not listen to his albums very often though. I guess this is in part because I would like to save his music for very special moments. But I can see why my friend thought that there was still beauty in all that sadness. Nick Drake will always be one of my favourite musicians, one of the few who can give me a sense of being alive in a world that is real. In such a world, people are able to experience the whole spectrum of emotions in succession, without feeling ashamed for that.

Alejandra Valero, Mexico

Grammar: adjectives and adjective order

9 Complete the sentences with the first word for each of the compound adjectives.

a Although no one called him handsome, everyone did agree that he was extremely ....-looking in his own way.
b He was so ....-minded that he kept forgetting things.
c He's extremely ....-minded. He never does anything unless he thinks it is a morally good thing to do.
d He's incredibly ....-sighted. He can't see anything which is a long way away.
e It's because she's so ....-skinned that she has to be especially careful in the bright sunshine.
f She was an ....-haired beauty. Her hair colour was somewhere between brown and red.
g The ....-tempered man just wouldn't stop shouting.
h They are so ....-minded. They just can't accept any new or interesting ideas.
i What I remember about her as a teacher is that she was very ....-minded. She treated all the children the same and never punished anyone unnecessarily.
j You can't complain if your hotel isn't great when you go on a ....-price holiday.

10 Write the adjectives in blue in the correct order in front of the nouns. The first one is done for you.

a black / old
an ...old black... briefcase
b black / frightening / huge
a .... storm cloud
c American / folk / haunting
a .... song
d Colombian / elegant / generous / tall
a .... woman
e 19th-century / operatic / unimpressive
an .... overture
f ancient / cooking / Mexican
.... recipes
g expensive / high-heeled / Italian
.... shoes
h blue-green / large / round
.... eyes
i beautiful / British / radio / small / talented
a ....
.... actress

Functional language: taking ourselves to be fixed

11 Complete the dialogue with phrases from the box.

a bit off the top ◆ How can I help you? ◆
I'd like a haircut, please ◆ if that's all right ◆
Just above the ears ◆ Mr Cartwright ◆
Oh I'm sorry, Mr Cartwright ◆
Oh, come on, Mr Cartwright ◆ Peter (x 2) ◆
That's not very convenient ◆
What would you recommend?

A: Good morning
B: Good morning sir. (**a**) ....
A: My name's Cartwright. I've got an appointment with Mr Smith.
B: (**b**) ...., Mr Smith has been called away on urgent family business. We tried to reach you but you didn't answer your phone.
A: Oh dear. (**c**) ....
B: But Paul Jones can see you (**d**) ....
A: Well I don't know ...
B: (**e**) ...., he's one of our most experienced haircutters.
A: Oh all right.

C: Morning, (**f**) .... What's your first name?
A: Sorry?
C: Your first name.
A: It's, umm, (**g**) ....
C: Right, (**h**) ...., what can I do for you?
A: (**i**) ....
C: Well yes, obviously. But how shall I cut it?
A: (**j**) ....
C: Well Peter, with hair like yours, I think you should have (**k**) ...., shorten the sides, and then ...
A: (**l**) .... ?
C: Yes, that's right.
A: OK. That's fine. Do your worst!
C: I think you mean my best, Peter.

70 unit nine

Writing: curriculum vitae

12 Complete the following tasks.

a List the schools, colleges and / or universities you have attended with the right dates. Put them in order where the most recent is first, and the first one is at the end of the list.

b Make a list of any full or part-time jobs you have had. Put them in order where the most recent is first, and the first one is at the end of the list.

c Make a list of the exams you have taken with the qualifications you obtained. Put them in order where the most recent is first, and the first one is at the end of the list.

d Make a list of your hobbies and interests. Put them in order where the one that 'sounds the best' goes first.

e Note anything else you might want to say to make yourself 'sound good'.

f Think of two people (ex-teachers, ex-employers, etc.) who you could ask to support your application (be your referees).

Use your notes to complete the following CV form.

Name:

Date of birth:

Address:

Schools / Colleges attended:

Exams:

Qualifications:

Employment record (including holiday jobs):

Hobbies and interests:

Additional information:

References:

Pronunciation: tone of voice (attitude)

13 Listen to Track 30. The speaker says 'Good afternoon, Mrs Clarke' seven times. Put 1 to 7 in the brackets depending on the speaker's tone of voice.

a The speaker has some bad news for Mrs Clarke. [ ]
b The speaker is thrilled to see Mrs Clarke again after a long time. [ ]
c Mrs Clarke owes the speaker money and has not paid it back. [ ]
d Mrs Clarke is a famous person and the speaker is very impressed to meet her. [ ]
e Even though it is a formal occasion, Mrs Clarke isn't wearing any shoes. [ ]
f The speaker has been waiting for Mrs Clarke since 11 o'clock this morning (when they had arranged to meet). [ ]
g The speaker is very tired. Mrs Clarke is the 10th person to come into the office. [ ]

Check with the answer key and listen again.

Culture and language

14 Re-write the following sentences so that they reflect your own reality, views or language. Who is 'we' in each case?

a According to research, we don't think blonde women are as intelligent or competent as women with darker hair.

b We drink a lot of coffee in various coffee shops which you can find in almost all towns and city centres.

c We have definite ideas about what makes people attractive.

d We often choose to marry people who look a bit like us or like people we know well (e.g. our family).

e We often judge people by their appearance.

f We often use a list of adjectives before a noun, and we have an accepted sequence for those adjectives.

g We seem to be keener than before on the idea of plastic surgery to make ourselves look 'better' or younger or 'different'.

h When we describe people, we often use words like 'a little' or 'absolutely' to modify our descriptions.

i When we have our hair cut, we often have long conversations with the hairdresser.

j When we write a CV, we include details of age, marital status, education, qualifications, work experience and interests.

Self-check

15 Put 1 to 10 in the brackets to show how difficult the following abilities are for you in English. 1 = 'I feel confident about this / I can do it', but 10 = 'I am not at all confident about this / I'm not sure I can do it'.

a Being able to describe people's physical appearance in a variety of ways [ ]
b Having a conversation in a place where people go to have their hair cut, or some other thing done (such as going to the dentist or a plastic surgeon!) [ ]
c Knowing when to use commas and when to use *and* when we have more than one adjective before a noun [ ]
d Making and using two-word (compound) adjectives [ ]
e Putting together a CV giving all the relevant information about education, experience and interests [ ]
f Reading various pieces of information about people's perceptions of blonde hair for women, and being able to share bits of information with classmates [ ]
g Recommending things in a number of different ways [ ]
h Sequencing a number of adjectives correctly when using them before a noun [ ]
i Understanding a 'dramatic' conversation about who people are attracted to – and being able to identify different points of view [ ]
j Understanding the meaning of different words that all describe the same kind of thing (e.g. thinness), but which have different connotations [ ]

Take the items you scored from 6 to 10 and look back at the appropriate place in Unit 9 of the Student's Book.

Test your knowledge

16 Translate the following sentences and questions.

a Leave him alone guys!

b He has thinning hair, deep-set eyes, a pointed nose and a weak chin.

c He's a little overweight, but he's extremely good-looking.

d Sport has never played a major part in my life.

e I was thinking of having my hair cut short.

f When I was a child, we had a rectangular pink tablecloth on the kitchen table.

g I'm going to give you a prescription for an aspirin.

h Can I give your name as a reference in my CV?

Did you have problems? If you did, go back to the relevant activity in the Student's Book to check on meaning and use.

The phonemic alphabet

17 Consult the table of phonemic symbols on page 125 and then write these words in ordinary spelling.

a /ˌgʊdˈlʊkɪŋ/

b /vəˈlʌptjuːəs/

c /ˌwelˈdrest/

d /ɪtsə ˈbɪtəvə ˈmes/

e /juːl ˈdæmɪdʒ jɔː kəˈrɪə prɒspekts/

f /ʃiːz ˈæbsəluːtliː ˈgɔːdʒəs/

g /ˈwɒt əjuː ˈtɔːkɪŋ əˈbaʊt/

Check your answers by listening to Track 31.

UNIT 10 Heavy weather

Reading: getting warmer

1 Look at these pictures from the movie *The Day After Tomorrow*. What is happening in the pictures? Did you see this movie when it came out, or have you seen it since?

2 Read the article from a San Francisco newspaper and answer this question.

According to the author, why is global warming such an important problem?

....
....
....
....
....

CLIMATE CHANGE 'MORE DANGEROUS THAN TERRORISM'

It was, and still is, one scary movie. Thanks to global warming, in *The Day After Tomorrow*, the world literally freezes over. Yet how real was the science behind one of the decade's big disaster movies?

'Climate change is a far greater threat to the world than international terrorism,' says the science adviser to the British government. 'Temperatures are getting hotter, and they are getting hotter faster than at any time in the past,' says the international weather expert. 'Climate change is poised to change our pattern of life,' says an African ecologist. But successive governments in the US and elsewhere won't listen.

The number of extreme weather events has doubled from the decade before: lethal heatwaves in Europe, floods in Africa, droughts in Asia and the United States. A record 300 million people flee their homes from natural disasters. Carbon dioxide in the atmosphere hits record levels. Warming increases the range and virulence of diseases. Trees die in New England. Glaciers melt faster in Alaska. There's a major influx of freshwater in the North Atlantic and a slowdown of ocean circulation below the Arctic Circle. Antarctic ice flows faster into the ocean.

What could be next? Rising sea levels swamp coastal cities. Famine in Europe. Nuclear wars for water. A million species threatened with extinction. The end of life on Earth as we know it.

Sounds terrifying, but these aren't scenes from *The Day After Tomorrow*. They're from the real world. Everything in the second and third paragraphs has happened or is the statement of a real person (including Sir David King, chief science adviser to the British government). Everything in the fourth paragraph is science-based speculation.

The movie itself exaggerates the speed with which global warming brings on a new ice age, but the paradox that more heat might lead to more ice is real. If cold water from melting glaciers really does change ocean currents like the Gulf Stream, Manhattan could get colder pretty quickly – though in a decade, not a New York minute, as *The Day After Tomorrow* would have it. But all by itself, heat is already causing problems like drought, crop failures, disease, violent storms – and is threatening much more as the century proceeds.

Meanwhile, why haven't we noticed all this? Why are we determined to be oblivious? While 72 per cent of Americans said they were concerned about global warming in 2000, by 2004 this had gone down to 58 per cent and only 15 per cent believed it had anything to do with fossil fuel consumption. The combustion of fossil fuels (such as when you drive your car, or fly in a plane) produces carbon dioxide that contributes to the greenhouse effect and releases particles that are dangerous to breathe. Surely Mums and Dads, at least, should be worried about the effect on their children's health and their grandchildren's world? But perhaps it's hard to get upset about something that sounds so moderate and nice as 'global warming'? Even the 'greenhouse effect' sounds decidedly unthreatening. Who's afraid of a greenhouse?

Whatever the reason for our apathy, the climate crisis is the keystone issue of our time. Addressing it means addressing virtually every other significant environmental and energy problem and it must be done soon, because what is newest and most challenging about global warming is that once its effects are clearly apparent, it's too late to stop them.

3 Read these sentences. According to the article, which of them refer to the movie (*M*), which of them refer to real life (*RL*) and which refer to scientific predictions (*SP*)?

   a Three hundred million people have to leave their homes because there are natural disasters. ....
   b Global warming brings on a new ice age. ....
   c There is a record level of carbon dioxide in the atmosphere. ....
   d People in Europe do not have enough food to eat. ....
   e Less than 20% of people in the US know about the effects of cars on the environment. ....
   f A million species of animals are in danger of extinction. ....
   g There are more diseases that spread more quickly. ....
   h Sea levels rise and flood cities that are near oceans. ....
   i New York becomes frozen in ice very quickly. ....
   j More than 40% of the US population are not worried about global warming. ....

4 Match the words and phrases from the text (*a–i*) with their meanings (*1–9*).

   a apathy   ....
   b flee   ....
   c influx   ....
   d lethal   ....
   e oblivious   ....
   f paradox   ....
   g poised to   ....
   h swamp   ....
   i virulence   ....

   1 about to very soon in the future
   2 cover with water
   3 escape from
   4 flow coming in
   5 killer
   6 lack of interest
   7 strength of harmfulness
   8 unaware
   9 illogical, unexpected situation

unit ten 75

Grammar: narrative (simple and continuous forms)

5 Circle the correct form to complete the sentences. In two of the sentences, both forms are possible.

a She was very tired because she had been painting / had painted the house all day.
b They were watching / watched TV when the explosion happened.
c Robert took a short break from writing emails. So far he had been writing / had written ten and he still had five more to write.
d When I had arrived / arrived home, I was finding / found that I forgot / had forgotten to turn the tap off when I left / had left for work. The tap had run / had been running all day.
e They knew that the weather was getting warmer. The temperature had been increasing / had increased by two degrees and the same was predicted for the following year.
f I wish you told / had told me about the problem before.
g Scientists noticed a pattern. Rainfall had been increasing / had increased by one inch every year for the last ten years.
h We have been living / have lived in this house for ten years, but now it's time to move.
i It had been snowing / had snowed for two hours and the snow was settling / settled in a thick layer on the ground.
j How long have you been knowing / have you known about this problem?

6 Put the verb in brackets in the correct tense. The first one is done for you.

John (**a.** look) *looked* around nervously as he got into his car. There (**b.** appear) .... to be no one following him, but he (**c.** not take) .... any chances, so he (**d.** take off) .... quickly and immediately (**e.** slip) .... down a side street, checking in his mirror all the while. As he (**f.** drive) ...., he (**g.** think) .... about the photos and why he (**h.** pursue – *passive*) .... None of it (**i.** make) .... sense. He (**j.** attend) .... the party as part of his job and he (**k.** take) .... the photos for the local newspaper. Since he (**l.** take) .... them, he (**m.** know) .... that someone (**n.** watch) .... him and his apartment (**o.** break – *passive*) .... into twice. What (**p.** can) .... be so important about the photos that people (**q.** be) .... prepared to watch him 24 hours a day and break into his apartment? He (**r.** hope) .... that Marlene (**s.** be able) .... to tell him when he (**t.** get) .... to the office. She was the one who (**u.** tell) .... him to take the photos. There (**v.** have) .... to be a good reason why she (**w.** not answer) .... his phone calls. John (**x.** be) .... afraid of what that answer might be.

Vocabulary: weather words

7 Match words from the two columns (*a–k* and *1–11*) to find words and expressions connected with the weather, either literally or metaphorically. Write them out in the spaces provided.

a	blazing	1	disposition
b	thunderous	2	lightning
c	torrential	3	wind
d	storm of	4	protest
e	howling	5	sun
f	gales of	6	pour
g	thunder and	7	struck
h	down	8	season
i	rainy	9	laughter
j	sunny	10	rain
k	thunder	11	applause

a ....
b ....
c ....
d ....
e ....
f ....
g ....
h ....
i ....
j ....
k ....

8 Now write one of the expressions from Activity 7 in each blank in this paragraph. The first one is done for you.

Julie stepped out into the (**a**) ...blazing sun... at 10 in the morning during the (**b**) .... in Mexico City. She spoke no Spanish, but with her (**c**) .... , she had no problem communicating with people and making friends. At about 2 in the afternoon, she noticed the clouds gathering and soon there was a (**d**) .... shaking the leaves from the trees. Then suddenly it started – a few drops at first and then (**e**) .... Then came the (**f**) .... lighting up the sky and causing the street dogs to run for cover. She ducked into a restaurant to escape the (**g**) .... and she was (**h**) .... at the noise. There were three different bands playing three different kinds of music and (**i**) .... coming from every table followed by (**j**) .... when each band ended a song. Julie looked on as a (**k**) .... broke out when the band wanted to stop playing.

Listening: weather forecast

9 Listen to Track 32. Write the number of the weather forecast on the picture of the weather it describes for tomorrow.

a   b   c
d   e   f

10 Listen again and choose the best answer for each forecast.

Forecast 1
In the next few days, there will be:
a ... a lot of clear skies and sunshine. [ ]
b ... strong winds from the north. [ ]
c ... a lot of heavy rainfall. [ ]

Forecast 2
The weather will be warm because:
a ... there is high pressure. [ ]
b ... there will be a light wind. [ ]
c ... of the time of year. [ ]

Forecast 3
The temperature in the day will be:
a ... minus 2 degrees. [ ]
b ... about 3 degrees. [ ]
c ... about 0 degree. [ ]

Forecast 4
The weather is:
a ... unusual for the time of year [ ]
b ... unsafe for driving. [ ]
c ... warmer than expected. [ ]

Forecast 5
The wind will:
a ... last until the following day. [ ]
b ... drop before night falls. [ ]
c ... be strong for two days. [ ]

Forecast 6
The flood:
a ... will take place in the highlands. [ ]
b ... has taken everyone by surprise. [ ]
c ... has caused people to leave their houses. [ ]

11 Listen to Track 32 again and complete these sentences with a word or expression from the forecasts.

Forecast 1
The only .... is that the wind is going to .... , so there'll just be a light .... from the north.

Forecast 2
Enjoy it while you can – it's not going .... and Tuesday will see a .... to cooler temperatures with .... of some rain.

Forecast 3
The day will start off .... and very cold and .... there'll be some .... later in the day ....

Forecast 4
We're expecting a pretty heavy .... during the night and going on into the day tomorrow with .... expected and plenty of drifting in ....

Forecast 5
Those winds will probably last .... into the night and .... in the early hours of the morning.

Forecast 6
Heavy rains are expected in the next 24 hours and .... in lowlands is expected as ....

Pronunciation: stress in weather expressions

12 Practise saying these sentences.

a This evening there'll be a light breeze from the east.
b The high pressure system is bringing good weather.
c After 5 this evening there'll be cooler temperatures.
d Temperatures will fall to below freezing tonight.
e There was heavy snowfall all day today.
f Ice on the road is creating hazardous driving conditions.
g There was bright sunshine all morning followed by light showers.
h The announcer gave an emergency flood warning.
i The mayor told the people of the town to make flood preparations.

Now listen to Track 33. Do the speakers there say the sentences in the same way?

Functional language: conversational gambits

13 Match the two parts of the dialogues. The first one is done for you.

a The weather's awful today.   9
b His new book is awful, so boring.   ......
c There's nothing good on TV tonight.   ......
d Don't you just love French restaurants?   ......
e To change the subject, isn't the latest Hollywood blockbuster ridiculous?   ......
f By the way, talking of Hollywood, have you ever been to Los Angeles?   ......
g Sorry to interrupt, but do you recognise that man over there?   ......
h Incidentally, did you hear about Rachel Morrison?   ......
i Miranda told me she didn't like her new job.   ......
j Graham's going on holiday for a month.   ......

1 Yes, but from another viewpoint, at least it's got great special effects.
2 And that's not all. He's buying a new car as well.
3 And as if that wasn't enough, she said the pay was too low! I think it's a good salary, don't you?
4 I did. Wasn't it terrible about her father?
5 Yes, I think he was in our class at school.
6 But on the other hand, they tend to be very expensive.
7 I have, and what's more I've even been to Hollywood.
8 Yes, but there again, his last book was great.
9 Yes, and to make matters worse the bus was late.
10 And that's not all – there's nothing good on all week!

78 unit ten

14 Complete this dialogue with a suitable expression from the box below.

> Hold on a minute
> looking at it from another angle
> on top of that
> Could I say something here
> if it wasn't enough to
> Incidentally, on the subject of
> if I just might make a point

PRESENTER: You're tuned to 'Face the Issue' where this week we talk about global climate change.

JANE GRAVES:
(a) .... ?

PRESENTER: Yes, Jane?

JANE GRAVES: Well, we've been talking a lot about the weather getting warmer, but
(b) .... about the causes. Fossil fuel consumption is …

MARTIN BROOKSTONE:
(c) .... !
There are other causes too.

JANE GRAVES: But cars are the most important cause of all and
(d) ...., the manufacturers keep making cars that use more petrol and pollute more.

PRESENTER: (e) .... cars, what kind of car do you both drive?

JANE GRAVES: I drive a hybrid electric car that pollutes less and uses less fuel.

MARTIN BROOKSTONE: I have to admit that I drive an SUV, but,
(f) ...., I have a big family and we really don't use the car much.

JANE GRAVES: This is precisely the problem, as
(g) .... own a car that increases the problem, the owners then try to justify why they need one!

Writing: weblogs and online journals

15 Read these letters to an Internet forum. Complete the characteristics of a blog and an online journal in the table below.

Friday November 19, 2004   Previous | Next
Ask Reeves

Dear Reeves

What are blogs, and are they the same as online journals?
Confused from Cornwall

Dear Confused:
As you probably know, 'blog' is short for 'weblog' and is usually defined as a personal or noncommercial web site that uses a dated log format (like a diary or journal) and has the newest entry at the top of the page. A blog contains links to other web sites along with commentary about those sites, which an online journal does not. A weblog is updated frequently and sometimes groups links by specific subjects, such as politics, news, pop culture, or computer issues.

Weblogs and online journals are often confused, and they can frequently overlap in content and style. But purists point out that a person writing in an online journal or diary is logging their life, not the web. Weblogs still exist to log what's going on around the world wide web.

Online diaries have become extremely popular over the past few years. From Russian filmmakers to Malaysian teenagers to London accountants, anyone can write about their daily lives and publish it for the world to see.

I hope this answers your question.

Reeves

	Weblog ('blog')	Online journal
includes the date	✓	
the most recent entry comes at the top		
the writer talks about her / his life		
the writer talks about things connected to the world wide web		
there are links to other websites		

unit ten 79

16 Read these extracts and say which one is a blog and which one is an online journal according to the definitions on page 79.

Saturday, August 21, 2004:

Sproglet has got cleaning disease. During this week that we have been on holiday, he has invited a friend round (twice) to tidy his bedroom, cleaned the television, his bike and the street in front of our house. While I was in the queue at the chemist's, he tidied up the children's play area. Yesterday, he refused an ice lolly, saying 'no, mummy, it will make me messy'. Who is this monster I have created? Isn't my lack of hygiene and general disregard for clutter good enough for him?

Liz Wright |1:55 PM|
http://twodumbblondes.blogspot.com/

> July 31, 2004
> **Bunny saved via Craigslist**
> Okay, remember Craigslist isn't about us, it's about what you do with it. Well, some folks did something really nasty to a bunny rabbit, then they blogged it, but other people reported it on Craigslist, and the bunny is safe.
>
> The Chron covered the incident and its aftermath.
>
> USA Today summarizes it nicely:
>
> Someone found the photos on one of the suspect's personal website and posted them on Craigslist, the popular Internet bulletin board, where the House Rabbit Society in Richmond saw it.
>
> Posted by craig on July 31, 2004 01:06 PM
> http://www.cnewmark.com/archives/000259.html

Note: The Chron = The San Francisco Chronicle

17 Read the extracts again and answer these questions.

Who or what:
a ... is 'Sproglet'?
b ... is concerned about Sproglet?
c ... is not good at cleaning the house?
d ... is 'Craigslist'?
e ... saved the rabbit?

18 Write your own short blog entry and an online journal entry for today.

Blog	Journal

Culture and language

19 Are things the same or different in your country? Circle *S* or *D*.

a In Britain, the weather is a very common topic of conversation. S / D
b In English, there are several special words and expressions to talk about the weather. S / D
c The summer months are hotter than the winter months. S / D
d There are special expressions that you can use in conversation when you want to interrupt someone politely. S / D
e In English, there are simple tenses and continuous tenses. S / D
f The past perfect tense is used to talk about an event in the past which happened before the main events in the story which are written in past simple. S / D
g People do not have to carry special equipment to deal with the weather (except an umbrella!). S / D

Self-check

20 Read the following statements and put a tick in the correct column.

As a result of studying Unit 10 …	Yes, definitely	More or less	Not sure
I can use expressions to describe weather conditions.			
I understand how to use weather words in various metaphorical expressions.			
I can use the correct tense and sequence of tenses when telling a story in the past.			
I can use expressions to reinforce and balance what has been said.			
I can write a diary entry and an online journal entry.			
I can use intonation to help me understand what someone means.			
I can use expressions to change the subject and interrupt politely.			
I can listen to song lyrics and identify what the singer is singing.			
I can recognise the meaning of words in context.			
I can talk about the weather using appropriate word and sentence stress.			

If you have ticked 'more or less' or 'not sure', go back to the appropriate place in the unit so that you can tick the 'yes, definitely' column.

Test your knowledge

21 Which of the following sentences are written in correct English? Put a tick (✓) or a cross (✗) in the brackets. If there is an error, correct it.

  a When I arrived, I was surprised to see that she talked on the phone to her sister. [ ]
  b I could see by her swollen eyes that she had been crying. [ ]
  c The chef took out the cake that she had been baking the day before. [ ]
  d Today there will be severe sunshine followed by a light thunderstorm. [ ]
  e The crowd broke out into thunderous applause. [ ]
  f For change the subject, do you like dogs? [ ]
  g I hate to interrupt, but have you seen my car keys? [ ]
  h She was completely oblivious to my cries for help and kept walking. [ ]
  i The escaped convicts decided to flee the country. [ ]
  j Accidentally, on the subject of dogs, have you seen my poodles? [ ]

The phonemic alphabet

22 Consult the table of phonemic symbols on page 125 and then write these words in ordinary spelling.

  a /təˈrenʃəl ˈreɪn/

  b /ˈdaʊnˌpɔː/

  c /ˈheviː ˈflʌdɪŋ/

  d /ˌɪnsɪˈdentliː/

  e /ˈfriːzɪŋ ˈtemprətʃəz/

  f /tə ˈtʃeɪndʒ ðə ˈsʌbdʒekt/

  g /ˈhæzədəs ˈdraɪvɪŋ kənˈdɪʃənz/

Check your answers by listening to Track 34.

UNIT 11 Famous for 15 minutes?

Reading: what to watch

1 Read the programme choices for May 28th on page 83. Which programmes are the sentences talking about? Write the letters of the sentences in the correct rows of the table below.

  a It has people who nobody knows.
  b It has six main characters.
  c It has three finalists.
  d It is difficult not to watch it.
  e It puts a group of people into a house.
  f It recreates scenes of how something was built.
  g In this one, people sing in order to win.
  h It's a 'situation comedy' (comedy series).
  i It's about a historical figure.
  j It's the first show in a new series of a popular reality programme.
  k It's the last show in a long-running series.
  l It's the last show of the third series.

  > Friends
  >
  > Art of the garden
  >
  > Big Brother: Live Launch Show
  >
  > American Idol

2 Read *Today's Choices* again. Who or what:

  a ... cried?
  b ... designed the gardens of Blenheim Palace?
  c ... have apparently chosen interesting people for their show?
  d ... have big and powerful lungs?
  e ... is an American version of a British TV show?
  f ... is going to have their own new series?
  g ... is in its fifth year?
  h ... is married to a nice man?
  i ... is sad and funny?
  j ... tells a story about a garden designer or architect?
  k ... was the owner of Blenheim Palace?
  l ... wears informal / casual clothes?
  m ... won the last series of *Big Brother*?
  n ... buys and sells fish in the north of Scotland?

3 Complete the sentences with these words and phrases from the text.

  > as dull as ditchwater ◆ bid their last farewells ◆ brickbats ◆ crowning achievement ◆ dark horse ◆ fell out with ◆ fool the eye ◆ pulls in big audiences ◆ talks us through ◆ there are no great fireworks ◆ tying-up of loose ends ◆ we'll just have to wait and see

  a A rather literary way of writing that they say goodbye is ....
  b When all of the story details are finally resolved, we talk of a ....
  c A way of saying that something is not fantastically exciting or dramatic is ....
  d Another way of saying 'he explains it' is to say 'he .... it'.
  e If there's a possibility that someone will win even if nobody expected them to, we can call them a ....
  f If two people who once were friends disagreed about something, we can say that they .... with each other.
  g If we want to explain that a TV show is watched by a lot of people, we can say that it ....
  h We often call sharp criticisms ...., especially when they are made about actors, singers, etc.
  i When we are tricked by things we see, we can say that they ....
  j When we don't know what's going to happen and we want people to know this fact, we can say that ....
  k When we want to describe somebody's greatest success in their profession, we can talk about their ....
  l A rather literary way of saying that something is very boring is to say that it is ....

82 unit eleven

FRIDAY 28 MAY

TODAY'S CHOICES

SITCOM
Friends *9.00pm*

All right, I admit it, I cried. Quite a lot, actually, as the friends bid their last farewells after ten years – and this final show like all the others will be shown all over the world again and again and again! But even though it's the last show (and they are difficult to pull off), this one gets it just right. There are no great fireworks – this is a neat and, in some ways, quite a low-key tying-up of loose ends to make a highly satisfactory finale. It's sad of course, but it's frequently funny too, and there are some great jokes. Fans of the series would expect nothing less from a comedy that has been so good over such a long period of time.

So tonight we're joining the six as they start their new lives. Joey, of course, is the character who will live on in a new TV series. Chandler and Monica are preparing to become parents and move to the country, and Phoebe is married to sweet Mike. There's just the small matter of Ross and Rachel whose on-off romance has been such a big part of the show from the very beginning.

Rachel is heading off for a new life in Paris, while Ross is trying to work out where his future really lies. Everyone is very tearful – yes, they look like real tears – as Monica's apartment is packed up and they all leave it for the last time. So go on, get out those paper handkerchiefs. Just this once.

Alison Graham

GARDENING
Art of the garden *9.20pm BBC2*

Diarmuid Gavin tells the story of the designer Lancelot 'Capability' Brown, often called the nation's greatest landscape architect. In his scruffy jeans and cord jacket, Diarmuid takes us to Capability Brown's crowning achievement, the gardens of Blenheim Palace, surely one of Britain's greatest 'stately homes', and talks us through the story of their construction.

From 1760, thousands of labourers worked for years to dig a huge artificial lake, make a mile-long river and plant tens of thousands of trees.

The reason for all this hard work was to create a landscape that was totally beautiful and natural and which, more importantly, looked as if it had always been there. And it did. No one would have guessed how much effort it had taken if they hadn't known.

And how much money! The Duke of Blenheim, who owned the house, nearly went bankrupt paying for his gardens, and for years all he could see was a muddy field. Perhaps that's why he fell out with Capability Brown and started arguing with him – and why the programme makers feel they can have actors pretending to be the two men. Much better are reconstructions of the work in progress, and the programme has some incredible special effects that fool the eye into believing we are really there.

David Butcher

REALITY
Big Brother: Live Launch Show *10.00pm C4*

Love it or hate it, it's almost impossible to ignore *Big Brother*, which, like its ITV1 cousin *I'm a Celebrity ... Get Me Out of Here!* fascinates viewers and media alike for weeks. Even when the participants are as dull as ditchwater and the footage veers from mind-numbingly boring to downright infantile, the series pulls in big audiences. So, reluctant though you may be to get drawn into the experience, chances are you'll dip in at least once to see what all the fuss is about.

Now in its fifth year, the format remains unchanged (a group of unknowns move into the house for the summer, we watch their every move and vote one out every week until just the winner remains), although it's alleged that the makers have tried to recruit more exciting housemates this time. We'll just have to wait and see ...

Jane Rackham

MUSIC
American Idol *8.30pm ITV2*

Pop Idol's brash American cousin reaches the end of its third run. There are still three divas left in at press time but, assuming Jasmine Trias is voted out before the final, it'll be Fantasia Barrino, a wonderful soul singer, versus the contest's dark horse, the psychotically perky Diana DeGarmo. Both have lungs like traction engines, and are immune by now to any brickbats thrown by their harshest critic.

Jack Seale

TV Insider
We've got our eye on him

Whatever happened to Cameron Stuart, last year's winner of the fourth Big Brother series? Well, he's still involved in the fish trade on the island of Orkney, off the north-east coast of Scotland. But the 33-year-old has done a few extra things since his win. He's appeared in a pantomime in Aberdeen, he's writing a motoring column for his local paper and he's done some radio presenting for BBC Radio Scotland. 'I'm resolving to have as much fun this year as last year,' he says happily. But he's not planning on leaving his day job just yet. 'All the other things are just extras,' he says. 'But they're great!'

unit eleven 83

Vocabulary: fame and notoriety

4 Complete this map of words and expressions connected with fame and notoriety.

be in the spotlight ◆ come into the limelight ◆ legendary ◆ fame ◆
stardom ◆ come into the public eye ◆ famous ◆ renowned ◆
notorious ◆ celebrated ◆ eminent ◆ be a VIP ◆ achieve notoriety ◆
notoriety ◆ eminence ◆ star ◆ legend ◆ infamous ◆ well-known ◆
be flavour of the month ◆ become a household name ◆ infamy ◆
hit the headlines ◆ renown ◆ celebrity ◆
have your name on everyone's lips ◆

Positive connotations   Neutral   Negative connotations

nouns   nouns   adjectives   nouns

adjectives   FAME   adjectives

expressions   expressions   expressions

5 Now complete this crossword with suitable words and expressions.

Across
1 The .... scientist rose to speak about his latest discovery.
2 Have you any idea who is .... of the month at the moment? I can't keep up with pop stars today.
3 Some people can't take the pressure of .... and prefer to remain unknown.
4 Clint Eastwood has been a household .... for over 30 years.
5 When did the singer Eminem first rise to ....?
6 Pele is a .... in the world of football.

Down
1 Would you like to be constantly in the public .... as famous people are?
7 I hate speaking in public – I just don't like to be in the ....
8 Al Capone was a .... gangster from the 1930s.
9 Some people cope well with .... while others can't stand the pressure.

84 unit eleven

Grammar: phrasal verbs

6 Read these sentences and say whether the verbs in blue are Type 1 (inseparable, intransitive) or Type 2 (separable, transitive) verbs.

a That music is very loud. Could you turn it down please?
....

b If you want something else, you really have to speak up, you know. I can't read your mind. ....

c At first, business was slow when we started the new restaurant, but now it has really taken off and we're full every night. ....

d Thanks for buying me lunch – that was silly of me to forget my purse, but I'll pay you back as soon as we get to the house. ....

e I'm very proud of my children. I brought them up to be very independent. ....

f The old cinema is being demolished. They're pulling it down next Tuesday.
....

g That was a very hard algebra problem, but the students eventually worked it out.
....

h I don't have time to finish the report today – I think I'll have to put it off until tomorrow.
....

7 Now replace the words in *italics* with one of the verbs in blue from Activity 6 to make new sentences that have the same meaning.

a She owes me $100. I hope she *gives it back to me* soon.
....

b People who *grow up* in cold countries are more used to the cold than people who are raised in a warm climate.
....

c This is a very difficult dilemma, but I'm trying to *find the right answer*.
....

d This old building should *be destroyed* as it's very dangerous and could fall.
....

e The meeting will have to *be postponed* until next week as an emergency has come up.
....

f Her acting career *is suddenly going very well*. She's appearing in two new movies this year.
....

g Could you *make the volume lower*, please – it's very high and it's hard to talk.
....

h You need to be more assertive and *give your opinion* or you'll be ignored.
....

8 Say whether these verbs in blue are Type 1, Type 2, Type 3 (inseparable, transitive) or Type 4 (inseparable, three parts).

I don't know how you (a) put up with your boss. You should really (b) look for another job.
....

They say that the boy (c) takes after his father. They both (d) get along with other people.
....

For their fifth wedding anniversary, they had hired a babysitter to (e) look after the baby and were (f) looking forward to a romantic dinner for two at a restaurant.
....

She had agreed to (g) come by to help me with my homework. On the way, she (h) ran into another friend and arrived too late. I was disappointed that she had (i) let me down.
....

Maria always (j) fell for the wrong type of guy and she always (k) broke up with them after a few weeks.
....

Pronunciation: stressing the right element in phrasal verbs

9 Look at these sentences and decide which words should be stressed. Practise saying the sentences.

a I don't know how you put up with it!
b The plane took off.
c Do you get on with her?
d I was sad when she turned me down.
e Will you please turn the radio off?
f Guess who I ran into today?
g They're going to pull it down today.
h I have to look after my sister.
i She's taking care of her grandfather this week.

Now listen to Track 35. Do the speakers say the sentences in the same way as you?

Functional language: checking and confirming

MECHANICA IN CONCERT
8.30 pm
The London Apollo
Friday 9th September
Doors open 7.30 pm

10 Put this conversation in the right order. The first line is given below.

a NICK: So, you've got the tickets, right?
b CHARLIE: Oh no! My parents said I have to be home before midnight.
c CHARLIE: Oh, but it'll last for about two hours, don't you think?
d NICK: Yeah. They're the best.
e CHARLIE: Do you mean to say we might not be home until after midnight?
f NICK: Oh, yes. Here they are. So, let's see what time it starts?
g NICK: Maybe not.
h CHARLIE: I guess so. After all, they are the greatest band in the world, wouldn't you say?
i NICK: No. It starts at 8.30.
j CHARLIE: No, I thought you had them. They're in your wallet, aren't they?
k NICK: Maybe, but remember the last time we saw them it lasted almost four hours.
l NICK: Well, you'll have to tell them the concert goes on longer, won't you?
m CHARLIE: It starts at 8, doesn't it?

a ....

11 Complete the dialogue with an appropriate question.

don't you ◆ did you ◆ haven't you ◆ Does that mean ◆ huh ◆ right ◆ would you say

INTERVIEWER: OK, Mr Blackburn. I need to verify some information before we begin the audition. You're Richard Blackburn, (a) ....?
RICHARD: That's right.
INTERVIEWER: And you live at 18 Mill Drive, (b) ....?
RICHARD: Yes, I do.
INTERVIEWER: It says here that you started dancing in 1994. (c) .... that you've been dancing for more than ten years?
RICHARD: That's right, yes.
INTERVIEWER: But you've only been singing for about five years, (d) ....?
RICHARD: Uh-huh.
INTERVIEWER: You didn't go to drama school, (e) ....?
RICHARD: No, I went to the local comprehensive school.
INTERVIEWER: So that school was where you learned to sing and dance, (f) ....?
RICHARD: Well, that's where I started and then I took extra classes as well.
INTERVIEWER: OK, Richard. Let's see you dance, (g) ....?
RICHARD: OK.

Listening: the price of fame

12 If you were famous, which of these things do you think would be a disadvantage and which do you think would be an advantage?

a people recognise you as you walk in the street		
b people try to take your photograph all the time		
c you get to travel a lot		
d meeting other famous people		
e having special privileges		
f having fans asking for your autograph		
g being constantly in the public eye		
h the pressure to produce great work		

13 Listen to the conversation between Brad and Diane on Track 36 and write *D* or *A* in the table above, according to whether they see it as an advantage, a disadvantage or both.

14 Now listen to Track 36 again and tick who agrees with these points, Diane, Brad or both.

	Diane	Brad	Both
a I'd like to be famous.			
b Everyone has a right to privacy.			
c I'd like to meet famous people.			
d It must be hard to make friends when you are famous.			
e I wouldn't like to have a bodyguard.			
f Famous people have to look good all the time.			
g Some famous people live on their past reputation.			
h You need to have a talent for something to be famous.			

15 Can you guess the meaning of these words and expressions from the conversation?

a paparazzi
  1 photographers who don't respect privacy
  2 fans who recognise famous people
  3 people who leave famous people alone

b it comes with the territory
  1 it's a part of your life
  2 your land belongs to you
  3 this is something unacceptable

c is entitled to
  1 has the right to
  2 has no right to
  3 wants to have

d hang out with
  1 spend time with
  2 share a house with
  3 work with

e groupies
  1 people who are interested in privacy
  2 people who like to be with famous people
  3 people who are very famous

f that would be a real pain
  1 it would be a good thing
  2 it would be annoying
  3 it would make my teeth hurt

g living on their past
  1 trying to be private
  2 using their reputation
  3 producing new work

h a late developer
  1 someone whose talent shows at a later age
  2 someone who is a child star
  3 someone who never shows any talent

unit eleven 87

Writing: researching for writing

16 Complete these tables about two famous people using the information below. The first one is done for you.

> March 14, 1879
> August 5, 1962
> Los Angeles, California
> 29, including *Niagara*, *The Seven-Year Itch*, *Gentlemen Prefer Blondes*
> Ulm, Germany
> Norma Jean Mortenson
> theory of relativity
> June 1, 1926
> April 18, 1955
> German, later became a US citizen

Marilyn Monroe

Date of birth: a

Place of birth: b

Real name: c

Movies made: d

Died: e *August 5, 1962*

Albert Einstein

Date of birth: a

Place of birth: b

Why famous: c

Nationality: d

Died: e

17 Now use the information above and any other information you can find to write a short biography of either Marilyn Monroe or Albert Einstein.

Culture and language

18 Re-write the following sentences so that they reflect your own reality, views or language. Who is 'we' in each case?

a We have a lot of famous musicians and actors.
....

b We don't expect famous people to have a lot of privacy.
....

c In English, we have many verbs that have more than one part (phrasal verbs).
....

d We can use multi-word verbs with literal and metaphorical meanings.
....

e We often use tag questions to check and confirm what we are saying.
....

f We use rising intonation and falling intonation to indicate whether the tag question is a real question or not.
....

g We have different words to talk about people who are famous for positive reasons and those who are famous for negative reasons.
....

h The most famous sportspeople we have are in sports like football, cricket and athletics.
....

Self-check

19 Put 1 to 10 in the brackets to show how difficult the following abilities are for you in English. 1 = 'I feel confident about this / I can do it', but 10 = 'I am not at all confident about this / I'm not sure I can do it'.

a Using vocabulary related to fame and notoriety to talk about people [ ]
b Identifying Types 1, 2, 3 and 4 phrasal verbs [ ]
c Using phrasal verbs correctly [ ]
d Identifying the stressed syllables in phrasal verbs and pronouncing them correctly [ ]
e Using different resources to find information on a topic [ ]
f Doing a piece of writing based on research [ ]
g Telling the difference between rising and falling intonation in tag questions [ ]
h Using questions to check and confirm information [ ]
i Listening and making notes about what I hear [ ]
j Writing a short biography of a person using information about her / his life [ ]

Take the items you scored from 6 to 10 and look back at the appropriate place in Unit 11 of the Student's Book.

Test your knowledge

20 Translate the following sentences and questions.

a On reality TV, we often see people criticise and humiliate each other.
....

b I have no qualms about singing in front of a crowd of people.
....

c The plane took off.
....

d My new business has really taken off.
....

e Michael Jackson has hit the headlines again.
....

f Many people hate to be in the public eye.
....

g The thieves achieved notoriety after the diamond robbery last year.
....

h The weather's awful today, isn't it?
....

Did you have problems? If you did, go back to the relevant activity in the Student's Book to check on meaning and use.

The phonemic alphabet

21 Consult the table of phonemic symbols on page 125 and then write these words in ordinary spelling.

a /ˌnəʊtəˈraɪətiː/
....

b /ˈɪnfəməs/
....

c /ˈɪn jɔː ˈfeɪs/
....

d /ˈget əˈlɒŋ wɪð/
....

e /pʊt ˈʌp wɪð/
....

f /ˈdəʊntʃuː ˈθɪnk/
....

g /ə ˈleɪt dɪˈveləpə/
....

Check your answers by listening to Track 37.

UNIT 12 Writing and writers

Vocabulary: writing, books and authors

1 Match the type of book (*a–l*) with the cover (*1–12*). Write the correct number in the space provided.

a mystery ....
b history ....
c romance ....
d science-fiction ....
e biography ....
f autobiography ....
g literature ....
h self-help ....
i textbook ....
j reference ....
k travel ....
l children's fiction ....

Which of the books are fiction (*F*) and which are non-fiction (*NF*)?

2 Complete the sentences with the correct noun or verb form of one of the words in the box.

play ◆ mention ◆ work ◆ report ◆ merit

a The author talked about her new .... , which was to be performed on Broadway in New York.

b I'd like to .... that apart from being a very funny book, this is a great piece of literature.

c His first novel won the Booker Prize and there is no doubt that it .... this award.

d The 2,000-word .... on the conference was due the next day and Christy had not yet started it.

e The poet took great delight in .... with words to get the exact effect that he was looking for.

f Writing a novel takes talent, but it also takes a great deal of hard .... , which is what a lot of people forget.

g I detest romance novels. The .... of handsome heroes falling in love with damsels in distress makes me close the book immediately.

h She is an acclaimed author who has written prizewinning non-fiction books of great

....

i This term in your literature class, we will study great .... like Tolstoy's *War and Peace* and Zola's *Germinal*.

j Her job at the newspaper was to .... on crime in the city.

90 unit twelve

Reading: *The Curious Incident*

3 Read the three blurbs and then read the extract from *The Curious Incident of the Dog in the Night-Time* on page 92. Which is the correct blurb?

a *The Curious Incident of the Dog in the Night-Time* is a science-fiction story unlike any other. The narrator is a 15-year-old robot-human, Christopher Boone. When Christopher finds a neighbour's dog murdered in the summer of 2217, the (cyber)police are called. Like all robot-humans, Christopher is keen on the police, but something goes wrong when he first meets the one assigned to the case. Christopher starts to investigate further, something robot-humans should not do under Galaxay code 57/6/53. But Christopher likes dogs, the last natural creatures on earth. His investigations take him deep into a galaxy-wide plot to change the universe, a journey that will challenge everything he has been programmed to think.

b *The Curious Incident of the Dog in the Night-Time* is a teenage romance unlike any other. The detective, and narrator, is 15-year-old Christopher Boone. Christopher has had a troubled childhood – made only bearable by a friendly policeman who lives at the end of his road. So when a neighbour's dog is killed, he is pleased to see his friend. But then things go wrong and Christopher gets into even more trouble as chief suspect in the dog-killing incident. Help comes from an unlikely quarter and the story of Christopher's friendship with Betty Shears, the neighbour's daughter, is a tale of loyalty, and finally love, which no reader will be able to resist.

c *The Curious Incident of the Dog in the Night-Time* is a murder mystery unlike any other. The detective, and narrator, is 15-year-old Christopher Boone. Christopher has Asperger's, a form of autism, the mental condition that stops people from communicating with or understanding other people. He knows a lot about facts and maths, and very little about human beings. He loves lists, patterns and the truth. He hates the colours yellow and brown and being touched. He has never gone further than the end of the road on his own, but when he finds a neighbour's dog murdered, he sets out on a terrifying journey which will change his life for ever.

4 Read the extract on page 92 again and circle the best answer in each case.

a The policeman thinks that Christopher is:
 1 ... unlike normal 15 year olds.
 2 ... older than most 15 year olds.
 3 ... younger than most 15 year olds.

b The policewoman:
 1 ... offers sympathy to the dog's owner.
 2 ... arrests Mrs Shears.
 3 ... goes to Mrs Shears' house to change her tights.

c Christopher becomes upset because:
 1 ... the dog is dead.
 2 ... the policeman is being nasty.
 3 ... he can't deal with too many questions at once.

d Christopher mentions the bakery because:
 1 ... he sometimes thinks of things getting crowded in his brain like bread in a bread slicer.
 2 ... his uncle Terry works there.
 3 ... it has a bread slicer that is sometimes too slow.

e Christopher makes a noise which:
 1 ... is like the white noise you hear on a radio.
 2 ... he always makes when he can't cope with everything people are saying to him.
 3 ... he always makes when he listens to the radio to make himself safe.

f The bakery and the radio are both:
 1 ... things that really matter to Christopher.
 2 ... things he uses to help us understand what is going on in his head.
 3 ... things that his father and uncle Terry worry about all the time.

g Christopher hits the policeman because:
 1 ... he hates being touched.
 2 ... the policeman thinks he killed the dog.
 3 ... the policeman lifts him to his feet.

5 Find (a form of) these words and phrases in the text.

> blockage ◆ fork ◆ to groan ◆
> I'd got that far ◆ leaf ◆
> to poke out ◆ scratch ◆ to slice ◆
> to squat ◆ to stack up ◆
> tights ◆ to tune

Now match the words and phrases with these explanations.

a a garden implement with three or four points ....

b a piece of clothing usually for women that covers the legs and goes up the waist ....

c a small cut on the skin ....

d to almost sit down, but without the bottom touching the ground ....

e I think I realise that. (sarcastic) ....

f to make a noise as if you are unhappy or in pain ....

g something that stops movement, usually in a small space ....

h to show a little bit (because some of it is still hidden inside or underneath something) ....

i to store in a pile ....

j to cut something into thin flat pieces ....

k to find a particular frequency on the radio when looking for a programme ....

l something found on trees ....

Extract from *The Curious Incident of the Dog in the Night-Time*

Then the police arrived. I like the police. They have uniforms and numbers and you know what they are meant to be doing. There was a policewoman and a policeman. The policewoman had a little hole in her tights on her left ankle and a red scratch in the middle of the hole. The policeman had a big orange leaf stuck to the bottom of his shoe which was poking out from one side.

The policewoman put her arm round Mrs Shears and led her back towards the house.

I lifted my head off the grass.

The policeman squatted down beside me and said, 'Would you like to tell me what's going on here, young man?'

I sat up and said, 'The dog is dead.'

'I'd got that far,' he said.

I said, 'I think someone killed the dog.'

'How old are you?' he asked.

I replied, 'I am 15 years and 3 months and 2 days.'

'And what, precisely, were you doing in the garden?' he asked.

'I was holding the dog,' I replied.

'And why were you holding the dog?' he asked.

This was a difficult question. It was something I wanted to do. I like dogs. It made me sad to see that the dog was dead.

I like policemen too, and I wanted to answer the question properly, but the policeman did not give me enough time to work out the correct answer.

'Why were you holding the dog?' he asked again.

'I like dogs,' I said.

'Did you kill the dog?' he asked.

I said, 'I did not kill the dog.'

'Is this your fork?' he asked.

I said, 'No.'

'You seem very upset about this,' he said.

He was asking too many questions and he was asking them too quickly. They were stacking up in my head like loaves in the factory where Uncle Terry works. The factory is a bakery and he operates the slicing machine. And sometimes the slicer is not working fast enough but the bread keeps coming and there is a blockage. I sometimes think of my mind as a machine, but not always as a bread-slicing machine. It makes it easier to explain to other people what is going on inside it.

The policeman said, 'I am going to ask you once again ...'

I rolled onto the lawn and pressed my forehead to the ground again and made the noise that father calls groaning. I make this noise when there is too much information coming into my head from the outside world. It's like when you are upset and you hold the radio against your ear and you tune it halfway between two stations so that all you get is white noise and then you turn the volume right up so this is all you can hear and then you know you are safe because you cannot hear anything else.

The policeman took hold of my arm and lifted me onto my feet.

I didn't like him touching me like this.

And this is when I hit him.

Listening: *Gladiator*

6 Read the following text carefully. Can you identify the people in each photograph?

Gladiator, starring the actor Russell Crowe, was one of the first great movie hits of the 21st century. It tells the story of a heroic Roman general, Maximus Decimus Meridius, who is captured by the evil emperor Commodus. He is forced to work as a gladiator, fighting for his life for the entertainment of the crowds. Commodus hates Maximus, because Commodus' father, the old emperor, Marcus, loved Maximus more than his own son.

7 The scene on Track 38 takes place early in the movie, and it partly explains why Commodus hates the gladiator. Marcus, the old emperor, sends for his son Commodus to see him.

Listen to Track 38. *True* or *False*? Write *T* or *F* in the brackets.

a Marcus makes Commodus the new emperor. [ ]
b Marcus wants Maximus to succeed him when he dies. [ ]
c Marcus wants Rome to be a republic (e.g. governed by the people, not an emperor). [ ]
d Commodus thinks that his father has always loved him. [ ]
e Commodus has always wanted the sun on his head. [ ]
f Marcus takes responsibility for any of Commodus' failings. [ ]

8 Match the words and the definitions.

a ambition ....
b butcher ....
c courage ....
d devotion ....
e fortitude ....
f justice ....
g resourcefulness ....
h smother ....
i temperance ....
j wisdom ....

1 desire to succeed
2 bravery when in danger
3 courage shown when you are in difficult situations
4 fairness in the way people are treated
5 intelligence gained through experience
6 ability to find ways of dealing with practical problems
7 love and loyalty that you show to someone
8 not drinking alcohol because of moral or religious beliefs
9 a verb which means to kill someone by putting something over their face to stop them breathing
10 a verb which means to kill someone or a lot of people in a cruel and violent way

Listen to Track 38 again. Which of the qualities were on Marcus' list? Which are the qualities that Commodus says he has?

Marcus' list	Commodus' list

9 Read the following acting 'directions' from the original film script.

a He kneels in front of his son.
   ....

b He stretches his arms out to Commodus, seeking forgiveness. Commodus slowly embraces him, together they weep.
   ....

c Holding his fingers to his lips
   ....

d In anguish and tears from the disappointment of Marcus' decision
   ....

e Marcus moves his hand to touch Commodus' face and Commodus pulls away.
   ....

f Marcus still kneeling, Commodus presses his father tightly against his body, smothering him, as Marcus struggles to be free, but fails. All the while, Commodus cries and moans in pain, as though a child.
   ....

g Surprised at Commodus' reaction, Marcus sits.
   ....

h The smile quickly vanishes, leaving in its place painful bewilderment.
   ....

i With a slight smile on his face
   ....

Listen to Track 38 again as you read the Audioscript. Match the directions with the numbers on the script where you think they occur.

Pronunciation: identifying syllables

10 Look at the words *a–j* from Activity 8 and write them in this chart according to the number of syllables they have.

Two syllables	Three syllables	Four syllables

Listen to Track 39 to check your answers.

Grammar: relative clauses

11 Match the beginnings of sentences on the left (*a–j*) with the best clause (*1–10*) to make complete sentences.

a Is that the girl ....
b I remember a time ....
c That's the couple ....
d That's the carpet ....
e I want to show you the town ....
f We ran into the neighbour ....
g It was the day ....
h She's the one ....
i Would you like a cushion ....
j I'm looking for an office ....

1 whose wedding was reported in the paper.
2 whose aunt wrote a book about her.
3 they came over to our house – last Friday, I think.
4 my sister moved to last year.
5 we bought for our living room.
6 when we didn't watch TV all night.
7 you can sit on?
8 where I'll be able to write.
9 you used to sit next to at school?
10 whose dog jumped into our garden.

12 In several of the sentences in Activity 11, the relative clause refers to the <u>object</u> of the sentence and so the relative has been omitted. Re-write in full those sentences that have the relative pronoun omitted.

....
....
....
....
....

13 Join these sentences using relative clauses. The first one is done for you.

a This is the woman. I told you about her yesterday.
   This is the woman (that) I told you about yesterday.

b Did you see that car? It has a flat tyre.

c He is the one who wrote this book. The book is about animals.

d Her parents live in France. My best friend Gemma has decided to work in Paris.

e We were living in London that year. That was the year my novel was published.

f This is the house. We grew up in this house.

g Do you like this hat? I bought it at the market.

h I remember that day. We went to the beach and it rained all day.

i That's the author. Her book is very popular at the moment.

Functional language: agreeing and disagreeing

14 Put these words in the right order to make 'agreeing' and 'disagreeing' sentences. The first one is started for you.

a good / do / that / was / Joaquin Phoenix / agree / I
   I do agree

b that / surely / suggesting / not / Russell Crowe / you're / right / was / role / for

c joking / must / you / be

d sometimes / point / take / I / being / your / about / not / right / actors

e disagree / have / on / I / one / to / that / with / you

f mean / see / about / I / Joaquin Phoenix / you / what /

g that / on / I'm / Larry / one / with /

h less / you / both / couldn't / I / with / of / agree

15 Now use the sentences in Activity 14 to complete this dialogue.

DAVID: So what did you think of the movie *Gladiator*?

SARAH: I loved it. I thought it had a great storyline and was well acted.

LARRY: Rubbish. (**1**) ...., Sarah. I thought the acting was terrible.

EMMA: (**2**) .... I think Russell Crowe was overrated.

SARAH: (**3**) .... I think he's great and he was wonderful in *Gladiator*. And what about Joaquin Phoenix?

DAVID: Absolutely, Sarah. (**4**) ....

EMMA: Yeah, but (**5**) .... ?

LARRY: Exactly!

SARAH: (**6**) ...., but I think he was perfect in *Gladiator*.

EMMA: Fair enough, (**7**) ....

LARRY: (**8**) ....! I thought they were both awful.

Writing: telling a story

16 Look at these jumbled paragraphs that make up the beginning of a story. Put the paragraphs in order. The first one is done for you.

a She turned to wave goodbye to Lucy Jacobs through the window as she walked down the office steps. Was it her imagination or did Lucy give her a look that seemed to be warning her of danger?

b It was snowing outside so she also took her umbrella, hoping this would help her to stay dry.

c She stepped out into the street where two dark figures appeared out of the shadows to join the people who were rushing to get home in the chilled night air.

d Janice had been working on the Bancroft account all day and had almost finished, but there was something very suspicious going on and she wanted to get to the bottom of it. Richard would know the answers.

e Janice rushed too, as she was planning to meet her boyfriend, Richard, who worked for Bancroft Inc. She was particularly anxious to see Richard tonight – she really needed his help.

f Janice Bloomfield had a strange uneasy feeling as she slipped on her coat, wrapped her scarf around her neck and pulled her hat onto her head.

....f.... ....

17 Look at the pictures that tell the second part of the story. Write the second part of the story in your own words.

Look at the model answer to check how close you were to the original story.

18 How does the story end? You decide. Write the end of the story.

Culture and language

19 Are things the same or different in your country? Circle *S* or *D*.

a There are many English books that have been translated into several languages. S / D

b There are many movies which are made from famous books. S / D

c Sometimes the same word in English can be used as a noun and as a verb. S / D

d There are different words and expressions to agree and disagree with someone according to how strongly you feel. S / D

e Reading is a very popular pastime when people are travelling to work on public transport. S / D

f We join sentences by using different clauses and pronouns like *who*, *which* and *that*. S / D

g Sometimes in spoken language, we shorten words by joining two syllables together. S / D

Self-check

20 Read the following statements and put a tick in the correct column.

As a result of studying Unit 12 …	Yes, definitely	More or less	Not sure
I can recognise and use words that can be both nouns and verbs.			
I can use words and expressions connected with books, authors and writing.			
I was able to identify the different parts of the blurb of a book, talk about the blurb and make decisions based on it.			
I can identify the number of syllables in a word.			
I can write a book report about a book I have read.			
I can identify and use subject and object relative clauses.			
I can recognise defining and non-defining relative clauses in both speech and writing.			
I can use several expressions to agree and disagree with people.			
I can write a narrative based on cues and pictures.			

If you have ticked 'more or less' or 'not sure', go back to the appropriate place in the unit so that you can tick the 'yes, definitely' column.

Test your knowledge

21 Which of the following sentences are written in correct English? Put a tick (✓) or a cross (✗) in the brackets. If there is an error, correct it.

  a She is a prolific author, who has written 48 novels. [ ]
  b A biography is a book in which the author tells the story of her or his own life. [ ]
  c He was only 16 when he drafted his first novel. [ ]
  d I don't mind admit that I'd love to be a writer. [ ]
  e This is my mother, which lives in Australia. [ ]
  f She's the kind of person loves adaptations of books. [ ]
  g I agree with you to a certain extent, but I think you need to consider the problem in more detail. [ ]
  h This novel is a great job of art. [ ]
  i Do you remember that time when we went to Paris and couldn't find a hotel room? [ ]
  j This is the girl who her mother is a dancer. [ ]

The phonemic alphabet

22 Consult the table of phonemic symbols on page 125 and then write these words in ordinary spelling.

  a /ˈlɪtrətʃə/

  b /ˌɔːtəbaɪˈɒgrəfiː/

  c /ðə ˈblɜːb/

  d /ˈfeərəˈnʌf/

  e /ˈrʌbɪʃ/

  f /ˈtemprənts/

  g /ˈɔːwɪnˌspaɪrɪŋ/

Check your answers by listening to Track 40.

UNIT 13 Crime and punishment

Listening: being robbed

1 Listen to Track 41. For each of the three stories, draw a line to connect the things mentioned. Warning: some of the objects don't appear in any of the stories.

2 Listen to Track 41 again. Who:

a ... had coffee with Jane?
....

b ... had a new mobile phone?
....

c ... bought more coffee?
....

d ... looked 'vaguely suspicious'?
....

e ... took the mobile phone?
....

f ... went to New York?
....

g ... had bought a new camera?
....

h ... didn't know what to do for a moment?
....

i ... wasn't frightened until later?
....

j ... thinks you can avoid crime by being sensible?
....

k ... made a silly decision for some reason?
....

l ... was pleased when two girls approached him?
....

m ... ended up looking rather silly?
....

98 unit thirteen

3 Complete the following extracts from Track 41 with one word for each blank.

a My uncle .... me up and arranged to meet me .... coffee close to the university library where I had been ....

b He was lurking .... looking vaguely ....

c And he .... at me in a really scary way and he was .... , 'well you can have it back then. If you want it that ....'

d Afterwards I .... if I'd done the .... thing.

e Quite .... , actually, but at the moment it .... , I didn't have time to feel ....

f … and before I .... what was happening, someone's got a hand .... my throat and something is .... to my neck, cold and ....

g He was .... absolutely shocked, his mouth just .... open.

h It was his pride and ....

i You have to keep your .... open, especially when you're .... away from home, in a .... country, for example.

j That seems like .... silly, just asking for .... I'd say, but maybe there was a .... , I don't know.

k He just felt .... flattered and stood up to .... to them and they had a great .... , lots of laughter and ....

l I'm .... sure he won't be .... in like that .... !

Vocabulary: crime and criminals

4 Complete these newspaper reports (1–4) with an appropriate crime word from the box below. Some words can be used more than once.

hackers • sentenced • arrested • accused • robbery • theft • convicted • hacked • guilty • embezzlement • shoplifting

1 Janet Hawkins was today (**a**) .... to two years' imprisonment for armed (**b**) .... She was seen entering the Granton Grocery Store with a pistol where she stole £200 from the cash register before escaping from the store. Ms Hawkins pleaded (**c**) .... to the crime.

2 At the Crown Court today, Richard Furley was (**d**) .... of (**e**) .... after he admitted diverting funds from his company Southern Insurance into his own bank account. He was (**f**) .... in June after the firm's accountant noticed discrepancies in the company's books.

3 At East Briarley Magistrates' Court today, Justine Marshall, 19, and Sandy Carter, 22, were found guilty of (**g**) .... The young women entered Holmes Department Store on 25th March and stole goods worth £700. The two were arrested as they left the store and (**h**) .... of (**i**) .... by the store detective.

4 Two young computer (**j**) .... were (**k**) .... yesterday in connection with an investigation into a bank (**l**) .... that took place last month. During the break-in, the young men allegedly (**m**) .... into the security system at the bank, disabling the security cameras and alarm system.

5 Now match the correct story (1–4) with the picture (a–d) that illustrates the crime.

1 .... 2 .... 3 .... 4 ....

unit thirteen 99

Pronunciation: noun / verb stress shift

6 Look at these sentences and underline the syllable that has the main stress in the words *convict* and *suspect*.

a The police expect the judge to convict the man today.
b The convict escaped from jail.
c He was convicted of armed robbery.
d Many convicts re-offend once they are released from prison.
e The main suspect in the case is a 24-year-old woman.
f The police suspect the woman of committing arson.
g The suspects had their fingerprints taken by the police.
h I never suspected her of cheating.

🎧 Listen to Track 42 to check your answers.

a What does the stress difference tell you about the different meanings of the words?
b Can you find other words like this in your dictionary?

Functional language: making deductions

7 Put this conversation in the correct order, starting with *c*.

a MIKE: I don't know. Maybe he's waiting for someone.
b CARLY: Yes, he is. Quick! Let's go into this cafe and call the police.
c CARLY: Look at that man over there!
d MIKE: It might be his car.
e MIKE: I think you're right. He's looking at us.
f MIKE: Where?
g CARLY: I don't think he's waiting for someone. He might be trying to see if anyone's watching.
h CARLY: The one standing next to the green car wearing a leather jacket.
i CARLY: There's no way that's his car. Why's he looking round like that?
j MIKE: What about him?
k CARLY: I reckon he's about to break into that car.

c ....

8 Solve this puzzle.

Everyone is telling a lie, so who stole the bike? Put a tick in the brackets as you discover who did not do it.

[ ] Richard Wright: Maya definitely stole the bike.
[ ] David Monk: Richard will tell you who stole the bike.
[ ] Clare Moseley: David, Richard and I could not have stolen the bike.
[ ] Brian Clarke: I have not stolen anything today.
[ ] Maya Jameson: I did not steal the necklace.
[ ] Erika Brookes: Richard must have stolen the bike, so David and Clare couldn't have.
[ ] James Pierce: I stole the bike, so Erika can't have.

Answer: Brian Clarke. Because everyone is lying, the statement 'I have not stolen anything today' is definitely false and we can be certain that Brian must have stolen something.

Reading: coughing for a million

9 Read the extract from the book *Judging Crime* by Peter Hedley. Who or what is:

a ... *Who wants to be a millionaire?*

....

....

b ... Chris Tarrant?

....

....

c ... Charles Ingram?

....

....

d ... Tecwen Whittock?

....

....

Who wants to be a millionaire? has been one of the most popular television quiz shows, not only in Britain, but also around the world. In the show, the host asks a question and gives the contestant four possible answers. If the contestant gets the right answer, they win the money – say £100 – and then go on to the next question for, say, £250. The money increases for each question until, if the contestant has answered all the other questions correctly, the prize for the final question is one million pounds.

In this extract from a show some years ago, the host of the show is television personality Chris Tarrant. Answering the questions is an ex-army officer, Charles Ingram.

TARRANT: What kind of garment is an 'Anthony Eden'? An overcoat, hat, shoe, tie?
INGRAM: I think it is a hat.
A cough from the audience.
INGRAM: Again I'm not sure. I think it is ...
Coughing from the audience.
INGRAM: I am sure it is a hat. Am I sure?
Coughing from the audience.
INGRAM: Yes, hat, it's a hat.

That answer – the name for a peculiar type of British hat that nobody wears anymore – earned Charles Ingram £250,000. Two questions later, he had won a million pounds, and the audience in the studio went crazy. But something wasn't quite right. As he progressed through the various stages, Charles Ingram didn't really seem very sure of himself; he obviously didn't know the answer at first, so he must have been very good at guessing. Unless he wasn't guessing. To many in the audience that night, it seemed as if he kept changing his mind and frequently repeated an answer as if waiting for a signal.

He was.

Charles Ingram's wife Diana was in the audience, and so too was a man with the extraordinary name of Tecwen Whittock. At first, people might have been sympathetic about Tecwen. He had a bad cough. But a man sitting next to him in the audience noticed that there was something strange about the cough. It was too loud, and it wasn't very regular. It only happened occasionally, almost as if he was coughing on purpose.

He was.

The three of them, Charles Ingram, Diana Ingram and Tecwen Whittock, had planned the whole thing. Whittock coughed to tell Charles when he had the correct answer. They began to notice it in the television control room, but at first they didn't believe it. In the end, though, it was just too obvious, and when tapes from the programme were played to a court in London a year later, there was no doubt. Charles and Diana Ingram were guilty of cheating on a game show. They were given prison sentences of 18 months and fined £15,000 each. Tecwen Whittock was sentenced to 12 months in prison and fined £10,000. None of them actually went to prison, however, because the sentences were 'suspended' – that means that they would not go to prison unless they committed another crime.

Did the Ingrams and Tecwen Whittock get an appropriate sentence? How 'bad' is it to cheat a television quiz show in which winning money is a matter of chance anyway? It is crimes like this that challenge our notions of what is right and what is wrong, and since administering justice in the courts means that we have to decide on how serious something is (is robbery more or less serious than driving too fast, for example), the case of the cheating Ingrams is an excellent one to consider.

unit thirteen 101

10 Find the names of people or things in the text on page 101.

a It was shown everywhere – not just in the UK.
b It is worth one million pounds.
c It is a kind of hat.
d It was worth £250,000.
e He didn't seem sure of himself.
f He coughed a lot of the time.
g They thought he was waiting for something.
h She was in the audience.
i He noticed that there was something strange about the cough.
j They had planned the whole thing.
k They were shown to people during the trial.
l They were fined a total of £30,000.
m He was given a 12 months' suspended sentence.

11 Complete each blank with one word from the text. Do not change the word in any way.

a A .... is someone who invites you to their house, or to a party, or who is in charge of an event like a quiz show.
b A .... is someone who takes part in a race or a game.
c If something gets bigger or more dangerous, for example, we say that it ....
d An .... is part of a whole.
e .... is a formal word for an article of clothing.
f If something happens every few minutes, with the same interval of time between each occurrence, we say that it is ....
g When someone does something because they want to do it, we can say they have done it ....
h When something is very clear so that anyone can understand it, we say that it is ....
i The word .... can either mean the place where a trial takes place or the people who are in the place where a trial takes place.
j If something is correct and suitable for a situation or an event, we say that it is ....
k Tina was in charge of .... the charity's budget of a million pounds.
l Those two students were copying each other's work in the exam. They were ....

Grammar: the passive voice

12 Transform these sentences so that they mean the same as the original sentence.

a The mechanic is fixing our car at the moment.
Our car
b This novel was written by Jane Austen.
Jane Austen
c Our car might have been broken into by a gang.
A gang
d Do you think the diamonds were stolen by someone at the store?
Do you think someone
e She can't have taken the clothes from the department store, because she was with me.
The clothes
f The judge is going to sentence the assassin now.
The assassin
g I'm sure the police are wrongly accusing that young man of murder.
I'm sure that young man
h The thief must have stolen the diamonds between the hours of 8 and 10 pm.
The diamonds

13 Change the style of these paragraphs, using the passive voice where appropriate.

a I put 20 grams of salt in a beaker and then I added 50 cl of water. Then I heated the mixture until I dissolved the salt. I boiled the water till it evaporated. There was salt left in the beaker.
Twenty grams of salt

b We asked 52 people what they thought about crime on TV. Fifty people said they thought that TV stations showed too much violence and crime on TV. Two people said they felt that TV stations showed the right amount of crime.

c Fifty people attended the meeting yesterday. One person proposed that we should change the time of the next meeting. Everyone agreed on this proposal. We're going to hold the next meeting at 6 pm instead of at 8 pm.

Writing: peer review

14 Read this piece of student writing and find the mistakes in it. Underline the mistakes.

Task: Write a review of your favourite crime film.

The Usual Suspects

My favourite crime movie of all time is *The Usual Suspects*, starring Kevin Spacey and Gabriel Byrne. The film has surprise ending, which I can't tell you. It is about a legendary gangster called Keyser Soze, who the police have never been arrested him. Everyone is knowing about Keyser Soze, but he has never seen by everybody. The movie begins when a boat blown up and there are only two survivors, Verbal Kint (Kevin Spacey) and a Hungary man. The Hungarian man is terrorist and he is badly injure. When he is be interviewed by the police, Kint is forced to tell whole story which began six weeks earlier. Kint tell the story of the powerful mastermind of the whole plot, name Keyser Soze. He tells us about a gang from five men who plan do their last robbery and about how that robbery go wrong. We also see the story of Dean Keaton (Gabriel Byrne), an ex-cop who becomes a criminal, but who is trying to start a life free of crime. The movie has lot of action and suspense and by the finish of the film you are dying to know who is Keyser Soze. But then comes the big surprise which I can't tell to you.

Carlo Benedetti

15 Now complete this questionnaire about the writing.

Name of writer:			
Checked by:			
	Yes	Not sure	No, not really
a Is the writing interesting and clear?			
b Is the writing well organised?			
c Does the writing contain enough information?			
d I think the writing could be improved by: • • •			

16 Write an improved version of the student's film review.

Culture and language

17 Re-write the following sentences so that they reflect your own reality, views or language. Who is 'we' in each case?

a There are several notorious criminals that everyone knows about.

b We see some crimes as much more serious than others.

c We have more sympathy for people who rob from the rich, such as the fictional British character Robin Hood, than for people who rob from the poor.

d In English, we have many special words and expressions that are used to describe crimes and the procedures related to law and the legal system.

e The passive voice is a commonly used structure when you don't want to say or don't need to say who did the action that you are talking about.

f The passive voice is often used in formal and / or academic writing.

g In English, we often use modal verbs to make deductions.

h When we make deductions, we can use different structures to indicate how certain we are of what we are saying.

i We have a lot of films and TV programmes about crimes and solving crimes.

Self-check

18 Put 1 to 10 in the brackets to show how difficult the following abilities are for you in English. 1 = 'I feel confident about this / I can do it', but 10 = 'I am not at all confident about this / I'm not sure I can do it'.

a I can use words and expressions related to crime and criminals. [ ]

b I can use the passive voice structure correctly and appropriately. [ ]

c I can read a story and tell the story to someone else. [ ]

d I can read a piece of writing and tell someone else what some of the problems and mistakes are. [ ]

e I can edit my own work and write an improved version of a piece of writing. [ ]

f I can make deductions which indicate that I am sure about what I say or unsure of what I say. [ ]

g I can discuss crimes and the seriousness of them. [ ]

h I can recognise and identify sentence stress in sentences using modal verbs. [ ]

i I can listen to news stories and understand the main points of the story. [ ]

j I can write about crimes that I've heard of. [ ]

Take the items you scored from 6 to 10 and look back at the appropriate place in Unit 13 of the Student's Book.

Test your knowledge

19 Translate the following sentences and questions.

a What was he arrested for?

b She was charged with embezzlement and convicted in court.

c She must have stolen the diamonds, because she was the only one who had the opportunity.

d President John F. Kennedy was assassinated, but no one is really sure who the assassin was.

e There was an attempted robbery at the local bank today.

f The woman is suspected of being a shoplifter.

g Bonnie and Clyde admitted committing their crimes.

h He couldn't have carried out the burglary, because he was in jail.

Did you have problems? If you did, go back to the relevant activity in the Student's Book to check on meaning and use.

The phonemic alphabet

20 Consult the table of phonemic symbols on page 125 and then write these words in ordinary spelling.

a /ˈgetəweɪ ˌkɑː/

b /ˈprɒsəkjuːtɪd/

c /ˈdjʊərɪŋ ðə ˈrɒbəriː/

d /ˈpɪkˌpɒkətɪŋ/

e /emˈbezəlment/

f /tə biː ˈtʃɑːdʒd wɪðə ˈkraɪm/

g /hiː ˈmʌstəv ˈdʌnɪt/

Check your answers by listening to Track 43.

UNIT 14 Stories from the heart

Reading: *Why Cat and Dog are no longer friends*

1 Read the introduction. Where did West Indian folk tales come from originally, and how were they changed?

....

....

When the Europeans brought West Africans to the West Indies to work for them, the Africans brought their stories with them, stories from the Ashanti people about Anansi the spider and all the other animals. But in the West Indies, these stories changed and new animals were added: Snake, Rat, Cat, Dog, Parrot, Tumble-bug and Turtle. These stories – or folk tales – are still told today.
One of the most popular stories is called *Why Cat and Dog are no longer friends*.

2 Read the paragraphs and put them in the right order. The first two are done for you.

[ ] 'Dog,' said one of the other cats, 'this isn't like you. Why are you shouting at us like this? It isn't dignified, and it's not a bit like you, and besides, I think you'd better get back to the house. It seems to be on fire.'

[ ] 'Good idea,' said Dog. 'Let's talk about it when I've finished making the dinner.' He left the room and went to the fire to complete the cooking. Meanwhile, Finger Quashy went to the pantry where she saw, to her delight, that there were two beautiful pears on a top shelf. She took them down, leapt out of the window, and hid them in the garden so she could take them home later. But unfortunately for her, Rat saw her take the pears and started yelling his head off. 'Dog,' he shouted, 'oh, Dog. Finger Quashy has taken your pears. Finger Quashy has stolen your pears.'

[ ] And that's why Dog and Cat are no longer friends. Dog blamed the four Cats for distracting him so that the house burnt down, and he suspected, anyway, that Rat had been right about Finger Quashy. Worst of all, all his clothes had been reduced to ashes in the fire and he only had one suit left – the one he was wearing (which was the one he was born in) – and which he would have to wear until he died.

[ ] But Dog wasn't having any of it. He was absolutely beside himself with fury and he had a great big stick in his hand. He was ready to kill somebody.

[ ] Dog looked back, and it was true. Flames were ripping through the kitchen and he could hear his young son calling for help. He ran back into the house, saved his son and ran back into the garden. The Cats had gone. Dog had to watch his house, with all his things, burn right down to the ground. It turned out that his son had been playing with the fire, and because he wasn't there he hadn't realised until it was too late.

[ ] Finger Quashy was right to be nervous. Dog was at his wits' end. Every time he put pears out to ripen in the sun, someone stole them. He swore that if he ever found out who the thief was, he would break their bones. So when the Cats arrived, dressed in their finest clothes, Finger Quashy said, 'Dog, it's a real problem about your pears. I reckon it's Rat who's taking them, and since I'm the fastest cat around, why don't you make me your watchwoman and then I can guard your pears and stop Rat getting them?'

[ ] One of the things that Finger Quashy liked stealing most were the avocado pears that grew in Dog's garden. They were the most delicious pears for miles – and pears were the favourite food of all the cats in the area.

[ ] The Cats didn't need to think about it. They shot straight out of the window and into the garden where they scrambled up into a tree. Dog ran out after them and stood at the bottom of the tree, swearing in the most reprehensible fashion.

[2] The reason that Finger Quashy was nervous was that she feared that Dog might just know her secret. This was – and there is no nicer or kinder way to say it – that Finger Quashy was a thief. She stole everything all the time, but nobody knew about this because she was the fastest cat in those parts, and ran like the wind.

[ ] This was looking pretty bad for Finger Quashy, but she was, as we know, pretty fast. So she ran back into the sitting room, and by the time Dog came in, she was sitting there looking sweet, just like her three companions.

[1] When Dog invited four Cats to dinner, they were very pleased. He made good dinners and they were looking forward to a very nice meal. But one of the Cats was just a little bit nervous. Her name was Finger Quashy.

unit fourteen 105

3 Answer the following questions on the text on page 105. Why:

a ... was Finger Quashy nervous?

b ... did Dog's house burn down?

c ... did all the cats scramble up into the tree?

d ... was Dog so upset even before the dinner started?

e ... did Finger Quashy run back and sit in her chair looking nice?

f ... did Dog think that Finger Quashy had taken his pears?

g ... were the cats pleased to be asked for dinner?

h ... aren't Cat and Dog friends anymore?

i ... was Finger Quashy such a good thief?

j ... did Finger Quashy steal pears from Dog's garden (rather than other gardens)?

4 Match the following definitions to words and expressions from the text in blue.

a a phrase that means that something is burning strongly

b a phrase which means that a thing burned so fiercely that now it is just dust

c a slightly old-fashioned word to describe the room where you keep food supplies

d a word that means 'behaving in a calm, serious and appropriate way'

e a word that means 'jumped in order to land in a different place'

f a word to describe behaviour which is very bad and which people will criticise

g a word which means 'taking somebody's attention away from something'

h a word which means 'shouting and using bad words to insult people'

i a word which means that you considered someone to be responsible for something bad

j a word which means 'travelled at a fantastic speed'

k an expression that means that it is not the way you usually behave

l an expression which means that someone just has no idea what to do because nothing works

m an expression which means 'shouting loudly in an uncontrolled way'

n an expression which means 'very very angry indeed'

Vocabulary: poetic effect

5 Use the words and phrases in the box to complete the poem.

days ◆ house ◆ longed for ◆ memory ◆ met ◆
nights ◆ re-told ◆ sad ◆ sound ◆ told

Parents

Summer (**a**) ....
White-painted (**b**) ....
gazing over the rolling cliff.

And the murmur of incoming tides.

The story told, (**c**) .... and heard so often.

The (**d**) .... of his voice,
lion growly in the fading evening air.

This is a (**e**) .... of holidays, a dog-eared
thought returned to whenever I am (**f**) ....

and need to think of how it was in those
summer-lazy (**g**) .... when we were young
and safe and he (**h**) .... the tale

of how they (**i**) .... ,
romantic still
in uneasy-living times.
Refugee hope.
And love, (**j**) .... by the young then, as now,
blossomed in the wartime dark.

Peter Hedley

Check your poem with the complete version in the answer key.

6 Complete the chart with phrases from *Parents*.

a Two-word 'sentences' with no verb	
b Compound adjectives (made from two words)	
c Past participles (underline the one that is repeated for poetic effect)	

Listening: in an art museum

7 Look at this list of events in the life of the painter, Vincent van Gogh. Listen to Track 44 and put them in the right order.

a Van Gogh meets the painter, Paul Gauguin. ....
b Van Gogh spends time at a mental asylum. ....
c Van Gogh moves to Arles in Southern France. ....
d Van Gogh slices off a piece of his ear. ....
e Van Gogh shoots himself. ....
f Van Gogh goes to live with his brother in Paris. ....
g Van Gogh spends time in a hospital. ....
h Van Gogh starts to experiment with new painting techniques. ....
i Van Gogh becomes a salesman in an art gallery. ....
j The painter, Gauguin, joins Van Gogh in Arles. ....
k Van Gogh studies theology. ....

8 Look at these two pictures and listen to the descriptions from the museum audio tour on Track 45. Write the number of the exhibit by the picture.

unit fourteen 107

9 Listen to Track 45 again. Are these statements *True* or *False* according to what you hear? Write *T* or *F* in the brackets.

a Van Gogh lived in Paris for three years. [ ]
b He had a lot of money at that time. [ ]
c He wanted to try different ways of painting. [ ]
d He did not find the colour grey interesting. [ ]
e He uses the colour red to create a special effect. [ ]
f In the felt hat picture, he is wearing fashionable clothes. [ ]
g Van Gogh never painted other people. [ ]
h A straw hat would not normally be worn with a suit at that time. [ ]
i The main purpose of picture number 28 was to paint a suit. [ ]

Grammar: direct and indirect speech

10 Report the following conversations. If you see the cellphone, report the words as if they were being spoken now. If you see the old-fashioned phone, report the words as if they were said yesterday. The first one is done for you.

a Jill: 'It was nice to see you both yesterday.'
   She says it was nice to see us yesterday.

b Caroline: 'I really enjoyed working with you in the recording studio.'
   ....

c Graham: 'I had a fantastic game of golf last week.'
   ....

d Helen: 'I haven't been able to read the report you sent me.'
   ....

e Martin: 'Are you going to come over for a barbecue on Saturday?'
   ....

f Patrick: 'I've just read the most fantastic poem.'
   ....

g Paul: 'I hope you'll both be able to come to the opening of my new exhibition next week.'
   ....

h Peter: 'I've never felt better in my life.'
   ....

i Simon: 'I was going to call you earlier but something came up and I couldn't.'
   ....

j Steve: 'Would you tell Mary that I'll be late for the appointment?'
   ....

k Tina: 'I really enjoyed meeting you.'
   ....

unit fourteen

11 Match the first half of the sentences (*a–j*) with their completions (*1–10*). Write the numbers in the spaces provided.

a He agreed ....
b He promised ....
c He said ....
d He says ....
e She promised ....
f She said ....
g She says ....
h She warned ....
i They insisted ....
j They told him ....

1 he had just finished a new painting.
2 he's finished a new painting.
3 me not to do anything I would regret later.
4 she would arrive about half an hour late.
5 she'll be here in about half an hour.
6 that he hadn't worked as hard as he could have done.
7 that he work harder in order to pass his exams.
8 that she would call him the next day.
9 to call her the next day.
10 to work harder if he wanted to do well in his exams.

Functional language: expressing likes and dislikes

12 Find B's correct replies to A's statements.

A's statements

a I absolutely loathe modern music. ....
b I adore modern art. ....
c I can't stand being in crowded trains. ....
d I don't have anything against sculpture. It's just not my favourite art form, that's all. ....
e I'm crazy about Pedro Almodovar's films. ....
f I'm quite keen on Mercedes cars. ....
g I'm warming to the new TV channel. ....
h I've grown to like Norah Jones' songs. ....
i I've really gone off those American 'dumb' movies. ....
j I've taken a liking to that girl. ....
k The fitness craze doesn't do much for me. ....
l There's nothing worse than tinned music in supermarkets. ....
m Van Gogh is the best! ....
n You can't beat a good hamburger! ....

B's replies

1 Don't be ridiculous. She's half your age.
2 I agree. You get claustrophobic. Especially in the summer when it gets really hot.
3 I can see that! But you could do with losing a bit of weight.
4 I love them. There's nothing wrong with silly films that make you laugh.
5 Oh come on! Surely it's not that bad.
6 Oh no! I much prefer Picasso's paintings.
7 Really? I liked them – her singing – from the very beginning.
8 Unless you're a vegetarian!
9 Well then, what is?
10 Well yes, I like them too, but not that much.
11 Yes there is. Tinned music in aeroplanes.
12 Yes, I would be too if I could afford them.
13 Yes, it is getting better, isn't it?
14 Yes, me too. Some of it is really fantastic.

unit fourteen 109

Writing: films and music

13 Put the scene description phrases in order. For each scene, put 1 for the first phrase, 2 for the second one, etc. The first three for Scene 1 are done for you.

Scene 1
a Bright sunshine. Areas of shade under trees. [ ]
b Exterior. [1]
c He keeps looking back. [ ]
d Main street in a small town. [ ]
e Midday. [2]
f The camera follows the figure as he runs past us. [ ]
g The present. [3]
h We see a man run down the street, shielding eyes from the sun. [ ]

Scene 2
i Exterior. [ ]
j He looks over his shoulder back towards the camera as if he is expecting to see something. [ ]
k We are behind the runner. [ ]
l We can hear his heavy breathing. [ ]

Scene 3
m A policeman and two bank employees are running after the man. [ ]
n Camera behind the runner. [ ]
o The camera pulls back and turns round to look at what the man is running from. [ ]
p Exterior. [ ]
q They have raised fists, and are shouting. [ ]

14 Write three similar scenes of your own. Keep the same sequence as in Activity 13, but change as many words as you can.

SCENE 1

....

....

....

....

SCENE 2

....

....

....

....

SCENE 3

....

....

....

....

Pronunciation: pitch

15 Listen to Track 46 and write *E*, *N* or *U* in the brackets according to whether the speaker sounds enthusiastic, neutral or unenthusiastic.

a I like poetry. [ ]
b Let's meet at about 8 o'clock. [ ]
c This painting is OK. [ ]
d Your sculpture is very good. [ ]
e You're learning to paint, are you? [ ]
f I'd love to hear your latest poem. [ ]
g I'm warming to his work. [ ]
h You can't beat Leonardo da Vinci. [ ]
i I'm really pleased to see you. [ ]
j He's asked me out for dinner. [ ]

Culture and language

16 Are things the same or different in your country? Circle *S* or *D*.

a American films are popular in Britain and in many other countries. S / D
b British people try not to be too direct when they say whether or not they like things – unless they want to be very emphatic. S / D
c Everyone learns – and learns about – poetry at school. S / D
d Many people write poetry but it is not read widely by the majority of the population. S / D
e Many poems are about love, death, regret or the countryside. S / D
f Many public buildings have modern sculptures outside them. S / D
g People argue a lot about whether modern art is really 'art' or not. S / D
h Poets can play around with language, sometimes inventing their own new words and grammar. S / D
i When we report what people have said, we use many other verbs apart from *say*, *ask* or *tell*. S / D

Self-check

17 Read the following statements and put a tick in the correct column.

As a result of studying Unit 14 …	Yes, definitely	More or less	Not sure
I can identify when a word like *were* is stressed and not stressed, and I know how to make the difference myself.			
I can read straightforward poems and stories aloud, with appropriate pauses, stress and intonation so that meaning is clear.			
I can recognise the different situations in which I can use informal language such as 'he's like, you OK?' or more formal language such as 'he asked me if I was all right.'			
I can report what people have said using a variety of verbs such as *insist*, *complain*, *promise*, *explain* and *order*.			
I can say what I like and dislike, using a range of words and expressions.			
I can talk about modern works of art.			
I can talk about things that I have come to like or dislike over time.			
I can use written devices such as verbless 'sentences', repeated past participles and compound words to create poetic effect.			
I can write brief descriptions of scenes that could be used in films.			
I was able to listen to a British speaker talking normally and at normal speed, and understand what she said about storytelling.			
I was able to understand and enjoy three poems written by living writers.			

If you have ticked 'more or less' or 'not sure', go back to the appropriate place in the unit so that you can tick the 'yes, definitely' column.

Test your knowledge

18 Which of the following sentences are written in correct English? Put a tick (✓) or a cross (✗) in the brackets. If there is an error, correct it.

a I always have one hard-boiled egg for breakfast. [ ]
b I can't put my finger on what makes him so special. [ ]
c He insisted that I am on time. [ ]
d They apologised in being late. [ ]
e She suggested going to an art gallery she knew. [ ]
f I don't have anything against reading poetry aloud. [ ]
g I've really gone out of Van Gogh's paintings. [ ]
h I've grown to admire the way he plays the piano. [ ]
i This is where we will need an exterior shot. [ ]
j I've finally taken a liking to learning English. [ ]

The phonemic alphabet

19 Consult the table of phonemic symbols on page 125 and then write these words in ordinary spelling.

a /ˈeərɪəlˌʃɒt/

b /skɔːtʃt/

c /ˈdraʊzɪŋ/

d /ˌhevi ˈbriːðɪŋ/

e /ə ˈtʌtʃəv ˈhəʊm/

f /aɪ ˈkɑːnt pʊt maɪˈfɪŋɡərɒnɪt/

g /juːv ˈfaɪnəliː ˈfɪnɪʃt ðɪs ˈbʊk/

Check your answers by listening to Track 47.

Audioscript

Track 1
a Where have you been?
b Would you like some cake?
c Who told you about it?
d He's French, isn't he?
e It's a beautiful day, isn't it?
f Did Susan tell you she was coming over?
g What's the matter with her?
h Do you know who painted that picture?
i He's pretty famous, isn't he
j It hasn't started raining, has it?

Track 2
WOMAN: Er ... So this woman gets on a bus for the start of a long journey from Paris to London. She soon finds out that the man she's sitting next to is a talker – he just won't shut up. And she just wants to sleep for the whole journey so she's a bit disappointed. The guy keeps asking her questions and then, to make matters worse, he turns to her and asks her if she'd like to play a game. She says 'No, thank you' as politely as she can and closes her eyes to go to sleep, hoping he'll get the message.

Track 3
WOMAN: ... to make matters worse, he turns to her and asks her if she'd like to play a game. She says 'No, thank you' as politely as she can and closes her eyes to go to sleep, hoping he'll get the message.

But the man is not put off easily and he insists, saying that the game will be fun and that it's very easy. Even though she couldn't care less, he tells her the rules. 'I'll ask you a question and if you don't know the answer you have to pay me £5 and then you'll ask me a question and if I don't know the answer I have to pay you £5.'

The woman can't believe her bad luck. This is the last thing she wants to do, so again she says that she's not interested and turns away from him to try to get to sleep. The man is getting more and more frustrated and desperate to play by this time, so he decides to change the rules to see if that will tempt her. 'OK,' he says, 'if you don't know the answer you only have to pay me £1 and if I don't know the answer, I'll pay you £20.'

So the woman analyses the situation and comes to the conclusion that the only way to get some sleep is to play this ridiculous game, so she finally agrees to the game. So as you can imagine, the man is all keen when he asks the first question: 'How far is it around the earth?' The woman doesn't say a word – she just reaches into her handbag, takes out £1 and gives it to the man.

So now it's the woman's turn. She looks him right in the eyes and says, 'What's green in the morning, blue in the afternoon and red in the evening?' The man looks shocked. He thought this was going to be a piece of cake for him – what could this woman possibly know that he doesn't know? He gets on his mobile phone and calls all his friends, gets on the Internet using his phone and searches every reference he can, but still can't get the answer. He sends emails to famous professors, but no one knows the answer.

Finally, after a couple of hours he wakes the woman (who's been sleeping soundly all this time) and admits to being beaten. 'I don't know the answer!' he whispers, weeping with despair. 'Here's your £20'. Without a word, the woman takes the money and puts it in her bag and goes straight back to sleep. So, the man is completely flabbergasted and through his tears he wakes her and begs her for the answer. 'Please put me out of my misery,' he pleads, 'what's the answer?' The woman reaches into her bag and gives him a pound.

Track 4
a penny-pincher
b withdrawal
c spendthrift
d extravagant
e reckless
f stingy
g bankrupt

Track 5
INTERVIEWER: Why are you called Hag?
HAG: Er because my surname is Hargreaves, Ian James Hargreaves, and when I was seven, six or seven at school, from Hargreaves you got Haggis, Hargreaves Haggis, which was shortened to Hag, simple as that and I kept it ... I didn't like 'Ian'.
INTERVIEWER: And you've been Hag ever since?
HAG: I've been Hag ever since but when I went to college I had to carry it with me of course because people started calling me Ian and I hated being called Ian because the only people who called me Ian were teachers, parents ...
INTERVIEWER: And Hag then became your professional name as well?
HAG: It did, yeah everyone knows me as Hag apart from a couple of annoying people.

Track 6
HAG: I suppose, broadly speaking, I'm an illustrative photographer er in that I illustrate ideas by putting images together by putting you know several negatives into the same picture, usually to make a coherent image rather than an abstract image although I have been working with abstract ideas recently.

INTERVIEWER: Can you give an example in words of the kind of thing you're talking about?

HAG: Er, well the one that immediately comes to mind is 'a storm in a teacup' er which is exactly what it says it is. It's a storm in a teacup but of course the storm in the teacup is actually the storm that's put in the teacup and the teacup's surrounded by a storm so this makes a storm in a teacup.

INTERVIEWER: And this is a number of different photographs blended into one?

HAG: Yes, five I think, four, four or five. It's done in a darkroom. I have, if I, I have got eight enlargers. It's like having a multi-track recording studio if you like. You've got eight enlargers. You put a negative in each enlarger and print the bit of the negative you need onto the same piece of paper and then move to the next enlarger and print the next bit you want onto that same piece of paper so you end up with an image that's, all the elements are printed from the original negative. There's no copying involved or anything. It's just a question of masking it right so they fit together perfectly.

INTERVIEWER: You make it sound very simple, but it isn't simple at all, is it?

HAG: Aah. No. It isn't simple at all. It's just, you have to be patient. You have to understand a few things.

INTERVIEWER: Who likes your combination pictures?

HAG: I don't know (laughs). People like them. I've sold hundreds and thousands of pictures throughout the world in posters and postcards and things. And people have bought those with their own money. It's not like an art director you know agency that, you know, thinks up I want to employ this trendy photographer. They actually have to put their hands, they have to walk into a shop, they have to like it, they have to put their hands in their pocket and buy it with their own money and that's very flattering.

INTERVIEWER: Because there've been … one or two have been very very successful posters, haven't they?

HAG: There's been, yes, yes, I've had some very successful posters er, unfortunately the most successful one that I don't really like which has been a dolphin picture, some dolphins leaping out of the water, that was made into all sorts of things like er duvet covers and pillowcase sets, watches, clocks, jigsaw puzzle, er there are other things apart from of course posters and cards and postcards. Yes, that kept me alive for a few years.

Track 7

HAG: When I moved four years ago and built a new darkroom which took me all summer and it was a terrible struggle, people said to me 'Hag, why are you bothering building a darkroom? Do it on a computer.' My answer was, well there's two answers. Firstly I'm not Hag without a darkroom. I have to have a darkroom. Doesn't matter whether I use it or not but it has to be there. I don't feel whole without it. The second answer is, these questions … often come up while sitting in a restaurant eating a meal in candlelight. Now when were candles redundant, when were they obsolete technologically? You know, 200 years ago? And there we are, still sitting around a table eating meals with candlelight because it's nice, because they have a certain quality that you cannot get anywhere else except by a naked flame and that live flame on the table has a certain essence that you do not get from a light-bulb. So we use we the technologies, we use the tools for the qualities they have. A computer does not produce an original hand-made print that's printed from the … from each element er onto that piece of paper. Now people will pay for that rather than buying a digital file that's been created on a computer and then printed, no matter how well. It is not the same thing, it is a reproduction of a digital file.

INTERVIEWER: So film isn't going to go away?

HAG: No.

Track 8

1 (Could you give me a hand?)
2 (Did you use to play football?)
3 (I'd rather not.)
4 (It changed the course of history.)
5 (It depends what it is.)
6 (It's not a patch on the real thing.)
7 (Of course I could.)
8 (They used to live on a farm.)
9 (Turn off that alarm clock!)
10 (You couldn't open the window, could you?)

Track 9

a newspaper
b mother tongue
c throwaway camera
d windscreen wiper
e It's a fact of life.
f not a patch on the real thing
g more than a moment

Track 10

INTERVIEWER: Welcome to *Face the Facts*, our weekly look at the world we live in, the environmental problems we face, and what we can do about them.

Today we're really fortunate to have in the studio with us Dr Caroline Hall, a representative of the World Conservation Monitoring Centre. The Centre was set up in 2000 as part of the United Nations Environment Programme, or UNEP for people who like initials and acronyms. The job of the World Conservation Monitoring Centre is, as its name suggests, to collect information on our biologically-diverse world, and to tell us how the many different species of animal and plant life are faring on our planet. It is thanks to the World Conservation Monitoring Centre that we know how many different species of plants we have lost in the last 50 years, and which are now in danger. It is thanks to their work that we know which types of animals face the possibility of extinction so that, armed with that knowledge, we can do something to protect them.

Dr Caroline Hall is a specialist on world animal species and it is a great pleasure to have her with us here in the studio. Welcome Dr Hall.

DR HALL: Thank you.

INTERVIEWER: Dr Hall, I wonder if you could start by explaining something that I find confusing, and I suspect many of our listeners do.

DR HALL: Of course, if I can.

INTERVIEWER: Well, it's just this. What exactly does it mean to say that a species – plant or animal – is endangered?

DR HALL: Well, that's a good question because we actually have various categories for animals threatened with extinction, but the threat is different for different animals.

INTERVIEWER: How so?

DR HALL: Well, for example, animal species that could go extinct in the very near future – they're the ones in the most danger of course – are classified as 'critically endangered'. Those in danger but with more 'breathing space' – those which are at risk of extinction, but that risk is not one that threatens them at this very minute – we call simply 'endangered'. And finally, we classify a species as 'vulnerable' if it is not in immediate danger of extinction, but which, in the medium term, faces a risk of disappearing forever.

INTERVIEWER: That's very interesting. It's a kind of time thing, then.

DR HALL: Yes, that's true. In a way.

INTERVIEWER: And how do you determine which category a species or an animal is in?

DR HALL: Well, scientifically, we consider three things: the number of mature animals that exist, the reduction in the species over the last ten years, and the projected reductions in numbers for the next ten years.

Track 11

INTERVIEWER: Dr Hall, can you give us some examples of animals in the three categories you mentioned – that is what, 'critically endangered' for the most serious one?

DR HALL: Yes, that's right.

INTERVIEWER: And then endangered …

DR HALL: Yes, that's right, and …

INTERVIEWER: And vulnerable, I think you said.

DR HALL: Yes, I did and the …

INTERVIEWER: So what kinds of animal are we talking about?

DR HALL: Well, umm, … the black rhinoceros is a critically-endangered species. There are only approximately 2,550 left in the world – so it's in big danger of dying out in the very near future. The black rhino is found in small pockets in Kenya, Namibia, South Africa and Zimbabwe, by the way.

INTERVIEWER: OK, so that's the black rhino …

DR HALL: Then we have the African elephant which is an endangered species. There are approximately 610,000 left in different parts of Africa …

INTERVIEWER: And 'endangered' means that these elephants are in danger of disappearing, but not right now.

DR HALL: Yes, yes, and finally we have the orang-utan, which we classify as a 'vulnerable' species. There are thought to be about 20–30,000 orang-utans on the islands of Borneo and Sumatra.

INTERVIEWER: Thanks for that Dr Hall. Now the question that occurs to me is, why are these animals in danger of extinction? What's gone wrong in their world? Can you tell us something about this?

DR HALL: That's a good question. Sadly, it is mostly because of human beings exploiting these animals that they are in danger. In the case of the black rhinoceros, for example, it has been exploited for its horn, which is used in a lot of traditional medicines as well as for decoration. In 1994, black rhinoceros horn was worth as much as $60,000 a kilo – a very valuable commodity and so poachers killed thousands of these animals just for that reason. As for the African elephant, this species is endangered because of loss of habitat, as more and more of their territory is being taken over by humans who are desperate for more land to support the increasing populations; and of course, their ivory tusks, just like rhino horns, are also extremely valuable, even though it is against the law to import and export ivory. There is even an international ban on killing elephants, but it still goes on illegally.

INTERVIEWER: That's terrible.

DR HALL: Well yes, and in the case of orang-utans, they are also vulnerable because of their loss of habitat. Huge areas of forest are being cleared and consequently these tree-dwelling animals have nowhere to live. Without the forest, they will not be able to survive.

INTERVIEWER: I'm talking to Dr Hall from the World Conservation Monitoring Centre. Join us in Part two when I'll be asking her why we should care if we lose the odd animal species, and, if we do care, what we ordinary people can do about it.

Track 12

a Be careful.
b I would think very carefully before I did that again.
c I wouldn't touch that computer if I was you.
d I'm telling you not to do that.
e If you don't get ready soon you'll miss the film.
f If you shout at my dog you'll live to regret it.
g Stop that right now.
h Treat him properly or else you'll be in trouble.

Track 13

a sadistically
b dog-eared
c sociable
d a wolf in sheep's clothing

e They're fishing for compliments.
f I smell a rat.
g hold your horses

Track 14

Welcome to the High Park Leisure Centre. If you know the extension of the person you are calling, please put in that number now. If you would like to become a member of the Centre, please press 2.

If you would like information about our facilities and opening hours, please stay on the line. You may hang up at any time.

The High Park Leisure Centre is your super centre for all types of leisure activities from ice-skating to tennis to swimming. Our opening hours are from 7 am to 10 pm Monday to Friday, 8 am to 10 pm on Saturdays and 10 am to 6 pm on Sundays. We are open every day of the year except 25th December and New Year's Day.

The Polar Bear ice-skating rink is open from the beginning of October to the end of April. Admission prices are £5 for children under 13 and £10 for adults. This includes skate rental. Children under five are not allowed to skate and all children under 13 must be accompanied by an adult.

The High Park swimming pool is open all year round and costs £3.50 or £1 for members of the High Park Leisure Centre. If you'd also like to use the gym when you come to swim, there is a special price of £5 which allows you all-day access to these facilities.

In the sports centre, tennis, badminton and squash courts are available for rent when the High Park teams do not have matches. Please call 01 800 6767 extension 54 for details of availability and prices.

High Park Leisure Centre classes run all year round and the new winter sessions begin soon on 15th January. This term we will be offering classes in aerobics, ballet, modern dance, modern jazz, judo, tae kwondo and tai chi. Our classes last for ten weeks. Please take advantage of our online booking service at www.highparkleisurecentre.co.uk to register for a class or to consult our full catalogue of classes. You can also pick up a catalogue at the Centre during our opening hours and special discounts are only available from our office when you register in person. Unfortunately we cannot take registration for classes over the phone.

That concludes this recorded information service. If you would like to hear this information again, please press 1. If you would like to speak to a Leisure Centre representative, please press 3. Thank you for calling the High Park Leisure Centre, your super centre for leisure and entertainment. Goodbye.

Track 15

a
He's been revising for his exams.
He's been revising for his exams.

b
He watched Sue take a photograph.
He watched you take a photograph.

c
I've always liked her.
I've always liked her.

d
I like life art.
I like live art.

e
I've lived in London for years.
I lived in London for years.

f
Please make it right.
Please make it light.

g
That's my cap.
That's my cab.

h
This is Peter's best.
This is Peter's vest.

Track 16

a binoculars
b potholer
c scuba-diving
d Don't lose your grip.
e nonchalantly
f She gets a kick out of it.
g It doesn't do much for me.

Track 17

RADIO ANNOUNCER: Good afternoon and welcome to our second programme called 'How do people learn'. The speaker is Professor Randy Onnix, head of Applied Linguistics at the University of Hameltown.

ONNIX: As I said last week, many people have tried to explain how we learn things, like how to drive, how to play a musical instrument, or how to speak a foreign language. There are many different theories for this, of course, and people are coming up with new ideas every day.

One of the most popular theories in the first half of the 20th century was called behaviourism, and its influence is still felt 100 years on. Indeed, I would go so far as to say that the central tenets of behaviourism are still present in much teaching and learning that goes on today.

The theory of behaviourism is this: if you make someone do something and give them a prize, a reward when they do it correctly, and if you do this again and again and again, then they will learn to do it every time, and once they have learnt to do it in this way it will, in the end, no longer be necessary to give them that prize. The whole theory of behaviourism, in other words, depends on habit formation – that is getting people so habituated to a task that they do it without thinking.

There are many examples of this kind of habit formation. The Russian researcher Pavlov, for example, taught his dogs that the sound of a bell ringing meant that were going to be given food. As a result, every time he rang the bell the dogs salivated – even, in the end, when there was no food. Then there were all the experiments with rats. When the rats saw a light, they had to press a bar in their cages. When they pressed the bar they got some food. They did it again and again and again. In the end they learnt to press the bar every time they saw the light.

But perhaps my favourite example of this kind of experiment happened in the United States way back in 1920. Two researchers, called Watson and Raynor, experimented on a young boy who had a beautiful pet rabbit. Watson and Raynor wanted to see if they could train Albert to feel differently about his rabbit and so every time he went near the animal they made a terrible noise and, quite naturally, little Albert became frightened. They did this again and again until the poor boy developed a phobia first just about rabbits, then about animals in general and finally anything with fur. Every time Albert came face-to-face with an animal or a fur coat, he would start to show symptoms of terrible fear, crying, feeling sick and feeling faint.

Watson and Raynor were really pleased! 'This just shows that our theory works!' they said. Then they talked to Albert's parents. 'Can we go on with the experiment?' they asked. 'We can turn it round and make Albert love rabbits again.' But Albert's parents told them, for some reason, to go away!

Watson and Raynor's experiment sounds absolutely terrible to us today, but the idea of conditioning is still around. If people do the same thing enough times and get continual encouragement (or discouragement), the doing of it will become automatic – they will be able to do it without thinking.

Not all learning is the result of conditioning though. Other researchers have said that intelligence and creativity matter too. But that's the subject of my next talk. Until then, goodbye.

Track 18
a Don't be so bad-tempered.
b I wish I'd been more careful.
c If only I'd got here earlier.
d Take it easy.
e Use your imagination.
f He's absolutely out of control.
g She drives me absolutely crazy.
h Why should I tidy my room?
i I wish I was a bit taller.

Track 19
a bad-tempered
b grumpy
c irritable
d really fed up
e calm down
f I feel trapped
g he gets on my nerves

Track 20
PRESENTER: On today's Ask the Expert, we look at the topic of space tourism. Yes, space tourism – just like going for a week to the Costa Brava or Bangkok, we'll soon be able to take a tour of space. Here in the studio to discuss this and take your calls we have Dr Brian Kenney from the Space Research Institute in Texas. Dr Kenney, how futuristic is this? Will we soon be touring space rather than lying on the beach?

DR KENNEY: Well, over the past few years there has been a lot of market research on this topic and it's becoming increasingly clear that this is something the general public wants. In the industrialised countries, most people have expressed a wish to be able to travel in space, so it doesn't seem unrealistic for business to be setting up the facilities to make this possible.

PRESENTER: Thank you, Dr Kenney. So now it's over to you, the listeners. Let's hear your comments and your questions for Dr Kenney. And on line 1 we have our first caller, John from Kent. John? Can you hear me? You're through to Dr Brian Kenney of the Space Research Institute.

JOHN: Hello, Dr Kenney. Well, I suppose my first question is when do you think we can start touring space? Will space tourism be available to the average person in the street or will it only be for the wealthy?

DR KENNEY: A very good question. At least at the beginning space travel will of course be very expensive – probably in the range of $50,000 and up, but the whole idea of space travel is that it will generate a lot of money which will then allow the price to come down and make it more available for more people.

PRESENTER: How's that going to happen exactly?

KENNEY: Well at the Institute we like to think of space tourism in three phases.

In the initial phase there will be very few customers, a few hundred a year at most. Accommodation in space orbit will be pretty basic and prices will be very high.

The middle phase is where the number will rise to thousands of people per year travelling to space and the facilities in orbit will improve greatly, including a variety of different types of entertainment. And finally we get to the popular stage where the price will be the equivalent of a few thousand dollars and millions of people will be visiting space every year.

PRESENTER: So, does that answer your question, John? Would you like to be a space tourist?

JOHN: Oh most definitely – but the price will have to be right of course. Thank you Dr Kenney.

PRESENTER: And now on the line we have Jenny from Cardiff. Jenny? You're through to Dr Kenney.

JENNY: Hello? Yes, my question is who's going to pay for all this? Dr Kenney, you talk about the money generated from space travel helping to bring down prices, but where is the money to start these programmes going to come from in the first place?

DR KENNEY: Yeah, that's another good question. Well, space travel and exploration are moving into a new phase. Previously all space travel was government funded. But governments have cut back a lot on their space programs and private industry is now stepping in to fund these space tourism programs. So don't worry, your tax dollars (or pounds) are not going to be paying for the development of space travel – these programs will all be funded by private companies, not the government.

PRESENTER: When is this going to happen?

DR KENNEY: Well, in actual fact there have already been some fare-paying space travellers. The first one was Dennis Tito in 2001 who visited the international space station MIR, so we could say that space tourism has already started. For the program to really take off (no pun intended), it's only a matter of a few years.

Track 21

a D'you reckon it'll rain tomorrow?
b D'you supppose he'll win?
c What d'you think will be the score?
d Did you see the game on Saturday?
e What d'you reckon she'll do?
f D'you think they'll get there before we do?
g Who d'you suppose will be there?
h Did you know they were going to be here?

Track 22

a overpopulation
b robot
c clairvoyant
d astrology
e space tourism
f the general public
g in the first place

Track 23

INSTRUCTOR: Well now, Mr ... er ... Radinski, have you ever driven a car before? ... You have? ... On your father's farm ... but you crashed into the gate and it had to be repaired ... and the radiator needs replacing because you drove into a wall ... and your father is buying some new wing mirrors because you drove too close to the fence ... how interesting ... yes, I hope it will be easier now too, Mr Radinski.

Right, let's start ... OK? ... Adjust your rear-view mirror ... good ... and what about your wing mirrors? Where? You see that button there, do you see? Yes, that one ... excellent ... Now make sure the car is in neutral ... yes, that's right. Now switch on the engine ... that's good ... Er, you can take your foot off the accelerator now, Mr Radinski ... good ... Now indicate to the right ... yes it is that little stick thing ... yes, you do pull it downwards ... yes, Mr Radinski, a little bit like that, but you didn't need to use quite so much force really ... yes, I'm sure we can get a new one. Now then, put your foot on the clutch ... good ... and put the engine into first gear ... good. Now press down on the accelerator ... no, you don't have to exaggerate ... that's better. Release the handbrake ... a bit more ... good, very good ... Accelerator ... check the rear-view mirror ... good ... accelerator ... accelerator, Mr Radinski, accelerator. Come on ... yes, that's better now. Er, clutch ... second gear ... foot off the clutch and accelerate ... oh good, Mr Radinski, very good, very good indeed. Now speed up a bit ... Er, you see that woman crossing the road ... Mr Radinski, that woman? Crossing the road? Mr Radinski? I think you should stop. Mr Radinski, stop ... stop ... STOP!

Yes, Mr Radinski, it is a good thing she jumped out of the way ... Concentrate on the road, please ... good ... Now as you can see, we are coming to a roundabout so we'll need to slow down and that means putting your foot on the brake and the clutch. OK? ... Brake and clutch ... Mr Radinski? ... Mr Radinski? ... There's a lorry on the roundabout ... right in front of us ... not the accelerator, Mr Radinski, the brake ... the brake, Mr Radinski ... the brake ... the clutch ... the brake! The brake! ... The brake ...

Yes, yes, Mr Radinski ... the truck driver was very rude ... Yes, I agree, he used some very bad words ... Yes, it was very unkind of him to suggest that you needed your head examining ... Yes, I'm sure he would have been more sympathetic if he had remembered what it was like to learn to drive ... Yes, you're right, we can always get a new car ... Yes, Mr Radinski, I think we are going to have to walk home ... Yes, yes, Mr Radinski, that is the end of this lesson.

Track 24

a accelerator
b gear stick
c radiator
d rear-view mirror
e steering-wheel
f wing mirror
g pedestrian
h roundabout
i engine
j neutral
k handbrake
l mirror

Track 25

a It needs mending.
b pedestrian
c metacognition
d I had my car washed.
e lime-green T-shirt
f careful analysis

Track 26

PRESENTER: Today on the Good Food Show we have something rather unusual for you all. Some exciting news about a food that we don't usually consider to be nutritious and healthy – chocolate. Yes, an extra special treat for all you 'chocoholics' out there – the benefits of chocolate to our health. Now, chocolate has been blamed for all kinds of ailments from obesity to headaches, tooth decay and even acne. Today, we want to set the record straight and look at some of the possible health benefits of eating chocolate according to the latest research and talk about some of the more unusual ways of eating chocolate. With us in the studio we have Dr Karen Mortimer, a researcher at the South East Nutrition Institute, who has been taking part in a series of investigations on the health effects of chocolate to the diet. Welcome, Karen.

DR MORTIMER: Thank you, it's good to be here.

PRESENTER: So, what's this all about? Can chocolate really be good for you?

DR MORTIMER: Well, first I want to stress that this research is relatively new and it will be some time until we have any really conclusive evidence, but the results that we are getting so far are very interesting indeed.

PRESENTER: So what have you found? Why do we generally think that chocolate is bad for us?

DR MORTIMER: Well, first of all, I think it's important to point out that chocolate, or cacao, has not always been seen as the decadent sweet item that it is today. The use of cacao as a medicine is well documented from when it was first introduced to Europe from the Americas in the 16th century. The kinds of things it was used to treat were emaciated patients to help them gain weight, people who had no energy in order to stimulate the nervous system and for patients who had some kind of digestive problem as cacao seemed to stimulate the kidneys and the digestive system.

PRESENTER: So, they were all given a bar of chocolate and told to go home and eat it? Sounds like a nice cure.

DR MORTIMER: (laughs) Well, no, not exactly. Until relatively recently people used to drink chocolate rather than eat it. The Mayas and the Aztecs in Mexico crushed cacao seeds and mixed it with water and then flavoured it with chilli peppers, honey or vanilla or flower petals, and then later the Spanish drank it with sugar and cinnamon and other spices, more like the hot chocolate we drink today.

PRESENTER: So where do chocolate bars come from?

DR MORTIMER: That was not until the mid-1800s when new machines made it possible to mass-produce solid chocolate bars, which consequently made it more affordable for the general public.

PRESENTER: OK, so you've told us a little about the history of chocolate, what about the latest research? What have you found?

DR MORTIMER: Well first of all, the good news is that there is no evidence of any connection between eating chocolate and skin outbreaks.

PRESENTER: So eating chocolate doesn't give you spots?

DR MORTIMER: No, there's no connection.

PRESENTER: So, what good can chocolate do?

DR MORTIMER: Well, chocolate is full of flavonoids for a start.

PRESENTER: That sounds nice. What's that?

DR MORTIMER: Flavonoids are also found in red wine, tea, fruits and vegetables and these are thought to have a good effect on the heart. These flavonoids also act as antioxidants which are thought to prevent or slow down damage to the body's cells and tissues, particularly important against cancer.

PRESENTER: Sounds good so far. So should we all be eating more chocolate?

DR MORTIMER: Well, the problem is, of course, that chocolate also contains sugar and saturated fat – two things that are not good for us, particularly milk chocolate.

PRESENTER: So what do you recommend?

DR MORTIMER: Well, certainly dark chocolate contains more of the benefits and less of the potentially harmful effects than milk chocolate and as yet our research does not tell us how much chocolate it is safe to eat without receiving the harmful effects.

PRESENTER: Why? Can chocolate be dangerous?

DR MORTIMER: Eating large quantities of fat and sugar is certainly not good for you. It can lead to obesity and of course the sugar is also bad for your teeth, but there are also claims that chocolate is somehow addictive like a drug. There are about 300 chemicals in chocolate including caffeine and the active ingredient THC that is found in marijuana, but these are found in such small quantities that you would need to eat about 25 pounds of chocolate at once to feel the effects, so a physical addiction is pretty much impossible.

PRESENTER: So what about those chocolate cravings that many of us experience from time to time?

DR MORTIMER: The cravings that people feel are far more likely to be culturally taught than physical and the 'highs' that people claim to feel after eating chocolate most likely come from the carbohydrates in the sweet which raise the serotonin levels in the brain and this is what makes you feel good.

PRESENTER: So all that chocolate advertising really works, huh?

DR MORTIMER: That's right.

PRESENTER: So, Karen, let's take our break here before we move on to look at some of the more unusual ways of eating chocolate. Stay tuned for some great recipes using chocolate, including the famous chicken mole from Mexico which has chocolate as its main ingredient. We'll be right back.

Track 27

I often have a craving for chocolate. I know that it's decadent, but I love to bite into a rich creamy bar of chocolate, the kind that are mass-produced for people like me who must have chocolate to give them a boost and stimulate them to get through the rest of the day. I don't care what they say about acne and tooth decay, but I do worry about my weight. Do those emaciated-looking models in magazines never eat chocolate bars?

Track 28

a cardiologist
b cool as a cucumber
c he saved my bacon
d chocolate
e emaciated
f I'd like to make a complaint
g manager

Track 29

I never felt magic as crazy as this;
I never saw moons knew the meaning of the sea.
I never held emotion in the palm of my hand
Or felt sweet breezes in the top of a tree.
But now you're here
Brighten my northern sky.

I've been a long time that I'm waiting.
Been a long time that I'm blown.
I've been a long time that I've wandered
Through the people I have known.
Oh, if you would and you could
Straighten my new mind's eye.

Would you love me for my money?
Would you love me for my head?
Would you love me through the winter?
Would you love me 'til I'm dead?
Oh, if you would and you could
Come blow your horn on high.

I never felt magic crazy as this;
I never saw moons knew the meaning of the sea.
I never held emotion in the palm of my hand
Or felt sweet breezes in the top of a tree.
But now you're here
Brighten my northern sky.

Track 30

1–7
Good afternoon, Mrs Clarke.

Track 31

a good-looking
b voluptuous
c well-dressed
d It's a bit of a mess.
e You'll damage your career prospects.
f She's absolutely gorgeous.
g What are you talking about?

Track 32

Forecast 1

NEWSCASTER: So, it's over to Jim at the weather center to tell us about what we can expect here in the Bay Area in the next 24 hours. Jim?

FORECASTER: Thanks Leslie, well, not much good news for people in the whole Bay Area I'm afraid. Although you may wake up to clear skies and sunshine, that's not going to last and you can expect heavy rain throughout much of the day and into the night. The only silver lining is that the wind is going to drop, so there'll just be a light breeze from the north, which will make things a little more comfortable. Things look a little better for the rest of the week, but my advice for the next few days is: don't forget your umbrella.

Forecast 2

FORECASTER: So that's how things look tonight. Now let's take a look at the next few days. Well, the high pressure coming from the east should keep the temperatures pretty warm – about 25–28 degrees celsius which is very warm for this time of the year, and there'll be no wind, so lovely weather for a picnic on the beach. Enjoy it while you can. It's not going to last, and Tuesday will see a return to cooler temperatures with a chance of some rain.

Forecast 3

FORECASTER: Here's the weather forecast for tomorrow in the South West. The day will start off cloudy and very cold and chances are there'll be some hail later in the day in the hills. The temperature will be minus 2 in the morning going up to about 2 or 3 during the day and going back below freezing by nightfall. From all of us here at Radio Westward News, we wish you a warm good night.

Forecast 4

FORECASTER: And finally your weather forecast for the Toronto area tomorrow. Well, no surprises here really at this time of year. We're expecting a pretty heavy snowfall during the night and going on into the day tomorrow with blizzards expected and plenty of drifting in rural areas. This is of course going to create pretty hazardous driving conditions, so take great great care on the roads if you have to drive tomorrow. We'll be back tomorrow. Good night.

Forecast 5

NEWSCASTER: Now it's over to the meteorology center for tomorrow's forecast.

FORECASTER: Thank you Jenny. Tomorrow should start off fine with some bright sunshine with temperatures going up to about 55 degrees Fahrenheit, but those temperatures are going to drop as the wind picks up and the cloud comes over with a chance of some scattered showers in the highlands. Those winds will probably last well into the night and ease off in the early hours of the morning.

Forecast 6
ANNOUNCER: We break into the variety show with an emergency flood warning. Heavy rains are expected in the next 24 hours and flooding in lowlands is expected as rivers rise. Many houses in the area have been evacuated and flood preparations are in operation. Please contact your local flood prevention service at 631 673, that's 631 673, to find out if your area is in danger and how you can prepare for the flooding.

Track 33
a This evening there'll be a light breeze from the east.
b The high pressure system is bringing good weather.
c After 5 this evening there'll be cooler temperatures.
d Temperatures will fall to below freezing tonight.
e There was heavy snowfall all day today.
f Ice on the road is creating hazardous driving conditions.
g There was bright sunshine all morning followed by light showers.
h The announcer gave an emergency flood warning.
i The mayor told the people of the town to make flood preparations.

Track 34
a torrential rain
b downpour
c heavy flooding
d incidentally
e freezing temperatures
f to change the subject
g hazardous driving conditions

Track 35
a I don't know how you put up with it!
b The plane took off.
c Do you get on with her?
d I was sad when she turned me down.
e Will you please turn the radio off?
f Guess who I ran into today?
g They're going to pull it down today.
h I have to look after my sister.
i She's taking care of her grandfather this week.

Track 36
BRAD: Look at that great party. I'd love to be famous.
DIANE: Would you? I'm not so sure I would. I mean it must be a nice feeling to walk down the street and to have people recognise you, but sometimes it must get really annoying
BRAD: Yeah, I suppose so, especially thinking about the paparazzi. Sometimes they must want privacy and then there's a camera in your face the whole time.
DIANE: That's the cost of fame, though. You just have to accept it – it comes with the territory.
BRAD: I guess, but at the same time I think everyone is entitled to a private life no matter who they are.
DIANE: Yeah, but think of all the cool things you get to do when you're a star. Like visiting places all over the world and meeting other famous people. Imagine meeting people who were your heroes when you weren't famous. That helps to make up for the disadvantages, surely.
BRAD: Well yes …
DIANE: And all the opportunities to do things that you would never be allowed to do or places you would never be allowed to go if you weren't famous.
BRAD: True. But what about friends? Would you still have a lot of friends? Do you think we'd still hang out with Darren and Susana if we were famous?
DIANE: Hmm … we'd have to make Darren wear some new clothes. I wouldn't want to be seen with him in that old sweater!
BRAD: Yeah, I wonder if famous people keep their old friends or make new ones?
DIANE: It must be hard to make new friends, because you don't know if people want to know you for you or for who you are – someone famous.
BRAD: Then there are the fans and groupies who hang around all the time – some of them are obsessed, you know.
DIANE: I hadn't thought of that – that would be a real pain, having to have a bodyguard 24 hours a day.
BRAD: And then there's the pressure of fame.
DIANE: What do you mean?
BRAD: You know, you can't just get up in the morning and go out, because there are people watching you: the press love to catch glamorous people looking a mess. You have to look good all the time and smile and say interesting things – you can never totally relax. It's open season on you and your whole life, all the time.
DIANE: And we haven't even mentioned work and the pressure to produce something great again and again.
BRAD: Oh, yeah, there's that too, but I see plenty of famous people living on their past and not really doing anything new.
DIANE: Mmmm, I guess that works for some of them, but not others. But anyway. What do you think, do you still want to be a world-famous guitar player?
BRAD: Yeah, I reckon it's worth it. I'd better start classes though! Maybe I could be a famous football player instead.
DIANE: Hmm, might be hard… You can't even make it into the local team.
BRAD: You never know – maybe I'm a late developer.

Track 37
a notoriety
b infamous
c in your face
d get along with
e put up with
f don't you think
g a late developer

Track 38

MARCUS: Are you ready to do your duty for Rome?
COMMODUS [1]: Yes, Father.
MARCUS: You will not be emperor.
COMMODUS [2]: Which wiser, older man is to take my place?
MARCUS: My powers will pass to Maximus to hold in trust until the Senate is ready to rule once more. Rome is to be a Republic again.
COMMODUS: Maximus? [3]
MARCUS: My decision disappoints you?
COMMODUS: You wrote to me once, listing the four chief virtues – wisdom, justice, fortitude and temperance. As I read the list, I knew I had none of them. But I have other virtues, Father – ambition, that can be a virtue when it drives us to excel; resourcefulness; courage, perhaps not on the battlefield but there are many forms of courage; devotion, to my family, to you. But none of my virtues were on your list. Even then, it was as if you didn't want me for your son.
MARCUS [4]: Oh, Commodus, you go too far.
COMMODUS [5]: I searched the faces of the gods for ways to please you, to make you proud ... One kind word, one full hug while you pressed me to your chest and held me tight, would have been like the sun on my heart for a thousand years ... What is it in me you hate so much? All I ever wanted was to live up to you, Caesar, Father.
MARCUS: Commodus, [6], shhhhh; [7] your faults as a son, is my failure as a father. [8]
COMMODUS: Father, I would butcher the whole world if you would only love me! [9]

Track 39

a ambition
b butcher
c courage
d devotion
e fortitude
f justice
g resourcefulness
h smother
i temperance
j wisdom

Track 40

a literature
b autobiography
c the blurb
d fair enough
e rubbish
f temperance
g awe-inspiring

Track 41

Jane's story

JANE: My uncle rang me up and arranged to meet me for coffee close to the university library where I had been working. We went to a café that most people use around there. It's just next to the BBC, well the World Service at Bush House anyway.

Anyway, so we met up and the place was pretty crowded. We had to talk quite loudly. But it was nice to see him. We talked about family things, holidays, about my cousins and all the sorts of things you talk to a favourite uncle about.

While we'd been chatting away, I'd seen this character out of the corner of my eye. He was lurking around looking vaguely suspicious. He was tall, a bit older than me, with fairly long hair. Wearing jeans and a sweatshirt. He had a woolly hat on even though it was in the middle of summer.

After we'd been talking for some time my uncle offered me a second coffee, so I said yes and he went off to get it. I reached into my bag to get a book I wanted to show him. I pulled my new mobile phone out first and put it on the table.

So, the situation: my uncle's at the counter getting the coffee and I'm watching him and then the tall guy walks past our table and as he passes he just picks up my phone and in a very unhurried way he makes for the door. Luckily, for once, my brain is actually working – and anyway I saw him do it. So, without thinking about it at all, I leapt out of my chair and reached him just as he got to the door. And again, I wasn't really thinking much when I talked to him. I said something like 'excuse me, I think you'll find that's my phone'. And he looked at me in a really scary way and he was like, 'well you can have it back then. If you want it that bad.' And he just threw it on the floor and walked out onto the street.

My phone broke open and I thought it was a gonner, but amazingly I managed to put it back together, and it's working fine. Afterwards I wondered if I'd done the right thing. You know, people are always saying you shouldn't tackle a thief, but hey I was really fed up. That's why, I suppose.

Angie's story

ANGIE: Oh yes, the camera incident. That was years ago. I'd completely forgotten about it. But it was quite an experience, I can tell you. Quite terrifying, actually, but at the moment it happened, I didn't have time to feel frightened. That came later. Some kind of delayed shock. I suppose I was lucky to survive really.

We were on our first big holiday. That's me and my first husband, and we'd got to New York which was great. I mean it was the first time I'd ever been there. So on our second morning, we decided to go for a walk in Central Park. It must be one of the most famous parks in the world. It was quite cold and I seem to remember I was wearing my red jacket and some new gloves I'd just bought. And just as we were walking past an area with trees, and there didn't seem to be many people around, this guy jumps out of the bushes and runs up behind me (I didn't see that bit of course) and before I knew what was happening, someone's got a hand round my throat and something is pressed to my neck, cold and sharp. Well of course I struggled for a second and a mean voice whispered 'don't even try lady' in my ear.

I can remember my husband's face. He was looking absolutely shocked, his mouth just hanging open. And then the guy says from behind me, 'hand over the camera buddy,' to my husband of course, 'hand over the camera buddy or your old lady gets it' – I can remember the exact words.

Now the thing was, David – that's my first husband's name – had just bought this expensive new camera and it was hanging round his neck. It was his pride and joy. So he looked at me and he looked at the camera, and his face went all confused, and then he said – can you believe this? – 'Angie' (that's my name) 'Angie, what should I do?' And I said, well you can imagine, 'give him the **** camera of course,' and he did and the thief ran away with it and David and I had an argument! Beginning of the end, really!

Michael's story

MICHAEL: Most people experience crime at some time in their lives. It can happen anywhere in the world, big cities, the country, anywhere. The thing is people just seem to like taking other people's possessions I suppose, or they need the money. But actually you can do your best to avoid crime just by being sensible. You have to keep your eyes open, especially when you're far away from home, in a foreign country, for example.

See, I heard this story once about a guy who was sitting on a beach on holiday in some exotic foreign location. It was the end of some kind of business trip and he decided to have a last look at the sea before heading off home. And he'd taken his things with him, passport, money, credit cards and air tickets to get home, all that kind of thing. All in his shorts. That seems like so silly, just asking for trouble I'd say, but maybe there was a reason, I don't know. But anyway, he took off his shorts and there he was sitting in the hot sun in his swimming things, a typical Brit, gradually getting sunburnt. And then these two beautiful girls came up to talk to him. I mean really beautiful. And it never even occurred to him to wonder why two people like that who must have been at least 20 years younger than he was should suddenly decide he was so fascinating. He just felt really flattered and stood up to chat to them and they had a great conversation, lots of laughter and smiles. Then they said they had to go but perhaps they'd see him again, he could easily find them at the beachfront café 'over there'. As he waved them goodbye, he felt pretty good. Until, that is, he sat back down on the sand and realised that absolutely everything had gone.

It was OK in the end, of course. He got a new passport, cancelled his credit card and didn't lose much money. But he felt pretty stupid walking back into the hotel and explaining what had happened to him. I'm pretty sure he won't be taken in like that again!

Track 42
a The police expect the judge to convict the man today.
b The convict escaped from jail.
e The main suspect in the case is a 24-year-old woman.
f The police suspect the woman of committing arson.

Track 43
a getaway car
b prosecuted
c during the robbery
d pickpocketing
e embezzlement
f to be charged with a crime
g he must have done it

Track 44
You're listening to the self-guided tour of the Van Gogh Museum in Amsterdam.

Vincent Willem van Gogh was born March 30, 1853, in Groot-Zundert, son of a Dutch Protestant pastor. He was a moody young man who was easily bored and by the age of 27 he had been in turn a salesman in an art gallery, a French tutor, a theological student and an evangelist in Belgium.

In 1886, Van Gogh went to Paris to live with his brother Theo van Gogh, an art dealer, and became familiar with the new art movements developing at the time. Here, Van Gogh began to experiment with the modern techniques that were popular at the time.

In 1888, Van Gogh left Paris for southern France, where he painted scenes of the fields, the peasants and lives typical of the people who lived in the countryside. During this period, living at Arles, he began to use the swirling brush strokes and intense yellows, greens and blues associated with some of his most famous paintings such as *Bedroom at Arles* and *Starry Night*.

In his enthusiasm, he persuaded the painter Paul Gauguin, whom he had met earlier in Paris, to join him. After less than two months, they began to have violent disagreements, culminating in a quarrel in which Van Gogh wildly threatened Gauguin with a razor. That same night, in a fit of deep remorse brought on by his many mental problems, Van Gogh cut off part of his own ear.

For a time, he was in a hospital at Arles. He then spent a year in the nearby mental asylum of Saint-Rémy, working between repeated spells of madness. Finally he left the mental asylum and lived for three months in a town called Auvers. Just after completing one of his most remarkable paintings, the ominous *Crows in the Wheatfields*, he shot himself on July 27, 1890, and died two days later.

During his life, Van Gogh wrote more than 700 letters to his brother Theo, and these letters give us a remarkable picture of how he approached his art, what he painted and when, and his state of mind. He left behind about 750 paintings and 160 drawings. He only ever sold one painting in his lifetime, but now his most famous works (such as *Sunflowers*) sell for millions of dollars.

Press the number on the wall to hear about the works that you now see in front of you.

Track 45

You're listening to the self-guided tour of the Van Gogh Museum in Amsterdam. These exhibits are numbers 27 and 28.

The two pictures you see before you were both painted when Van Gogh was in Paris from 1886 to 1888. In that two-year period, he painted 27 self-portraits. This was because he often could not afford models and so painted himself in order to experiment with colour and different techniques.

The first picture, number 27, shows Vincent in an elegant suit and hat. It seems that Vincent used this picture in order to study grey. The picture is full of varying tones of grey and even the eyes, which are normally green, are painted in a dramatic blue-grey tone. The hat is made of felt. The red in his face and particularly in the beard makes the head stand out from the background. The kind of clothes he is wearing suggest fashionable Paris at that time and it seems that he is also advertising himself as a portrait painter. Van Gogh was always looking for customers for portraits as an important source of income.

The second picture, number 28, shows Van Gogh doing a study of colour yet again. Here, he seems to be looking at the effect of yellow against a blue background. Note also the range of colours in the jacket, bow-tie and background. The straw hat seems a strange combination with the suit that he's wearing, and this makes it clear that the purpose of the picture was to experiment with colour.

Please press 29 to hear about the next painting or 0 to hear more information on the life of Vincent van Gogh.

Track 46

a I like poetry.
b Let's meet at about 8 o'clock.
c This painting is OK.
d Your sculpture is very good.
e You're learning to paint, are you?
f I'd love to hear your latest poem.
g I'm warming to his work.
h You can't beat Leonardo da Vinci.
i I'm really pleased to see you.
j He's asked me out for dinner.

Track 47

a aerial shot
b scorched
c drowsing
d heavy breathing
e a touch of home
f I can't put my finger on it.
g You've finally finished this book.

Table of phonemic symbols

Consonants

Symbol	Example
p	please
b	better
t	truth
d	dark
k	class
g	go
f	finish
v	very
θ	thin
ð	that
s	sing
z	zoo
ʃ	shop
ʒ	measure
h	help
x	loch
tʃ	children
dʒ	join
m	some
n	son
ŋ	sing
w	wait
l	late
r	read
j	yes

Vowels

	Symbol	Example
short	ɪ	sit
	e	said
	æ	bat
	ɒ	top
	ʌ	luck
	ʊ	foot
	ə	again
long	iː	sleep
	ɑː	car
	ɔː	forward
	uː	school
	ɜː	heard
diphthongs	eɪ	lake
	aɪ	tie
	ɔɪ	joy
	əʊ	go
	aʊ	wow!
	ɪə	peculiar
	eə	air
	ʊə	cruel